Date Due

FEB 2 4 1978		
JUN 1 0 1983	DEC 1 1 2003	
	DEC 0 7 2004	
OCT 3 1 198	SEP 2 4 2005	
JAN 2 6 1989		
JUN 2 3 199		
JAN 2 9 1993		
2 9 199		
SEP 2 9 199		
DEC 2 3 1994		
NOV 1 7 199		

BRITISH COLUMBIA

THE PIONEER YEARS

T.W. PATERSON

STAGECOACH

STAGECOACH PUBLISHING CO. LTD.
P.O. Box 3399, Langley, B.C. V3A 4R7

Typesetting, layout and design by
Mainland Graphics Ltd., Langley, B.C.

Printed in Canada by
D.W. Friesen & Sons Ltd., Altona, Manitoba

First Printing — October 1977

Canadian Cataloguing in Publication Data

Paterson, Thomas W., 1943-
    British Columbia : the pioneer years

    Bibliography: p.
    ISBN 0-88983-013-4
    ISBN 0-88983-015-0 pa.

    1. Frontier and pioneer life - British Columbia.
2. British Columbia - History. 3. British Columbia -
Biography. I Title.
FC3811.P38   971.1   C77-002218-9
F1087

Contents

BRITISH COLUMBIA
THE PIONEER YEARS

The famous and the forgotten—so many have contributed to the building of British Columbia during the past two centuries.

The careers of some have been given due tribute in recent years by historians and writers. But so many, many more are unhonored, unmourned, their roles on the provincial stage totally overlooked. While this may be inevitable in the march of progress it also is regrettable.

Not all have been statesmen, empire builders or heroes. Some, to use an expression of the past, were "rogues and vagabonds." But each, in his own unique way, contributed to the British Columbia that we enjoy today.

Many others were ordinary people of the day: men and women who were willing to forsake family, friends and country to brave the unknown of a New World in search of personal fulfillment. Gold seeker, homesteader and merchant, they made their way to British Columbia, by steamer, Red River cart, horseback, canoe and on foot. Each was seeking his own El Dorado, be it a gold mine, a piece of land or a new lifestyle.

Most found what they were looking for in the former Hudson's Bay Company domain and crown colonies. Some fell by the wayside, victims of an inhospitable wilderness or their own failings. Yet, among the latter, Victoria's town crier, John Butts, remains as one of the province's most hilarious characters. Idler, drunkard and scamp he undoubtedly was; but, at the same time, he did more to enliven a city than any of his contemporaries and, if ever there is a Hall of Fame (or Infamy!) for the dastardly, surely John Butts must be its leading luminary.

At the opposite end of the scale, there is the like of Minnie Paterson who sacrificed her health to bring help to shipwrecked mariners in the once-dreaded "Graveyard of the Pacific" off Vancouver Island's west coast. Jack Fannin survived an ordeal in the northern British Columbia wilds to found our present-day provincial museum in Victoria. Nellie Cashman followed the lure of gold from the American Southwest to British Columbia's Cassiar to the Yukon and Alaska. Wherever she went, she brought a warm smile and outstretched hand to all down on their luck. When she died, thousands wept for their tiny saint of half a century.

Walter Moberly dedicated his life and his fortune to the quest for a "true" Northwest Passage that would forge a commercial link between Canada, the British Empire at large and the Orient by way of British Columbia. He not only devoted his career to this goal but succeeded—and has been virtually forgotten for his troubles.

Another martyr to posterity was Rev. Robert Staines, who battled the monopolistic Hudson's Bay Company for representative government. He was eccentric, vain, arrogant—and right.

So many, many others have been overlooked over the years, their triumphs and tragedies filed only in archives and newspaper morgue. BRITISH COLUMBIA—The Pioneer Years is a token attempt to give some of these heroes and heroines a belated moment of recognition. For it is one of the satisfactions of an historian that he has the ability to dust off yellowing file and hold up to the light the events of the past which helped to build the province as we know it today, and the people who made the events. It is not a question of exploitation, or feasting on the dead, as this writer was once accused, but of acknowledging a longstanding debt to the tens of thousands who came before.

Many significant events have also been lost in the passage of time, as major disasters, epic engineering feats and personal struggles against overwhelming odds have joined their actors in obscurity. It is with a great measure of personal satisfaction that the author is enabled to make this small tribute to many of these forgotten characters and the struggles which made—or broke —them.

VICTORIA'S GREAT FIRE

"Swift and sudden, with no warning, and like lightning out of a clear sky, one of the most serious conflagrations in the history of Victoria, broke out yesterday afternoon about 2:30 o'clock. . . ."

THIS was Victoria's "Great Fire" of Tuesday, July 23, 1907, which, in four devastating hours, rampaged through entire blocks of buildings and homes, caused an estimated $200,000 damage, and entered the record books as the worst in city history up to that time.

When the city's beleaguered fire department, with its obsolete, inadequate and ill-functioning equipment battled the inferno to a stop, "scores of families (were) rendered homeless and a portion of the city had been entirely blotted out."

The conflagration began on the west side, in a block between Herald and Chatham Streets, igniting in a wooden lean-to adjoining the boiler house of the Albion Iron Works, in mid-afternoon. Within minutes, it was out of control, and racing through surrounding wooden structures. Aided by a strong southwesterly wind, the blaze was soon a voracious monster, leap-frogging eastward to Quadra Street. Leaving small islands of homes undamaged, through the efforts of their occupants and firefighters, the flames devoured a number of homes on the south side of Herald, between Douglas and Blanshard Streets, then jumped Chatham near the corner of Store and began burning on a second front.

According to one report, the fire "had three stages: one when commencing at 2:30 o'clock it blotted out the block between Store, Chatham, Government and Herald, with the exception of four small houses on the south side of Chatham near Store; a second when about 3:30 o'clock it had reached Calvary Baptist Church near the corner of Herald and Douglas . . . and a third which had its origin almost simultaneously with the second when it destroyed eight residences on Green Street."

City firemen were virtually helpless, being unable to use their scanty equipment effectively due to a water pressure described as being "practically nil." Due to a two-week period without rain, the wooden frame structures were tinder-dry, almost exploding into flame when wind-blown sparks soared over hastily-drawn firelines, and this flying fifth column ignited one home and building after another.

Only twice did the flames meet stiff opposition in

their march eastward: on Pioneer (North Park) Street, when desperate firefighters tore down five cottages so as to prevent their being consumed; and when they reached the brick home of James Townley, on Green Street. Here, fortunately, development had not yet caught up, that part of the city remaining in meadowland.

But, by 5 o'clock, firefighters battling the flames on the western front were forced to retreat towards Blanshard Street. An hour earlier, 30 soldiers under Lieutenant Vien joined the firefighting lines after

having been called in by Mayor Morley. The mayor and most of his council, for that matter, did their own part, being in the front lines.

Ironically, when black smoke had first begun pouring from a disused boiler room between Fisher's blacksmith shop and the Albion Iron Works, the initial alarm "did not attract much attention." But, because of the wind blowing off the harbor, and the dry state of surrounding buildings, the blacksmith shop was soon ablaze.

When the fire brigade responded, they had found their hands tied for want of water pressure, a single hose yielding but a pitiful trickle of water—and Fisher's shop had vanished in flames. Three neighboring buildings and the old Indian Mission Church, all of wood, and bone-dry, had been the next victims, roaring into a single, giant, terrifying column of flame and smoke. Because of inadequate equipment, and insufficient water pressure, firemen had been unable to save the four, and had turned instead to an adjacent Chinese laundry.

(Left) A fire engine of the type used to fight the blaze. (Bottom) Victoria fighters were paralysed by lack of water pressure.

Later, armed with hindsight, there were those who bitterly criticized the fire department for not having destroyed the Indian Mission so as to contain the fire. But, as officials explained, at that critical moment the full gravity of the situation had not been realized; an unfortunate fact, as it had been the sparks blowing from the old church's steeple which blitzed neighboring structures and transformed the fire from a serious blaze to a major disaster.

"The ground between Herald and Chatham Streets is, or was," the record continues, "largely occupied by small frame dwellings little better than shacks, and the flames spread northwards among these with frightful rapidity, and, with a high wind blowing it soon became evident that a conflagration was inevitable. Lower Chatham Street is occupied exclusively by cribs (houses of ill fame) and there were many painful scenes among the terror-stricken denizens. Women in scanty attire fled into the streets imploring aid, which was cheerfully rendered, though it turned out to be of no avail. Their furniture was piled out on the roadside and for a while seemed to be in safety, but the devouring flames spread across the street and eventually their entire effects were consumed. Despite all efforts to stop it the fire literally licked up everything in the block as far east as Government Street."

Despite the fact that further battle was useless, the heroic firemen did their best to slow the monster in its march by pitting useless hoses against a solid wall of flame and heat which almost blinded them and forced them to retreat behind obstructions from which they sniped with hoses and buckets.

One touching scene, described as "pathetic" by a reporter, but which, at least today, has a touch of comedy, concerned a lady of the evening who had lost her every possession in the flames. Sobbing bitterly in the street, she wailed to all around that this was the second time she had been wiped out by fire, the first disaster having occured when plying her profession in San Francisco. The double tragedy, she sobbed could only be an act of Providence, and henceforth (vowed she "amid heart-broken sobs which left no doubt of her sincerity") she would change her evil ways.

Not all, happily, were left destitute. A Government Street blacksmith named Mellor, warned that there was no chance of saving his shop, had time to remove his precious tools to safety. Then the flames swept over Government Street, igniting first the grass, then igniting a vacant lot crowded with scrap lumber and crates.

But here, marvelled a reporter, "one of yesterday's many miracles were recorded. The cottages on the north side of Herald Street, east of Government, were untouched, although the houses to the back of them on the south side of Chatham were all consumed, as were the houses from St. John's Church east on the opposite side of the next block, in the same Herald Street."

When all was said and done, it was the wind, rather than the fire itself, which wreaked havoc from Store Street to where the Curling Rink now stands— one-half mile. For, displaying an almost playful mood, the wind fanned the flames at whim; first here, then there, spreading sparks—and instant destruction—indiscriminately; here, on one side of a street, there, on the other, and often leaving homes, or blocks of homes, untouched. This, too, was one of the "miracles" of the Great Fire of 1907.

Within an hour of the first outbreak, most of the city was without electricity, and St. John's Church, at the corner of Douglas and Herald, was a mass of flames which danced, virtually unnoticed, for an hour before firefighters could give its ruins some attention. Then the red scourge galloped onward, along the south side of Chatham Street towards Blanshard.

"It started with the little hardware store on the corner, and wiped out everything on the south side of the block. But the frame of the new building on the northeast corner of Government and Chatham, next (to) the brewery, was untouched, as were the buildings of the lower half of the block adjoining. All the houses on the east half were destroyed, notwithstanding unusual efforts to save them.

"Thus almost the entire block bounded by Store, Herald, Chatham and Government Streets, and most of the block immediately to the east are today a desolate waste with only a chimney standing here and there to mark the site of former human habitations."

Curiously, two homes on Green Street, to the east, were spared "in a most remarkable fashion: There was a fire to the right of them and fires to the left of them, but happily they were out of range and escaped the heat to an extent which enabled dampened roofs to triumph."

And so it went, the wind, with neither rhyme nor reason, choosing one victim, and sparing the next. For four tortuous hours, Victorians fought with little effect until, finally, due to the increasing distances between buildings in the "suburbs" east of Douglas Street, the fire began to subside. As in other areas, the wind played favorites here also, having spared entire blocks of homes on Quadra before devouring the homes of J. Mellhutsch and Fred Garnham. Then, veering from the south, the wind whipped its fiery columns along the north side of Quadra, and more homes fell victim.

It was on Pioneer Street that firemen, soldiers and hundreds of volunteers made their last stand. As they had waited, the fire charged eastward to Blanshard, paused, then dispatched two "advance couriers of destruction." One stalked up Green Street, leaving the ashes of 12 homes in its wake, as the other attacked the north side of Pioneer.

For an agonizing eternity, it appeared that the defenders were to be routed again, as their famous Deluge fire engine stood, useless, beside a fire

The aftermath of Victoria's Great Fire. Inset: Some were able to save some of their possessions.

hydrant—unable to raise enough water pressure to fire its boiler.

"But Victoria had had enough," the *Colonist* noted with triumph the next day. "Pluck and brawn can at a pinch do without water and it mastered the fire yesterday afternoon. The soldiers from the Esquimalt garrison, commanded by Lieutenant Vien, were there and there were hundreds of willing Victorians. They, with the help of the fire brigade, sufficed."

When it became apparent that the first blazing home and its immediate neighbor were doomed, hopes of turning back the holocaust were centered upon No. 22 Pioneer Street, a small cottage. If they could demolish it in time, the fire would run out of fuel and find itself contained. Within minutes, firemen and civilians, armed with axes and ropes, reduced the "dainty" cottage to a pile of rubble, which was watered down.

But the wind, not to be thwarted, suddenly increased in fury, fanning sparks farther ahead of the main advance of flames, and firemen saw that the sacrifice of No. 22 was not enough. "The call was nobly responded to and the houses (adjacent) were desperately attacked. Despite the intense heat the neighboring buildings were partly demolished with axes and then pulled down by ropes.

"One young man in particular, whose name could not be learned, mounted the tottering roofs, and at imminent risk to himself attached the ropes. Dozens of men manned the ropes, and, pulling together at the word of command, dragged down the tottering roofs and shaky walls amid the cheers of the spectators who densely thronged the streets."

And there, on Pioneer Street, the fire's main advance was finally checked.

At 6:30 that evening, sufficient water pressure was raised for the old Deluge engine to go into action, watering down those structures yet threatened, and extinguishing those ruins still smouldering. Then it was over.

Throughout the battle, Fire Chief Tom Watson had sped from skirmish to skirmish in his shiny Oldsmobile which, hours after, was so blackened with soot that it was unrecognizable.

Once the crisis had passed, weary officials set relief machinery in operation for 250 residents who had been left homeless, and took toll of the damages. In all, five city blocks, and more than a hundred homes and buildings, had vanished in four hours, the initial damage estimate being placed at $200,000. Only the direction of the capricious wind, which had been from the southwest, saved most of the city. Had it been blowing from the north, with firemen paralysed by nonexistent water pressure, much of the downtown business section undoubtedly would have been consumed. (As it turned out, this small miracle was but a reprieve, much of that section of town going up in flames just three years after).

Such was the fateful day of July 23, 1907—the day of Victoria's Great Fire. ●

(Left) When Captain W.H. McNeill led a second expedition to Gold Harbor his men succeeded in exposing a promising vein. But this time the Indians, resentful of the HBC's competition, stole the traders' tools and ore samples. When they became openly hostile, McNeill decided it wise, after only three days, to abandon the venture for the time being.

(Right) Captain William Moore was the most colorful of B.C. stern-wheeler skippers, taking part in every B.C. gold rush, including the Queen Charlottes in 1852.

The QUEEN CHARLOTTE GOLD RUSH

EL Dorado! This, it was claimed, was the vast, unknown hinterland of British Columbia in the 1850s.

Overnight, with the discovery of yellow pebbles in a mainland stream, this wilderness became alive with fortune seekers from around the world and British Columbia's future, as crown colony and Canadian province, was assured.

Yet the resulting stampede of humanity to the banks of "Fraser's River" was not our first gold rush. This history-making claim belongs to the Queen Charlotte Islands.

"Two pieces of gold, nearly pure, weighing 4½ and 1½ ounces, and a piece of auriferous quartz"—wrote James Douglas to his superiors in the Hudson's Bay Company's London office, in mid-August of 1850, had been discovered by Indians on the west side of "Queen Charlotte's island, near Englefield Bay and Cape Henry." Samples delivered to Fort Simpson understandably aroused the company's interest, although it was not until May of the following year that Chief Factor John Work visited the scene, to make four exploratory blasts and to gather samples. A subsequent expedition led by Pierre Legarre was less successful, the men failing to find the "mine," but discovering that "Queen Charlotte's island" was, in fact, a group. Work then returned to the site with Captain W.H. McNeill aboard the company vessel *Una,* with men and equipment.

Despite their efforts of almost a week, this party found little. Situated on the beach, noted Work, the diggings seemed to extend below the water's edge, as indicated by the fact that the best samples, in the form of "loose stones," were found below the tideline. Local Indians had been the most successful, having found one rock containing nearly two pounds of almost pure gold, and a second weighing six ounces. These, they offered to sell the traders at an exhorbitant price, when Work and party returned to Port Simpson.

By this time, word of the strike was getting around—despite efforts by the company to keep knowledge of the Moresby Island mine to itself. Shortly after Work's second visit, the sloop *Geo. Anna,* Captain Rowland commanding, arrived in Olympia with "very interesting news from the gold mines on Queen Charlotte's islands." Not only did Captain Rowland have a story for the Oregon *Spectator,* but samples as well: "Some beautiful specimens of virgin gold bearing quartz, the latter of the richest quality that (the correspondent, A.M. Poe) ever saw."

After testifying to Rowland's credibility—he was "a gentleman of veracity and experience"—Poe described the "mines" as being "equal, if not superior to anything of the kind yet discovered. The gold is found on the surface of the ground near the beach, and is dug by the natives in great quantities, without anything like a pick or shovel—having nothing but such tools as they can make themselves, they manage to get from two to eight ounces per day. They are very friendly to the whites and are anxious to have them come and trade and dig with them."

Late in October, the *Una* returned to the scene, Captain McNeill directing his men in the work of blasting away the overburden. Upon their exposing and tracing the vein, they found that it seemed to lead up the hillside. More than ever, the mine looked promising. But, this time, the Indians—the same ones who had been reported as being friendly and anxious to have the whites trade and dig with them—were not as gracious. Resentful of the HBC's competition, the natives became decidedly unpleasant, stealing the trader's tools and ore samples. When the whites protested, their hosts drew knives, and McNeill decided it wise, after only three days, to abandon the venture for the time being. The *Una* then sailed for Fort Victoria—and near-disaster.

Driven ashore on Neah Island during a gale, the vessel was looted and burned by Indians, Captain McNeill and company having to be rescued by the American vessel *Susanna*.

But if the HBC was having its difficulties in mining, there were those willing to risk any hazard. Captain Rowland's arrival in Olympia had coincided with the general realization that the boom of California had at last peaked. Gone were the golden days of '49, and more and more disheartened prospectors returned to their homes. Although disappointed, they were alert to any rumors concerning new strikes, and reports of gold in the Queen Charlottes aroused the entire West Coast. Before long, the schooner *Exact*, loaded with Oregonian adventurers, cleared Portland for the treasures of Moresby Island which, the *Spectator* assured its readers, promised to be a sure thing.

Few paid heed to the fact that, among those aboard the *Una* when she stranded, were the men of the American vessel *Georgianna*—Captain Rowland commanding—which had outfitted at Olympia and sailed for the new gold fields. Outbound, the vessel spoke the *Demaris Cove*, commanded by another '49er, Captain Lafayette Balch. Informed as to the nature of their expedition, Balch enthusiastically agreed to join them as soon as he rendezvoused with the brig *George Emery*. In due course, the goateed mariner-miner learned that the *Georgianna's* company, rather than finding their fortunes, had been wrecked and taken captive by the Indians. Balch immediately notified Colonel Simpson Moses, collector of customs in Olympia, and urged the formation of a relief party.

In turn, Moses alerted the army commandant at Steilacoom, and sought the assistance of Factor Work; that HBC official assuring him that, due to the time of year, the Haidas likely would not agree to transporting the castaways to Fort Simpson. Dissatisfied, the collector commissioned Captain Balch to sail for the north with authorization to pay whatever ransom was demanded, and with a seven-man detachment of soldiers. Seven weeks later, the *Demaris Cove* returned with the shipwrecked

prospectors, and an intriguing story of shipwreck and ordeal.

The wreck of the *Georgianna*, according to one of its company, has resulted from Captain Rowland's refusal to heed the advice of an Indian chief named John, who had been employed (upon high recommendation of an HBC official) as pilot. Choosing his own anchorage, the captain apparently enjoyed such faith in his anchors and cables that he ignored a worsening gale and his exposed position. In the early hours of the following morning, the *Georgianna* began to drag her anchors, then broke loose. When her frightened crew attempted to make sail, "everything blew away as fast as it was set," and the beleagured vessel struck the rocks. At first she shipped no water, although the waves made a clean sweep of her decks, as her crew huddled below "to save ourselves from exposure" amid the "greatest order and coolness."

With daybreak, a volunteer made his way to shore with a lifeline, while those aboard chopped away the mainmast. Suddenly relieved of this weight, the *Georgianna* "bilged and fell immediately," when Rowland and several others drifted ashore on the mast. When it became apparent that the vessel, by this time floating freely although mortally wounded, could not be saved, the remainder of her company escaped to the beach, where they were met by a growing assembly of Indians.

This welcoming committee, some 150-strong, "taking advantage of our exhausted condition after coming through the surf, plundered us of our caps, weapons, and such clothing as they could pull off us." Those who resisted were threatened with knives and tomahawks. Fortunately for the castaways, their pilot remained loyal and offered them the sanctuary of his home. After being shuttled by canoes, the men were "well received at John's house."

Once there, however, John showed his true colors by demanding that they build him a house! In exchange for a structure 36 feet square, and built in the "same manner as the HBC house," John would kindly take them to Fort Simpson. This, his unwilling guests refused to do, "considering it as the first step towards slavery. After a long conversation, John agreed to furnish us with a scanty supply of bad provisions until a favorable opportunity occurred to send an express to Fort Simpson. From the 20th of November to the 4th of December we had a succession of heavy east gales, with passing showers of rain. Passed the time in the most miserable manner, and received great annoyance from the Indians, over whom the chief seemed to have but little power."

Twice, notes were dispatched to Fort Simpson, as the shipwrecked fortune hunters waited impatiently for rescue. On the second occasion, they had succeeded in pursuading John to canoe five of their party to the HBC post, where Captain McNeill was in charge. Despite the fact that McNeill provided these men with provisions and clothing, the Americans received the distinct impression that he was in no way eager to send for their "suffering companions." "He promised," the *Georgianna's* log continued, "to send, but made no seeming attempt to do so. The Indians in the neighborhood of the fort were threatening to make war on the Haidas, and he seemed to be more anxious for his own safety than to relieve those who were in more imminent danger, although they were people of his own kind."

Rightly or wrongly, McNeill took all of four weeks to see to their relief. The five men who stayed at the fort, in lieu of payment for the goods and food provided them, were made to stand guard duty for the duration.

Throughout this period the Americans suffered cold, hunger and the unbecoming conduct of their hosts. Almost naked (their clothing having been stolen upon their reaching shore), they shared accommodation with 10 Indian families, consisting of 60-odd persons, and a host of dogs in a cedar-planked longhouse. Not all of the prisoners were mistreated (at least not in the accepted sense of the word), one of their number making himself quite popular with the natives by entertaining them. He soon regretted his acceptance when one old woman, having adopted him as her son, insisted upon chewing his food for him.

Finally the *Demaris Cove*, with Captain Balch and company, arrived from Olympia to ransom the captives for five blankets each. The only hitch in negotiations came when most of the Indians (particularly the "mother") demanded that the talented crewman remain with them. At length this was resolved and the *Georgianna's* ill-fated company released.

No sooner had details of this outrage by the Haidas been reported in American newspapers than the *Oregonian* renewed the excitement by stating that a crewman of the *Una* had displayed some of the gold he had recovered with nothing more than a cold chisel. In half an hour the seaman had obtained an ounce of the "richest quality we have ever seen."

The rush to the Queen Charlottes—whatever the mood of the Haidas—was on!

In a period of two months, six American vessels cleared Californian and Oregonian ports for Moresby Island, as many more planned to join them. Among the first to return was the *Eagle*, whose crew expressed disappointment. They had not found any gold themselves, that which they brought back having been purchased from the Indians "at quite double its value." They did, however, offer hope to others by remarking that gold, as evidenced by the quantities in possession of the Haidas, must exist in quantity on the islands.

Throughout this excitement, the Hudson's Bay Company, legal claimants to any mineral rights, had watched the situation with mounting concern.

Douglas regarded the American fortune hunters as invaders and, so as to circumvent further incursions by the miners, he ordered Chief Trader J.F. Kennedy and 40 men to sail for the minesite aboard the company vessel *Recovery*. But, for all of their efforts, they found gold only in a pocket near the beach, this vein quickly petering out. While there, they were joined by HMS *Thetis*, Admiral Moresby having arrived to preserve order.

It was then that the Schooner *Exact* arrived in Victoria, its company having spent "a hard winter" exploring the Queen Charlottes. Alas, their attempts at mining had been brief. After a single blast, they found they would have to fight for everything they got. With insufficient tools for mining, and inadequate strength to guard against the Indians, they spent much of their time surveying the islands' harbors, mountains, lakes and rivers. Although they were convinced that "there is plenty of gold there," the only precious ore which they had seen for themselves had been in the possession of some Indians—who had taken it from the *Una's* crew.

As time passed, and more seagoing prospectors visited the islands, the Indians became bolder. On September 26, 1852, Captain McNeill reported that the schooner *Susan Sturges*, British-owned but sailing under American colors, had been "plundered and burnt" by the Haidas. None of the seven-man crew, he wrote, "were lost on the occation (sic), and she had $1500 on board in gold and silver and a complete trading outfit all of which fell into the hands of the natives."

McNeill had had to ransom Captain Rooney and company, then clothe them upon their rescue as all had been robbed of their clothing. This time, there had been no suggestion that McNeill had tarried in seeing to the relief of the hostages, a Portland newspaper acknowledging the "commendable promptness" with which the Ss. *Beaver* had been dispatched to their relief. Unfortunately, upon Chief Factor Work's arrival at the Haida village, the tribe refused to surrender one of their prisoners. When they resisted all pleading, bribery and threats, "it was thought that he has been butchered by them ere this time."

Sporadic interest in the so-called gold mines of the Queen Charlottes continued until the undeniably great strikes of the Fraser River. Although Douglas had been appointed lieutenant-governor of the islands in the autumn of 1852, as a claim to British sovereignty, most Americans had abandoned the rush for fear of the Haidas and in disgust due to the poor returns. Subsequent surveys confirmed what some veteran miners had suspected from the beginning: that the "mines" of Gold Harbor were nothing more than a freak orepocket. Once this had been exhausted, they said, there was no more. A quarter of a century after, the great gold rush of the Queen Charlottes—with its shipwrecks and Indian pirates—was history. ●

(Left) The lawmen who brought the legendary Bill Miner to bay on the road at Murray Creek, 1906.
(Below) Arrival of Bill Miner and company at the Kamloops provincial jail.
(Opposite page) The old Grey Fox himself, Bill Miner, as photographed upon his capture at Kamloops.

THE GREY FOX

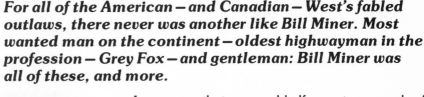

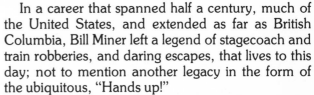

For all of the American — and Canadian — West's fabled outlaws, there never was another like Bill Miner. Most wanted man on the continent — oldest highwayman in the profession — Grey Fox — and gentleman: Bill Miner was all of these, and more.

In a career that spanned half a century, much of the United States, and extended as far as British Columbia, Bill Miner left a legend of stagecoach and train robberies, and daring escapes, that lives to this day; not to mention another legacy in the form of the ubiquitous, "Hands up!"

William A. Miner's apprenticeship in the precarious trade of highwayman seems to have begun in California, when he was just 16 years of age, and fresh from his father's ranch in Bowling Green, Kentucky. Whether it was the old story of falling in with bad company, the record does not show. But, for young Miner, the die was cast when, with two older companions, he robbed a stage of $75,000.

The gang made a clean getaway, Miner later stating that, because of his age, he had enjoyed little of the loot. For that matter, it does not seem to have lasted his partners too long, either, as, before long, they waylaid their second and third stagecoaches; about which time the long arm of the law caught up with them. Bill's share in the crime spree netted him three years in the hellish confines of San Quentin Penitentiary. The 19-year-old felon had served but a matter of months when, belatedly convicted of another robbery, his sentence was extended by a further two years. Thus it was not until after he had served four years and three months that Miner was released, in the summer of 1870.

Incarceration, however grim it had been, had not had the desired effect of rehabilitation as, within months of his return to the "street," Bill was back to holding up stagecoaches. This time, he displayed greater expertise and managed to elude one posse after another as he struck time and time again, and left the authorities with nothing more than a description and what was to become a trademark: his gentlemanly, soft-spoken—almost apologetic—behavior throughout the course of each holdup.

But, as before, his reign of terror was short-lived, and he was again sentenced to San Quentin; this time, for 13 years. The memories of his previous confinement in this castellated pest-hole drove him to desperation and, before long, he was on the run. Recaptured within hours, he was whipped until almost unconscious, then thrown into the dungeon-like cellblock known as the hole, where the prison's most hardened criminals were confined. And there he remained until officials were convinced that he would behave. As further discouragement of future escapes, he was made to wear the "Oregon boot;" this fiendish contrivance, straight out of the dark ages, slowing him to a shuffle and assuring his good behavior.

But it did not break his spirit.

Finally, in July of 1880, after 13 years in the horrors of San Quentin, Miner was awarded his freedom for the second time.

He was then 33-years-old, and embittered. A century after, it can only be concluded that his contempt for authority had been hardened. Whatever the case, Bill Miner's single concession to the power of the law was to seek fresher pastures. Moving to Colorado, where he was unknown, he teamed up with another veteran outlaw by the name of Bill Leroy, and immediately resumed his career as a highwayman. Several more stagecoaches fell to his command of "Hands up" before a posse stretched poor Leroy from a tree branch, and drove Bill on to the more civilized climate of Chicago, where, for a time, he posed as a successful miner from California.

But, once his ill-gotten means were gone, it was back to business—and back to Denver with a new partner. As before, however, the Colorado lawmen were soon on the scent, the outlaws fleeing before a hail of bullets. Finally cornered in a canyon, it looked like, this time, Bill's career was about to be ended. Although his partner managed to hold off the lawmen by wounding three with his Winchester, Miner realized that it was only a matter of time before they closed in and, vividly remembering the fate of Bill Leroy, the veteran highwayman—now known as the Grey Fox—slipped away into the night. Rather ungallantly, he left his accomplice to face the music.

But Miner's latest respite from justice, and return to his old California stamping grounds, was short-lived. Arrested for robbing the Sonora stage of $4,000 he was sentenced to 25 years in San Quentin.

And there, he remained; for no fewer than 20 years. When, for the third time, he was released, he was 60-years-old, grey and slightly stooped. More importantly, his generation behind bars had seen a world of change on the outside. The Wild West of his youth was now a maze of railroads and telegraph lines, the stagecoach virtually having gone the way of the covered wagon, and his oldtime opponents on the side of law and order now dismissed him as being nothing more than a harmless anachronism.

Bill's daring, his Winchester and bandana, they were convinced, would no longer keep the authorities awake at nights.

They did not count upon Miner's dauntless spirit, or his willingness to change with the times. With two new partners, he simply switched from stagecoach to train. Boarding the Oregon Railroad & Navigation Company express just outside of Portland, the masked trio forced the engineer at gunpoint to bring the train to a stop. Bill's inexperience with trains, however, almost proved to be his undoing when he set a dynamite charge to blast his way into the baggage car. Inadvertently using too much TNT, he almost demolished the car. Miraculously, an express messenger survived the charge and opened fire on the robbers. When one of his men was hit, Miner, thinking him fatally wounded, fled into the night.

His accomplice, in fact, lived—and talked—with the result that the third holdup man was shortly captured. Bill managed to make good his escape, despite the fact that the authorities now knew that their old nemesis was back in action, and mounted a full-scale manhunt throughout Oregon and Washington. Aided by the Pinkertons, lifelong enemies of Miner's, lawmen followed numerous leads without success, being unaware that the aging outlaw had achieved international stature by fleeing over the Canadian border. This, according to the record, is the first time Bill ventured outside the continental United States although, interestingly enough, some contemporary American lawmen believed him to have been born in Canada. Whatever the case, Miner was in British Columbia, temporarily safe in the Nicola Valley ranching region as a semi-retired American rancher going by the name of George Edwards.

There, his genuine fondness for children, his soft-spoken manner and gentlemanly way won new friends for the Grey Fox. With his tall, slightly stooped figure, Stetson, cavalry moustache, and piercing eyes, he was a commanding figure, even at the age of 60. Few who met him disliked him, and when, in due course, his real identity became known, many were shocked to think that the courtly George Edwards of their acquaintance was the most wanted man on the continent.

Apparently of independent means (this, despite the OR&N fiasco), Edwards enjoyed the role of retired rancher, and kept eyes and ears alert as to stagecoach and railway schedules, and money shipments. His interest, upon learning that Bullion's annual gold cleanup was to take place in a matter of days, can be imagined!

Thus it was hardly a matter of coincidence that, on the dark night of September 10, 1904, the CPR transcontinental was boarded and halted by three masked men, several miles outside of Mission. A Colt revolver pointed at his head, Nat Scott, engineer of locomotive number 40, numbly obeyed the command to stop, when, screeching in protest, the transcontinental braked. When the locomotive and express car were unhitched from the rest of the train, the ringleader, described to police as a slender man in mackinaw and broad-rimmed stetson, curtly instructed him to move a mile or so down the track, where, threatened with being blown up when the gang dynamited their way into the car, the frightened express manager unbolted the door.

The Big Rock, now known as Bill Miner Rock, where the mail car was cut off the Imperial Limited. (Right) The dead or alive wanted poster issued for Bill Miner and his pratners after the robbery of old '97, May 8, 1906.

Within minutes, Canada's first train robbery was history, and the outlaws—and $7,000—vanished.

Crossing the Fraser by small boat, Miner and his accomplices fled to Bellingham. By the time the alarm was raised and a dragnet organized, their trail was cold.

Months passed, without another clue as to the perpetrators of the robbery, when both Canadian and American authorities were rudely reminded of the case by another train-robbing trio which held up a Great Northern express near Ballard, Wash. This time, the haul was an impressive $30,000. As before, the outlaws eluded all pursuit, although Seattle Pinkerton head P.K. Ahearn expressed the opinion that the daring Ballard job had all of the earmarks of yet another Bill Miner job.

Back in Princeton, kindly old George Edwards continued to win friends and to enjoy his retirement, sharing a ranch with another oldtimer named Jack Budd. Although popular with young and old alike, Edwards preferred to keep pretty much to himself, but for the constant company of sawmill hand, William "Shorty" Dunn. Unlike Edwards, Dunn was known to be close-mouthed and distant, some whispering that he had been involved in the slaying of a lawman in the States. For their own part, Edwards and Dunn did little to invite questions; seeming to prefer their own company during a number of prospecting trips. (When "Edwards" true identity became known, several locals recalled that, incredibly enough, both he and Dunn had been prospecting at the time of the Ballard holdup).

As time passed, a third character joined the Edwards-Dunn circle, Louis Colquhoun, a handsome, goateed, and tubercular, teacher from back East

$11,500.00 REWARD

The Canadian Pacific Railway Coy.

areward of $5,000 (Five Thousand Dollars) for the capture, dead or alive, of the three robbers who held up train 97 between Ducks and Kamloops on the morning of the 9th inst., or $1,000 (One Thousand Dollars) for the capture, dead or alive, of any one of the robbers.

The Dominion Government

Also offers $5,000 (Five Thousand Dollars) on the same terms as the above.

The Provincial Government

Offers One Thousand Five Hundred Dollars (Five Hundred Dollars for each man) for capture and conviction.

DESCRIPTION.

LEADER: About 5 ft. 7 in. in height, slim build, about 50 years of age, wore a grey stubby moustache, face and hands very much sun burnt, eyes somewhat inflamed, wore glasses, tattoo mark on back of right hand, wore a black slouch hat and a blue-black overcoat.

SECOND MAN: About 5 ft. 7 in. in height, medium build, weight about 170 lbs, black hair, dark complexion, very clear and distinct voice, with slight Cockney accent, wore an old blue sweater.

THIRD MAN: Age about 40 years, about 5 ft. 10 in. in height, light or reddish moustache and thin face.

Kamloops, B.C., May 12th, 1906.

By Order.

with a petty theft conviction, becoming an inseparable companion. And so it went, until the historic night of May 8, 1906. As CPR locomotive No. 97 puffed through the darkness north of the little British Columbia community of Ducks, engineer Callin suddenly turned to find himself threatened by two armed, masked men. Clambering over the coal tender, one of the intruders waved his pistol under Callin's nose and quietly, firmly, told him to stop the train.

When Callin numbly obeyed, and No. 97 screeched to a halt, a third man ran from the shadows and the outlaws ordered the fireman to uncouple the locomotive and mail car, and to move several hundred feet farther down the track. There, after two mail clerks inside the car opened the door, the gunmen began to search for the registered mail. But, much to their surprise and disgust, they realized that they had the baggage car, rather than the express car.

This indignity was too much, even for the gentlemanly Miner, who cursed; his temper deteriorating even more when he found only $15.50. Fuming, the outlaw ordered Callin to drive them several miles down the line, when the three rode off into the darkness, unaware that, in their haste, they had overlooked several innocuous parcels in the baggage car which contained $40,000.

Miner, for all of his legendary exploits, had erred before. But surely the Ducks robbery was his most dismal failure. Not only had he mistaken the train's cargo, but (whether due to age, or the fact that he was beside himself with disappointment and rage), he left a clear trail for his pursuers. Even worse, the outlaws had lost their horses!

Within hours, a determined posse led by Constable W.L. Fernie had little difficulty closing the gap

(Above) Shorty Dunn, Bill Miner's accomplice, in 1906. (Below) Bill Miner's preliminary trial underway in the old Kamloops courtroom before Mayor Gordon, with Attorney-General Fulton acting as prosecuting attorney.

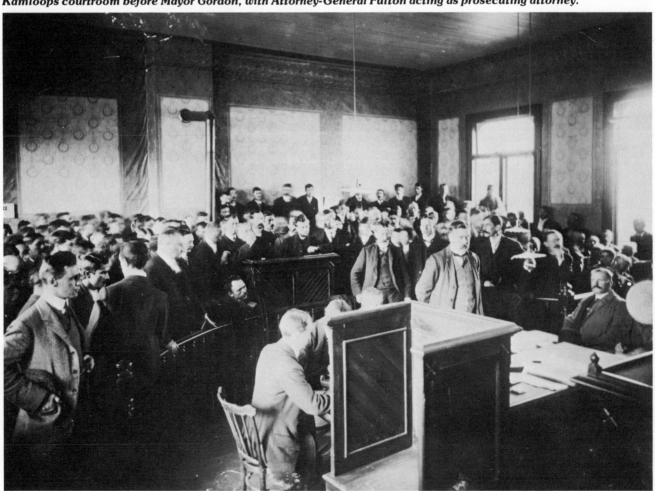

between themselves and the wanted men.

As it became apparent that they were making for the border, Fernie ordered his men to spread out. Miles later, it was Fernie himself who sighted three men in the distance and reported his discovery to a NWMP patrol which was also in the area. When the Mounties closed in, they found the strangers eating lunch. Spokesman for the three, one George Edwards, expressed amusement at the idea that they could be train robbers, and, for several moments, the officers began to wonder if they had the right party. The puzzle was solved by Shorty Dunn, who, panicking, drew his revolver, fired, and made a break for the bush. A Mountie bullet in his hip ended his flight and answered the question as to their involvement, when a search of the campsite uncovered a rifle and six handguns.

Within a matter of days, provincial police officers were amazed to learn that their prisoner, George Edwards, was the most wanted stagecoach and train robber on the continent, the old Grey Fox himself—Bill Miner.

In due course, the celebrated outlaw went on trial for the Ducks holdup. After the first jury ended in deadlock, a second trial convicted him and he was sentenced to life imprisonment. For shooting it out with arresting officers, Dunn also got life, Colquhoun receiving a mild 25 years. (Ironically, only the tubercular Colquhoun served "life" by dying behind bars, as Miner made his getaway and Dunn was eventually paroled).

This time, the authorities on both sides of the border were absolutely convinced: Bill Miner was finished. Yet, for all of his years and hardships, he did not look his age. At his trial in Kamloops, a reporter had described him as being "a rather striking looking fellow, with grizzled hair and moustache, erect and active, who doesn't appear to be within 10 years of the age credited to him on prison records. He claims to be 63, but looks more a man of 50, and moves like one of 30."

In short, the authorities had underestimated the Grey Fox yet again.

Sentenced to wheelbarrow duty in the New Westminster penitentiary's brickyard, Bill soon noted that, at one spot in the yard, he was obscured from the guard tower's vision by a tall smokestack. That was all he needed. With the help of three other inmates, he made trip after trip to that magic spot with his wheelbarrow, cautiously scratching a hole under the fence. At the right moment, he and comrades were under and into the woods, guards in hot pursuit.

The other three were soon recaptured, but Miner was gone from British Columbia forever. Making his way to the southern states, he held up an express train near White Sulphur, Georgia. The take this time was $60,000, and Bill must have thought the old magic had returned. But it was to be his last job. Picked up for routine questioning, he was identified

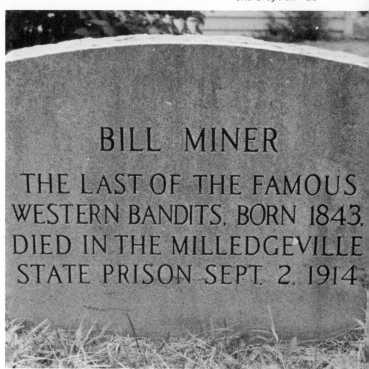

End of the trail for Bill Miner: his Milledgeville, Georgia, headstone.

by one of the officers as Bill Miner. Although "George Anderson" protested strongly, the Pinkerton agent who had spotted him by use of one of his agency's wanted circulars, was not to be denied. The oldest highwayman in the business had pulled his last job.

Which is not to say that he was finished—far from it! For, sentenced to 20 years in Millidgeville State Prison, Bill — now 68-years-old — bided his time for seven months on the prison farm — then headed for the timber. By overpowering a guard, he and a younger convict made it to the swamps. There, he was forced to finally concede that the old Grey Fox just wasn't what it used to be. Age, and half a lifetime in prison, had taken their toll. Exhausted, hungry and disheartened, the escapees hid in a boxcar. When the posse was alerted as to their hiding place, the manhunt was over. This time, however, Miner did not surrender without a fight, answering the posse's fire with a pistol until his companion was killed.

Shackled to a ball and chain, Bill waited eight months. Then, with two cellmates, he hacksawed his way through the bars of his cell!

But, after battling his way through snake-infested swamps and quicksand, he walked right into the arms of a posse. Old and weak, his latest ordeal was too great. Placed in prison hospital, Miner clung to life for another year but the old stamina was gone. On the evening of September 2, 1913, Bill Miner—master criminal of the American West, Grey Fox, and originator of the phrase, "Hands up!"—made his final escape from all worldly woes. ●

Ss ISABEL
STORMY CAREER
OF A LOVELY
LADY

The pioneer sidewheel steamer **Isabel** *made history in her 30 years: an active quarter of a century during which the liner, freighter, tugboat and "man-o'-war" became a household word in earlyday British Columbia ports.*

(Left) Captain Edward Stamp, owner of the Isabel, *upon his ship's "rescuing" the* Moneta *at Hastings Mill, promptly presented her master with a bill for $10,000. When Captain Turpin ignored his ultimatum Stamp obtained a court order authorizing the seizure of the* Moneta — *and the battle was on!*

(Right) The good ship Isabel *at Nanaimo. For more than a quarter of a century, as a liner, freighter, tugboat — and "man-o'-war" — she was a household word in the Pacific Northwest.*

LAUNCHED July 25, 1866, for Alberni lumber tycoon Captain Edward Stamp, the *Isabel* had drawn a large crowd of well-wishers to her baptism at Trahey's yard in Victoria. On shore and in small boats "crammed to their capacity," spectators eagerly awaited the ages-old ceremony to begin at 4 o'clock that Saturday afternoon.

Festivities had to be finished in record time when workmen noticed that the shoring holding the *Isabel* fast in her cradle was giving way, and the "last 'dogs'" had therefor to be quickly knocked away so as to give the restless craft a chance to make her first marine plunge.

"The shout, 'She's off!' soon resounded from all sides and away glided the *Isabel* down the ways amid the loud plaudits of the assemblage, re-echoed by those on board."

So sudden had been her launching that Mrs. J.G. Shepherd barely accomplished breaking the traditional bottle of champagne across her retreating bows. Even more surprised was the "jolly skipper" who had been mounting a ladder resting against her side when she began to move, plummeting him to the ground. Uninjured, he sheepishly dusted himself off and joined the others in celebrating the suc-

cessful, albeit premature, launching.

One hundred and 46 feet long, 275-ton *Isabel* cost the then awesome amount of $50,000. Built of the "finest timber ever put into a vessel on this coast," her frame was of unblemished pine, her keel carved from a single giant fir from Burrard Inlet. So fine was the new sidewheeler, in fact, that one newspaper thought her "almost too good to be engaged as a tug at the Burrard Inlet mill for which she was designed."

Named after a company director's wife, *Isabel* was moored alongside the Hudson's Bay Company wharf to await installation of her English-made boiler.

Once the machinery was installed the completion of her superstructure advanced rapidly in following weeks. Apparently Captain Stamp had agreed with the newspaper's observation as to the duties *Isabel* was to perform for, besides being equipped as a tug, she was outfitted to accommodate 50 passengers and 200 tons of freight. Rumor had it that she would enter the lucrative San Francisco trade.

On October 25, Ss. *Isabel* steamed at nine knots out of Victoria Harbor into the Strait of Juan de Fuca for a trial run. To Captain Stamp's delight, the

new steamer performed admirably.

Two weeks later, she returned to Victoria from her maiden voyage, having towed the bark *Deleware* to Nanaimo in only 12 hours. Stamp reported that all on board had been pleased with her handling. Then, instead of entering the California passenger and mail competition, *Isabel* tried her hand at the Victoria-New Westminster run. This decision soon created excitement in Victoria. When, on the morning of April 13, the *Isabel*, with 20 passengers and 40 tons of freight, slipped her mooring from her Inner Harbor berth, a cheering crowd was on hand. For it had been rumored that she would race the rival steamer *Enterprise* to New Westminster. Bets were made as Captain Stamp slipped his lines and gained a slight advantage on the *Enterprise* which had to back from her wharf. Then, funnels belching black smoke and mighty paddles churning the water white, they sped out of harbor, the *Enterprise* snorting in the *Isabel*'s foaming wake.

Captain Stamp maintained his slight lead around Trial Island and out of sight, when the gambling fraternity had endured a 12-hour wait for results of the contest. Finally a telegram reported that the *Isabel* had docked 10 minutes ahead of Captain

Swanson's command.

By April 29, the rivalry between the sidewheelers had degenerated to open hostility, with passengers travelling between Victoria and the Royal City enjoying considerably reduced fares during a brief rate war.

It probably had been Captain Swanson's supporters who spread the insidious rumor that the *Isabel* lacked adequate accommodation for passengers— to which a Vancouver resident, undoubtedly at Stamp's inspiration, replied that he had personally inspected the ship and had been "quite astonished to see the amount of room, convenience etc., provided by this misrepresented steamer. She contains an elegantly furnished saloon and a spacious lower deck; the saloon itself would contain a nice excursion party. There is a splendid clear upper deck the whole length of the vessel; this deck will be furnished with a strong railing and cushioned settings for about 200 people. A personal visit to the vessel will dispel all doubts as to her want of capacity."

One factor which suggests that this endorsement was something less than unsolicited is the fact that the May 24 holiday was but a week distant and the *Isabel*, like most steamers of her day, hoped to cash

(Above Left) Upon Captain Stamp's obtaining a court order for the Moneta's seizure, High Sheriff A.C. Elliott sailed aboard the Isabel *for Hastings Mill. But he returned empty-handed when the Moneta's master, "though an Englishman, used the most unbecoming language." When Elliot attempted to take the Moneta by storm, her captain responded with considerably more than unbecoming language, one of Elliott's deputies having to be hospitalized when wounded with a red-hot iron. (Right) Coal baron Robert Dunsmuir bought the aging liner-freighter-tugboat in December of 1888. During the trial trip to Comox the old workhorse attained her old-time record of nine knots. She was then 22-years-old and approaching the end of her career.*

(Below) Hastings Mill. Here, Captain Tom Pamphlett, master of the tugboat Isabel, *rescued the merchant vessel* Moneta *from destruction by fire — by driving her onto the beach.*

British bark *Moneta* anchored off the Burrard Inlet sawmill community of Hastings Mill to load lumber. All proceeded as usual until the next morning when a crewman detected smoke. His cry sent the crew running to their emergency stations, ripping off hatch covers and manning the pumps. The seamen battled heroically but Captain William Turpin realized almost immediately that the flames were spreading throughout his ship.

It was at this providential moment that the *Isabel* steamed into view with the French bark *Deux Jules* in tow. Captain Tom Pamphlett assessed the *Moneta*'s danger in an instant. Bawling orders for his men to cut the towline, he wheeled the *Isabel* toward the helpless Briton. Minutes latter he had his line secured as the *Moneta*'s crew struggled to raise anchor. This accomplished, Pamphlett towed the freighter toward the nearest beach—where she came to a shuddering halt on the rocks.

Seams ruptured, the *Moneta* flooded in minutes. Although it seems to have been a drastic course of action it was effective. As Captain Pamphlett had planned the blaze was extinguished!

But if Captain Turpin was less than happy with his savior's methods he was even sadder when he received owner Stamp's bill.

"Ten thousand dollars!" he roared. "She's only worth $15,000!"

However, upon reflection, Turpin grudgingly offered $2,500. But Stamp was adamant: $10,000 or he seized the ship. When Turpin ignored his ultimatum, he obtained a court order authorizing High Sheriff A.C. Elliott to seize the *Moneta*, and that official dutifully hastened to Burrard Inlet. He returned empty-handed, Turpin, "though an Englishman, (having) used the most unbecoming language."

The disrespectful Briton had, in fact, threatened the sheriff with worse than words.

Undaunted, Elliott headed back to Hastings Mill aboard the *Isabel* with reinforcements. Upon arrival, he was shocked to notice that the *Moneta*, despite her injuries, was gone and, ordering *Isabel* about, Elliott charged across the Gulf of Georgia in search of his rude prey. He found the *Moneta* limping through Porlier Pass, two and a half miles from shore. Pulling alongside, Elliott hailed Turpin to surrender his ship.

In wide-eyed innocence, that mariner shouted back that Elliott had no jurisdiction and that he could not board. When the marshal continued to make arrangements to seize his ship, fiery Captain Turpin bellowed, "Now, boys, come on, defend the ship, allow no man to come on board!"

Brandishing an evil looking sword over his head, the crusty skipper exhorted, "Knock any man down who attempts to come on board," and attacked.

Said the Victoria *Colonist*: "There was then a general howl, *every* man calling out, 'Down with the damned piratical rascals!' They were all armed with

Towboating was a precarious business a century ago, as the stranded tugboat Lorne *and her tow illustrate here. The* Isabel *was not immune to trouble either, as she clearly showed in March of 1868 when two sailing vessels she was towing were stranded on Discovery Island.*

in on the popular excursions to San Juan Island. Came the holiday, hotel proprietor Nicholas Bailey had the refreshment concession aboard her. For between 25 and 50 cents relaxing Victorians could enjoy a delicious lunch complete with ice cream. For the men, Mr. Bailey had stocked an adequate supply of the "best wines, ales, liquors and segars."

Then it was back to towing as the *Isabel* hauled the lumber ship *Australind* from Burrard Inlet to Cape Flattery.

By November of 1867, Captain Stamp was again casting a hungry eye at the California trade, then the monopoly of the California, Oregon and Mexico Steamship Company. He approached colonial authorities for a subsidy of $750 per voyage, two-thirds of which would be paid by the colony, the balance by the Admiralty. During negotiations, the *Isabel* continued at the task of towboating.

Captain Stamp's application seems to have failed for the record makes no mention of the *Isabel* heading for southern ports. When next the sturdy sidewheeler made the news, she was the lady of the hour—an honor she was soon to regret!

This raucous chapter in provincial maritime lore began early in June of the following year when the handspikes, harpoons, swords, and other like weapons, and every man had a quantity of ground pepper in his hands which was liberally bestowed on those who attempted to board the vessel. Some blew horns, others yelled, and as it was afterwards proved, not a few were armed with iron weapons red hot, with which they wounded both Mr. Elliott and Officer McMillan, one of the party of the *Isabel*."

Heroic Elliott had been the first over the side, four officers at his heels, when a thrust from a heated weapon seriously injured McMillan in the chest and fellow officer Stephens dragged him to safety. Immediately upon landing on deck, Elliott had had his warrant torn from his hands and thrown over the side. This unfriendly gesture had been followed by a lunge with a red-hot pitch-fork which burned him on the hand.

But, already, the battle was almost ended and, officers entrenched on her bloody deck, *Moneta* was impounded, her sails furled. *Isabel* then towed her to Esquimalt.

"Amongst the most determined defenders of the *Moneta*," reported the *Colonist*, "was Susannah, the maid in attendance on the captain's wife, who brandished a pair of rusty tongs over her head, and loudly exclaimed she would brain any man who dared come on board the ship. And to prove she was in earnest, she applied the tongs with great force to the shins of the unfortunate marshal, who yelled loudly from the pain produced by so formidable a weapon."

Bruised but victorious, Elliott and company returned to Victoria. Captain Turpin and his crew remained in Esquimalt, in navy cells. Officer McMillan had needed intensive medical treatment before he was pronounced to be in satisfactory condition.

Finally hauled into Admiralty Court, a grinning Captain Turpin joyously heard Justice Joseph Needham award Captain Stamp only $1,000 — less than half the sum that Turpin had offered in the first place, and a quarter of which was to be paid to the *Isabel*'s crew. However, in observance of the *Moneta*'s poor manners, Needham assessed Captain Turpin costs.

March of 1868 brought yet more action to the busy steamer. She had been towing the Hawaiian bark *Rosalia*, laden with 150,000 tons of lumber, from Burrard Inlet when she encountered the 900-ton British ship *Fanny* and took her in tow also. The little convoy proceeded steadily across the Gulf of Georgia as far as the San Juans when caught in a sou'easter. Within minutes, all three ships were in trouble.

Before long the *Rosalia*'s hawser parted and she drifted astern until 5 o'clock the next morning when she struck on Discovery Island. The *Fanny* had continued for a time with the *Isabel* when her cable also parted and, before sail could be set, she too was driven onto Discovery Island.

"Both vessels," it was reported, "beat heavily all night long. The *Rosalia*, lying on the southerly side of the island, was exposed to the full sweep of the wind, and before day dawned her bottom was knocked completely out. The position of the *Fanny* is on the easterly side of the island and less exposed, but owing to her heavy cargo she soon settled down on the rocks and was full of water before the captain and crew left her. All hands landed in the ship's boats."

In one disastrous night, Captain Pamphlett had lost two charges, the *Rosalia* being a total wreck, the *Fanny* severely injured. This regrettable turn of events not unnaturally led to another appearance in Admiralty Court for owner Stamp, the *Rosalia*'s owners claiming $20,000. The case took more than a month, the court finally ruling that the *Rosalia* had been victim of "want of seaman-like skill on the part of (her) captain."

Isabel then returned to towboating until October of 1869 when she stranded in English Bay after striking Ninepin Rock in dense fog. Refloated without serious injury, she was patched up at Burrard Inlet, her scarred bottom being properly repaired in Victoria two months later.

The busy sidewheeler was then sold to the Starr Brothers of Puget Sound who ran her between Victoria and Port Townsend, connecting with the Oregon Steamer *Alida* twice weekly with mail and passengers. When the new service proved to be popular the Starrs had her passenger facilities opulently refurbished.

It seemed like old times in September of 1870 when *Isabel* raced the *Eliza Anderson* from Victoria. As in her contest with the *Enterprise*, *Isabel* had beaten her opponent to the punch by slipping her lines first. By the time the *Anderson* boiled past what is now Fishermen's Wharf, *Isabel* had rounded Ogden Point, leaving only "a long streak of black smoke to mark her progress."

Fascinated spectators watched the bucking steamers until they rounded Beacon Hill Park. When last seen Captain E.A. Starr was increasing his lead with "space-devouring strides."

Isabel ran steadily between Victoria and Puget Sound, with an occasional voyage to Nanaimo, and behaved for the most part respectably and without incident. In August of 1871, she enjoyed a moonlight excursion to Esquimalt with a happy company of 200 Victorians. At the naval base they enjoyed dancing to the band of HMS *Zealous* then returned to town.

The occasion had almost been marred by tragedy when William Crockford, perhaps more relaxed than his companions, fell overboard at the pier. But Crockford "struck out manfully" and reached the wharf where eager hands soon hauled him to safety.

Then it was back to towboating, the *Isabel* hauling the collier *Remijio* from Nanaimo to Flattery. With 1874 she joined the booming Cassiar gold rush trade, hustling miners and freight to Stikine River

Two different views of Hastings Mill.

before returning to her familiar Puget Sound run.

Later that year the Starrs had her completely overhauled, her machinery being rebuilt and her passenger capacity increased to enter the Alaskan trade. Six months after, while towing the bark *Empress Eugenie* off Discovery Island, the scene of her disaster with the *Fanny* and *Rosalia* six years before, she ran aground and stuck fast, stranding the *Eugenie* at the same time. The tug *Grappler* succeeded in floating the bark then effected *Isabel*'s release. She was no sooner freed than Captain Dan Morrison went below to survey her damage — when she again grounded in the narrow passage.

This time he took no chances and transferred his cargo to the *Grappler*. Lightened, the *Isabel* floated free and returned to port, blushing, although Morrison blamed the misfortune on Pilot McKinnon.

May of 1876 brought her owners a suit for $7,544.85, the owners of the ship *Grace Darling* having charged the *Isabel* with having towed their carrier from Departure Bay the previous November — right over a reef. It took the Hon. Sir Matthew Baillie Begbie and a Royal Navy assessor but two days to dismiss the case, decreeing that the *Darling*'s

officers had contributed to the mishap through their negligence.

There were many other voyages in following years, the *Isabel* experiencing the frigid, foggy waters of Alaska and the bustling marine highways between Victoria and New Westminster and Puget Sound. But, by 1888, she was nearing the end of her career. The Starr brothers finally laid her up at Gig Harbor when their new ship the *North Pacific* was delivered from the builders.

In December, 1888, the gallant old liner-freighter-tugboat and "pirate" was purchased by coal baron Robert Dunsmuir. During the trial trip to Comox the aging workhorse attained her old-time record of nine knots.

She continued as a passenger liner between British Columbia ports for eight more years until she was replaced by the new steamer *Joan*. In 1894 she was reduced to the ignominious but useful role of floating plant and quarters for fishermen, her powerful engines having been removed. Two years later she was converted into a steam barge.

In 1898 the ancient laborer was towed back to Esquimalt Harbor and left to rot on the beach. ●

John "Jack" Fannin

Jack Fannin's pioneer efforts have resulted in Victoria's recently opened $10 million museum-archives complex. In the new museum (opposite page) each wildlife diorama alone occupies more space than the entire area of his first provincial museum.

JACK FANNIN

Pioneer Extraordinaire

John "Jack" Fannin, first curator, and virtually creator, of the British Columbia Provincial Museum, was a remarkable public servant. Few who knew the stocky, white-bearded figure with the braying laugh and twinkling eye realized he had once survived one of the most terrifying ordeals in British Columbia history. . .

"HE was fond of the woods, and the mountains, liked to fish, hunt and all that kind of thing," said one who knew him well. It is a simple epitaph for a complex man who excelled as natural historian, adventurer, explorer, surveyor, shoemaker, miner, musician, author, poet, prophet, composer —and great Canadian.

Little is known of Jack Fannin's early years beyond the fact that he was born July 27, 1837, in the Ontario hamlet of Kemptville. It is apparent, however, that young Jack grew up in the dense woods surrounding his little community. As he grew older, every tree, stream and blade of grass became a source of constant wonder and study. Plant, animal, insect and mineral: Jack watched and marvelled at all of Mother Nature's mysteries.

Another fact known in later years was that Jack's passion for the outdoors caused his school work to suffer, for he was compelled to begin again. He taught himself all that he had missed in class and considerably more; and he even obtained a position as school teacher.

In 1862, when the strapping young woodsman was 25, he heard wondrous tales of a gold strike in the Cariboo district of faraway British Columbia. When hundreds of people, including many of his neighbors, threw down ploughs and axes to follow the rainbow, Jack decided to join them. Thus he became a veteran of the fabled "Overlanders," qualifying for this select company by doing just that—hiking from Winnipeg to British Columbia.

After six months of unspeakable hardship, Fannin's party stumbled into Fort Kamloops. In Red River carts, on horseback, afoot, and on flimsy rafts, they had battled 1,000 miles of prairie, swamp, mountain and murderous river rapids.

For the next 12 years he labored with pick, pan and sluicebox throughout much of the province without success. Disheartened at last, he turned to the less exciting but more rewarding trade of shoe-

maker at New Westminster until, because of his experience as a prospector, he obtained a job with the provincial government and became head of the surveys department.

His first major assignment as surveyor was no less than "ascertaining the character and area of unoccupied lands in the valley of the Lower Fraser (River)." With characteristic vigor, he undertook the huge task. The enthusiastic report he sent back came to the attention of Victoria's daily paper, the *Colonist*. As the paper commented, the report is "so highly readable that we are induced to place considerable portions of it before our readers.

"It is so much out of the dry and trodden track of official reports that we must congratulate its author upon the success with which useful information is conveyed in a popular form."

Jack's prowess with pen, and his power of prophecy, are vividly illustrated in the following excerpt in which he describes the panoramic view of the Lower Fraser:

"Every settlement along the river can be readily seen through its windings 80 miles to the gulf, and looks still and motionless in the distance. New Westminster can be seen with the naked eye, and every settlement along the river can be readily distinguished. Sumas and Chilliwack, the former 17, the latter 12 miles away, appear almost at our feet.

"Here also can be seen in the country between Chilliwack and Cheam new openings made by recent settlers, looking upon which as new signs of awakening prosperity the imagination wanders into the future, when this green plain shall be dotted with herds and the tangled growth of forest which now covers the virgin soil of the uplands shall yield to the hand of hardy industry and fields of waving corn shall take its place; when the eye from this spot will rest on many a hamlet and the sound of human voices and human industry will fill the space where

now is silence and solitude.

"Fanciful as this picture may seem, and I have no doubt those whose experience have never led them beyond the beaten lines of travel through this district may think it very fanciful indeed, yet it is not only possible for this state of things to come about, but the time is not so dimly marked in the future when this very picture will become a living reality. For it can scarcely be consistent with the natural course of events that this beautiful valley will remain long, as it is, a comparative wilderness while so many of our fellow beings are struggling for a miserable existence in crowded homes of the Old World."

When next the *Colonist* had occasion to praise Jack Fannin, it was with blood-chilling headlines: *Amid the frosts of Stickeen! Horrible sufferings of the government explorers! Cold, hunger and grim death on every side!*

The story behind these headlines is one of incredible hardship and raw courage—typically Jack Fannin.

In October of 1874, the government dispatched Jack to explore the headwaters of Stikine River for signs of gold. Four months later, he and French Canadian George Florrence were brought, near death, into Wrangell by an Indian who had found them. Their story, as told by Jack's diary, is one of sheer terror.

Twice the surveyors attempted to beat upriver with supplies. The first time, their Indian boatmen turned back after encountering thick ice. The second canoe attempt was defeated by the same obstacle. Retreating to Wrangell, Jack decided to await a complete freeze and try again on foot.

On December 5, "having positive information that the ice had formed, and that travelling between the mouth of the river and the Boundary Post was safe, and hoping to get over that part of the journey before the heavy fall of snow," Jack and Florrence started out. They estimated the 60-mile trek would take four days and, to be safe, they packed eight days' grub. Their journey was to last three weeks!

Soon after leaving the mouth of the Stikine, the explorers encountered the worst storm of Jack's life. For 15 days it continued with scarcely an hour's intermission: snow, rain and hail, accompanied by a wind so penetrating that there were moments it was utterly impossible to face it. During all this time they travelled with heads bent forward, one following in the tracks of the other, their snowshoes sinking a foot at every step.

On the twelfth day their grub gave out but, on that day, there was a lull in the storm. The fog and mist which accompanied it lifted above the mountain peaks and showed them their whereabouts. They were still a few miles below the "Ice Mountain," scarcely halfway and their provisions gone!

The men faced each other in mute horror. When finally he was able to speak, Florrence suggested retreat. They looked back over the glittering waste of snow through which it had taken 12 days to walk and Fannin, shaking his head, refused to attempt it, but proposed to abandon everything—sleds and blankets—and push on to the Post.

Keeping only an axe, they began the mad race against certain death. That night they spent ceaselessly marching about their campfire to keep warm. Then, with morning, they pressed onward once more, to encounter new—and grimmer—obstacles.

Broken ice meant wading through frigid water or constructing crude pole bridges and the shivering adventurers became weaker with every step. Somehow they pushed on, "weak and exhausted, making little headway till the morning of the third day since leaving their blankets, when shortly after starting they came to a point where further travel was blocked."

The river was open from bank to bank with high and perpendicular bluffs on either side. Their position was grim. They could go no farther. Florrence, taking Fannin by the arm and pointing down the river, said: "We will go back to our blankets and have a good sleep." Faint and perishing from hunger, they commenced retracing their steps.

By nightfall, Florrence could hardly stand. His desire to lie down in the snow and sleep was overpowering. All through that lonely, haunted night, Jack talked to his comrade—talked and talked and talked until his tongue was swollen and stiff—anything to keep Florrence awake. During this nightmare, Florrence collapsed in their campfire but was hauled to safety without harm.

The next day, while they were travelling by an open slough, Florrence stopped suddenly. Taking off his snowshoes, he plunged into the water, returning almost immediately with a salmon grasped so tightly that his fingers met through the quivering flesh.

This tiny windfall lasted five days, Fannin rationing every scrap—fins, gills, bones and all. Finally reaching their abandoned sleds, they took one blanket apiece and staggered blindly downriver. On Christmas Day they were within five miles of Wrangell but were stopped by open water. With precious axe and benumbed fingers, they constructed a flimsy raft, finishing at dusk. Unable to wait for dawn, they set off in the darkness and had gone about a mile when they struck a rock and Jack was pitched into the river. Miraculously, he scrambled back aboard.

Now they had to land and build a fire so that he could dry out. The next day they set to work building a sturdier raft, again finishing at dusk. They were just about to shove off when an Indian in a canoe chanced along. The awed savior rushed his grotesque wards to Wrangell where Florrence "became delirious and had to be taken in charge by his friends."

Thus ended five bitter days "without eating

New Westminster where John Fannin, first curator and virtual creator of the British Columbia Provincial Museum, worked as a shoemaker.

anything and five nights without blankets in the middle of an almost Arctic winter." A week later, Jack Fannin and a fresh party "started back fully equipped to have it out with the elements."

In 1877, Jack had retired once again to the less rigorous trade of custom shoemaker at Hastings on Burrard Inlet (now Vancouver). Between shoemaking assignments, he indulged in his life-long passion for natural history by adding the art of taxidermy to an already impressive list of accomplishments. The bearded bachelor in the little shop crowded with bird, fish and mammal specimens became a favorite of neighborhood children who haunted his cluttered quarters in hopes of having him sing, entertain with his organ or cornet, or tell a fascinating tale of woodlore. On other occasions he led crab-spearing excursions and nature hikes about the area.

Also during this period he became internationally known as a big game hunter and guide. Then, in August of 1886, he eagerly accepted the post of curator of the newly-founded provincial museum in Victoria. To start the museum off properly, he donated his entire collection of prize specimens.

October 25, 1887, was a special occasion in his busy career. That day marked the official opening of the new museum in a little 15x20-foot room adjoining the provincial secretary's office in the main building of the famous "birdcages," the nickname given to British Columbia's original, wooden parlia-

ment buildings. Here Jack collected, assorted and preserved the flora and fauna of the province.

"So limited was the space here," wrote a colleague, "that when the black wolf, which is still a treasured specimen of the museum, was brought to Mr. Fannin he had to take it home to his own house and mount it in an empty room, where I can remember going to see it in the course of preparation."

Within three years he had outgrown his cluttered office several times over. When the new courthouse was completed in Bastion Square, the delighted curator moved, lock, stock and specimen, into the vacated James Bay courthouse. During this time he helped several prominent citizens form the Natural History Society to "assist in collecting and preserving natural objects for the provincial museum."

Society field trips were frequent, its prosperous members hiring a steamer and dredging for "deep sea shells and other specimens," to name but one project. Over the years the little museum's collections of butterflies, moths, shells, fossils, plants and mosses were increased extensively, classified and catalogued.

Of this phase Mr. Fannin's colleague wrote: "From the time that the museum was moved into the old courts of justice, the collections grew so fast and specimens multiplied so rapidly that the curator had literally both hands full. Mr. Fannin mounted almost all the large animals before going into the

The Legislative Buildings, Victoria. Known as the "Birdcages," they were the original, wooden parliament buildings. On October 25, 1887, British Columbia's first provincial museum was formally opened in a little 15 × 20-foot room adjoining the provincial secretary's office in the main "Birdcage." "So limited was the space here," wrote a friend of Fannin, "that when the black wolf, which is still a treasured specimen of the museum, was brought to Mr. Fannin he had to take it home to his house and mount it in an empty room, where I can remember going to see it in the course of preparation. . . ."

new buildings, and the collection of large mammals is very nearly complete and will always remain a lasting memorial to his skills as a naturalist and taxidermist...

"The beautiful cases of animals and birds in their natural habitats are also due to Mr. Fannin's artistic skill and painstaking care."

In 1898 the bulging museum, by then world-renowned as excellent for its size, was again moved, this time to the east wing of the present-day Parliament Buildings. On opening day, May 24, 1898, H.D. Helmcken, MPP, presented the proud curator with a beautiful pipe in appreciation of his immense work. Several years before, the government had sent him on a tour of American and European museums.

But Jack was reaching the end of the trail. After so many years of dedicated work, so many adventures, so much activity, he was stricken with illness and for his last years was a semi-invalid. Yet he did not retire until February 23, 1904. Jack Fannin, grand old man of British Columbia's vast outdoors, died four months later. He was 66.

"In the death of John Fannin, late curator of the provincial museum," said the Victoria *Daily Times*, "British Columbia lost not only one of the best known of her pioneers but one whose life's work will go down to posterity as among the most useful and conspicuous in the history of this century.

"A love of hunting, adventure, the insatiable craving of the man to study nature's laws, particularly as seen in animal life, a rare intelligence for comprehending things, and an artistic faculty for imitating them, were but some of the chief characteristics of the deceased. But this is not all that makes the memory of the late Mr. Fannin so fresh in the minds of many surviving him. He has left behind monuments to his skill and energy which can never be disassociated with the history of the pioneer days of B.C."

Many Victorians mourned the old man in white beard whom they had seen so many times, standing like a statue near Beacon Hill Park, listening intently to robins singing, or watching them flit from branch to branch as his jovial face beamed with the joy of an ever-new discovery. Others recalled his "air-cleaving" laugh which, "once heard, could be recognized from the Rocky Mountains to the Coast."

A quarter of a century later, the Geographic Board of Canada acknowledged Jack's enormous contribution to posterity by naming after him a lake, a creek and a group of mountains near Burrard Inlet. In northern British Columbia an intermediate subspecies of the stone sheep was named "Ovis Fannini" after him. But probably the most satisfactory development to Jack Fannin is the fact that the collection he started in a 15x20-room has grown into a magnificent, multi-million-dollar museum that annually attracts hundreds of thousands of visitors. ●

VANCOUVER ISLAND'S SKELETON CAVE

The late Tom Ilstad of Quatsino, discovered the cave with its gruesome mystery.

According to the hunters, the remains of no fewer than 35 men, women and children littered the cavern floor. One expert who examined a skull stated that its owner had been white, young and murdered.

A Skeleton story with an air of mystery, one writer has termed Raft Cove's collection of bones.

Situated between Kyuquot and Cape Cook on the west coast of Vancouver Island, about 14 miles southwest of Quatsino, the little cove is accessible only in favorable weather at high tide, or by hiking overland through dense wilderness. Not unnaturally, the inlet has few visitors.

But its story of a cave filled with human remains has popped up more than once during the three-quarters of a century since it was discovered by two Quatsino pioneers. Although a check with the appropriate authorities would seem to indicate that there is no real mystery—and never was one in the first place—several intriguing questions remain unanswered.

It was back in the spring of 1905 that Tom Ilstad and Philip Nordstrom stumbled upon the lonely cavern while hunting a wounded cougar. Said to be as "wild and desolate a bit of country as a man could find himself in," this stretch of coast is a jungle of 12-foot-high salal and devil's club, and the hunters had to follow their prey on hands and knees. For some time, they threaded their way through the maze of growth, when they suddenly found themselves crouching before the entrance to a cave.

Stepping gingerly into the cliffside, they waited for their eyes to adjust to the gloom. When they were able to see, they were astonished to note that the mud floor was littered with human bones.

Promptly forgetting their cougar, Ilstad and Nordstrom lit a fire and examined their find. After some examination, Ilstad, who was widely known for his extensive private library, estimated that the 40-foot-long cave contained the remains of no fewer than 35 men, women and children. Both men were familiar with the practice of Pacific Northwest Indians who disposed of their dead in sea caves, and that should have been the obvious answer to their find at isolated Raft Cove.

But, observed Ilstad, the skulls did not resemble those of Indians and the teeth were not ground flat through the abrasion of sand in food; a common condition with aboriginal remains. Whatever the nationality or origin of the cave's occupants, they had been there for a long time, as the bones showed signs of being encrusted with limestone crystals.

Before leaving the cave to its ghostly inhabitants, the men gathered up four skulls. Then they returned to Quatsino, where they showed their grim souvenirs to Carl Christensen, the local schoolteacher. Christensen, sharing their intrigue, suggested that they send one of the skulls to Dr. C.F. Newcombe in Victoria. There, the famous anthropologist and Indian expert supposedly pronounced the skull to be that of a Caucasian male. About 19- or 20-years old at the time of his

death, the anonymous youth had died from an axe blow to the head.

In the meantime, Ilstad had asked Quatsino residents if they knew of the cave at Raft Cove. Much to his surprise, neither Indian nor white had ever visited or even heard of it, let alone knew its secret.

And that, for 60 years, was the end of the story. Several had conjectured as to the identities of the 35 men, women and children, but early records of shipwreck along this dangerous stretch of shore failed to suggest who they were, how they died, or when they were entombed in the cave.

Fifteen years ago the late Guy Ilstad, son of the cave's co-discoverer, reported that, to his knowledge, the skeletons were there yet. Familiar with the story, he said, "I think there can be little doubt that *if* they were whites, it was the work of Indians, who murdered some shipwrecked people and then put the bodies in the cave to hide the crime. And if they are the skeletons of women and children it would help date the time of the kill because the Spaniards had neither women nor children with them when they were on this coast."

In 1938, he continued, another visitor to the cave found the skeletons were "only a scattered jumble of bones, with not a single skull left," these having been carried off by a settler. Mr. Ilstad, however, did not think that the skeletons were those of whites, stating that a skull had been "sent for examination in 1905 and. . .they reported it was Indian, although of course it's risky for me to hark back almost 60 years. Besides, at that time, I was not interested in anthropology."

Rather, his interest in his father's gruesome curio was in rigging it on a "make-shift ghost" and setting it up in his sister's bedroom. Unfortunately, he chuckled, he underestimated the power of a woman as, if he succeeded in scaring her, he never learned. His sister tossed "skull, white sheet and all out of the upstairs window!"

Returning to the possible origin of the skeletons, Mr. Ilstad marvelled that, in all of his years on the north-western coast of Vancouver Island, he had never seen an Indian village site that lacked protection from the open sea, where canoes could be launched: "Since the natives derived their living from the sea, it is rather obvious that they'd never select a place where they couldn't launch a craft for weeks on end because of winter storms.

"What I mean is that there couldn't have been an Indian village in Raft Cove. Nor is there any sign that there was. These sites are revealed by a pile of clam shells. In the Quatsino village the clam shells are over 10 feet in depth. So it makes one wonder why 35 persons would be assembled in such a remote and very unlikely place for a native village.

(Opposite page) Could this crumbling totem pole near Quatsino tell the secret of the "Skeleton Cave?"

"And if the victims were killed elsewhere it would mean a fairly calm day with high tide to convey the bodies to the cave... There is no decent shelter for miles around Raft Cove, and the cove itself cannot be entered except at high tide—and in good weather."

Adding further to the mystery is the reputed discovery, in 1917, of an 80-foot-long oak keel which was observed, half-buried in the sandbar in Raft Cove, by a timber cruiser of Mr. Ilstad's acquaintance.

Did the broken keel have any connection with the bodies in the cave? As the most likely source that Messrs. Ilstad and Christensen would have contacted was the Smithsonian Institution in Washington, D.C., that museum's division of physical anthropology was queried in 1964. In his reply, Curator J. Lawrence Angel stated that "...The specimens in our collection which most closely fit the description in your letter are two skulls which, according to our files, were collected by Mr. H.O. Bergh (onetime Quatsino postmaster) in the neighborhood of Quatsino, B.C., and presented to this museum through Dr. A.K. Fisher of the Biological Survey. The specimens were received here on Oct. 21, 1905.

"One of the skulls is an adult, probably female, and the other is a child about eight years old. Neither one of them shows any signs of violence or injury which could have resulted in death. They are both covered with stalagmite, which would seem to corroborate the story that they were found in a cave. These two individuals are not Caucasians, however, and their skulls show definite Mongoloid features. Although there is a remote chance that they were shipwrecked Japanese, it is more reasonable to assume that they were Indians native to the area."

And, unfortunately, there the trail ends; it being impossible at this late date even to state definitely that the two skulls in possession of the Smithsonian came from the cave at Raft Cove. And no existing records of shipwreck shed any light on the identity of the wreck that the timber cruiser saw there in 1917.

Half a century after his father's discovery, Guy Ilstad found his own "skeleton cave" in this desolate region. While exploring a cave, he discovered a human thigh bone, in good condition, beside the remains of an old fire. He carried the bone to his home, but later discarded it. Asked if he had any theory as to its origin, he replied that he thought it to be the remains of an American airman who survived the crash of a United States Navy PBY during the Second World War. The plane crashed about six mile south of the cave and, when found, contained the remains of all of its crew but one, who had covered his comrades with wreckage, then tried to hike out. He was never found and Mr. Ilstad conjectured that his lonely ordeal ended in the little cave that he visited in 1955.

Just one more unsolved mystery from British Columbia's colorful past. ●

(Above) Nanaimo. Days after paddling from Victoria, the Homfray expedition passed the coal mining settlement and made their final camp before crossing the Gulf of Georgia. Halfway across the Gulf, "It began to blow, and it looked as if a severe storm would overtake us before we could reach the opposite side... Several whales crossed our bow, which frightened us very much. Our canoe was often buried in the waves; however, we finally succeeded in reaching the opposite shore, our canoe leaking badly."

*"Presently we heard a loud war-whoop
sounding along the water. Our death
seemed now certain; a cold perspiration
came over me. Neither of us spoke. A
short time later another war-whoop
sounded, louder and longer than before.
We resigned ourselves to our fate. . . ."*

*(Below) From this dock, in 1861, Robert Homfray and
six companions set out for the unknown of Bute
Inlet. Upon their eventual return to Victoria, they
landed on the same wharf where they were met by Alfred
Waddington, who expressed amazement at their
ragged and half-starved condition.*

A WINTER JOURNEY IN 1861

FOR more than 30 years, Robert Homfray refused to publish his account of a dangerous surveying expedition to the Cariboo in 1861.

Finally, in 1894, at the insistence of his friends, he agreed to tell of this epic "winter journey (of) 1861," when he and six others had braved innumerable hardships in an attempt to survey a new, shorter route to the gold fields of the Interior by way of Bute Inlet.

Commissioned in Victoria by the Hudson's Bay Company, Homfray had agreed to take charge of the expedition despite the warnings of many who were convinced that he would never return alive. His friends, in fact, had been quite explicit, arguing that "it was madness to attempt it in the middle of such a severe winter.

"They also pointed out the great danger of navigating the Gulf of Georgia for so long a distance in a frail canoe, on to the head of Bute Inlet, up an unknown river, and through an unknown country, among mountains covered with snow, surrounded by fierce and savage tribes who had never seen a white man; besides the great risk of being buried under avalanches, attacked by hungry wolves; not to mention the ever-to-be-dreaded grizzly, with the off-chance of perishing miserably in the snow from starvation and exposure…"

As Homfray admitted with a smile, so long after, such advice did little to cheer him. But the challenge of "new and strange sights" and the fortunate possession of "a fair amount of courage" were sufficient to over-ride the most strenuous of objections and he looked forward to the adventure.

(Any question as to the secretary of the Philharmonic Society's courage had been answered several months earlier, when he had surprised two burglars attempting to break into his home in Trounce Alley. Upon Homfray's answering their call with a cocked six-shooter, the men had fled into the night).

Throughout the voyage by canoe to Bute Inlet, Homfray's aide, Cote, would be in command, Homfray acting as "captain" when ashore. Described as the HBC's best French Canadian voyageur and recognized as an expert with a canoe, Cote brought with him two other voyageurs, Balthazzar and Bourchier, a man named Harry McNeill and two Indians. As they would be travelling light, their outfit consisted of one canoe, two tents, two muskets and ammunition (a curiously small arsenal under the circumstances), and some beads and trinkets for trade. Each man was allotted two blankets, two axes, a hatchet, a spade and a small supply of provisions.

Their personal outfits had been kept to a minimum also, as all would have to be back-packed when they encountered snow.

When all was ready, they paddled from Fort Victoria on a fair October morning and made good time before putting in to shore to camp for the night. Upon getting underway early the next morning, they encountered heavy seas which opened the seams of their canoe and necessitated repairs; a routine of buffeting and patching which would become a ritual by the time they reached Bute Inlet.

After days of paddling against wind and tide, they passed Nanaimo and reached their final camp before crossing the Gulf of Georgia. With a night's rest they prepared to sail, Homfray noting in his journal that the morning "was fine, although the appearance of the Gulf was far from encouraging. When we were nearly half-way across it began to blow, and it looked as if a severe storm would overtake us before we could reach the opposite side... Several whales crossed our bow, which frightened us very much. Our canoe was often buried in the waves; however, we finally succeeded in reaching the opposite shore, our canoe leaking badly."

Nine days from Victoria, the weary adventurers reached Bute Inlet, having survived near-disaster during one violent gale. Here, the wind rushed through the fjord-like inlet with hurricane force and with the terrifying "roar of a cataract." Adding to this awesome symphony was the continuous rumbling of one avalance after another as the mountains shed their snowy capes.

Yet for all of Bute Inlet's rugged majesty they were not alone, as they came upon a party of Indians who were transporting a cargo of dried salmon in four canoes which they had lashed together with poles. Immediately upon sighting the strangers, the natives pulled for shore where, having landed their women and children, they paddled in pursuit, muskets levelled.

"Very greatly alarmed," Homfray instructed his two Indian packers to signal the others not to fire. After several long and tense moments they succeeded in assuring the fishermen that they were peaceable, when the others lowered their muskets and accepted small peace offerings in the form of some trinkets.

"Next day we saw a large canoe coming directly at us from a dark chasm in the mountains across the inlet, paddling hard. We regarded it with suspicion, and as the canoe came near us, Cote called out to McNeill, 'Down with the sail! Down with the sail!' "

Cote's abrupt command so unnerved one of their Indians, seated behind Homfray, that he fired his musket into the air and almost upset the canoe when the others, thinking themselves under attack from the rear, wheeled about.

Within minutes the strange craft, occupied by six half-naked Indians, all of whom were armed with muskets, came alongside. One of the grim-faced natives boarded their craft and pointed to the "chasm in the mountains from which they had appeared, and made signs to us to paddle hard. None of us spoke but quietly resigned ourselves to certain death.

"As we came near to the shore there were deep mutterings among the half-naked Indians, and they picked up their muskets as they were just landing."

Convinced that they were about to be massacred, the captives waited in silence, when a "loud war-whoop" was sounded from across the water, then was repeated several times. Homfray immediately noticed a change come over his captors, the Indians seeming to be undecided as to what to do next and, looking behind him, he saw a tall, powerfully built Indian in a canoe. Waving his paddle in the air and yelling, the stranger approached rapidly, the prisoners taking advantage of the diversion to stand "shoulder to shoulder on the beach, determined to die together."

With both muskets empty, they did not stand a chance of escape and waited for the end when, to their amazement and relief, their captors leaped into their canoe and beat a hasty retreat as the newcomer landed. Introducing himself as chief of the powerful Cla-oosh tribe, he explained that the pirates belonged to a distant tribe which made their living by robbing and murdering the occupants of any canoe that fell into their hands.

The gracious chieftain then escorted his guests to the village where, "very weak and exhausted," they feasted upon mountain sheep, bear and beaver meat. In turn, they made him gifts of trinkets and inquired as to a pass through the mountains.

He admitted that there was such a route, but that it was deep in snow and ice at that time of year, and guarded by the ferocious grizzly bear.

Despite their courting with murder, the explorers were eager to push on and plied the chief with gifts and flattery until he agreed to show them the way and, in freezing weather, they proceeded inland. At the head of Bute Inlet, they camped upon the debris of an avalanche half a mile wide, then proceeded up the Homathko River. Far in the distance they could see a snow-capped peak where, said their guide, the river had cut its way through the mountains.

At a glacier nearby they dug a deep hole as a cache for some of their provisions for the return trip, covering it with logs, dirt and snow. They then headed upriver against fierce rapids, two men remaining aboard the frail craft and keeping it off the rocks with poles as the others struggled along the riverbank with a towline.

"At last we came to a great 'embassus' formed of drifted logs piled on top of each other by the winter floods, about 20 feet high and half a mile long, stretching across the river. The water surged between the logs with great velocity. We had a dangerous task to perform as we had to lift the canoe over (and) into the water on the other side.

"The logs were very slippery and covered with snow. Any misstep would have precipitated us into the raging torrent..."

Digging a pit in the snowdrifts, they pitched their tent inside where they were sheltered from the icy winds which shrieked across the glacier without pause: "The noise of the avalanches falling night and day were deafening. It snowed hard; wolf and bear tracks were constantly seen on the banks on both sides of the river."

When they pushed on they found the carcass of a grizzly being devoured by vultures, their progress being watched by black bears and wolves.

It was at this point that their saviour and guide urged them to turn back. After consultation, and having decided that "it would show great want of courage if we did not go on," they bade farewell to the chief, who headed downstream, all arguments to make him stay having failed. Onward and upward they went, poling and pulling their canoe through the rapids. Wading in the icy stream, they virtually wore the clothes from their backs. But still they pressed forward, Homfray's log noting the grandeur of the glistening mountaintops, mountain sheep and glaciers.

Time and again, they courted disaster in the rapids but, always, they escaped. At least they did not suffer for want of food, their two Indian hunters keeping the expedition well-stocked with mountain sheep, deer and the surprisingly delectable beaver. For that matter, the ever-present bear did not fare as well, having to rely upon nightly visits to the river in quest of salmon.

"The river was now full of rapids, 13 feet rise in 100 feet, and intensely cold. Then the tow rope snapped, sending the canoe shooting down the rapids like an arrow. We had great difficulty in recovering it. The men were almost lost, and we found it quite impossible to proceed any further in the canoe.

"We realized too late that we should have followed the Indian chief's advice and turned back with him. We could now see a great canyon in the distance where the river came through the Cascade Mountains, but how we were going to get there we could not say..."

Once again they resolved to push on. After burying their canoe in the snow and tying themselves together like mountain climbers, with sounding poles in hand, they forded the river several times in the course of a day, "as it was so crooked." Within seconds of leaving the water their drenched clothing would freeze solid, their beards and moustaches also freezing to the point that they could not open their mouths to speak. Now too weak to carry their tent, and carrying only a blanket each and some food, they forced themselves to clamber over boulders which were coated with ice and gave the appearance of enormous glass balls.

For mile after mile they struggled over glacier and mountain peak, their strength steadily failing. By this time all were aware of their danger as they must soon become exhausted. Their only hope, said Cote, lay in encountering some Indians—an ironic turnabout from their arrival at Bute Inlet, when they had camped without fires so as not to attract the attention of any hostiles.

The days passed, each man watching desperately for the least human sign. But always their only reward was yet another view of virgin snow and ice. And so it went, the surveyors laboring forward as their strength diminished until, upon rounding a point of rocks, an overjoyed Homfray spotted a fresh moccasin print in the snow.

"We kept close together in a single file," he wrote, "one musket in front and one in the rear. Suddenly we saw a tall, powerful Indian and his squaw standing on the river's edge, looking cautiously about, having evidently heard us."

Despite the cold the brave was almost naked, his body being protected from the frigid wind by no more than a coating of jet-black paint; an appearance made all the more ferocious by large vermillion-colored rings about his eyes. Immediately upon spotting the strangers the Indian shielded his wife with his own body and aimed his bow and arrow at them, as he danced up and down and warwhooped loudly.

At Cote's advice, the surveyors rested their heads upon their shoulders to show that they were tired and opened and closed their mouths to indicate they were hungry. Advancing all the while, they halted within several feet of the wary native when Homfray, "being not afraid...went slowly up to him. He immediately seized me in his arms, and I was helpless in his powerful embrace.

"Cote ran up, saying, 'Don't fear, sir, he shan't kill you.' The Indian then slackened his hold, lifted up my arms, looked into my mouth, examined my ears, to see if I were made like himself. He had evidently never seen a white man before…"

Upon satisfying himself that Homfray was indeed "made like himself," the native decided that they were friendly and pointed towards a canyon. After drawing a sketch in the snow with an arrow, he waved them on upriver. They followed his instructions and continued upstream, when several Indians suddenly appeared from "different holes in the ground, which startled us very much."

Also armed with bows and arrows, they repeated the first Indian's war dance and whooping, when one, apparently the chieftain, walked with dignified step towards the explorers. As he neared, covered all the while by his men, he turned and retraced his steps until he came to a bush, when he "hung something of a red color on a branch." At this Homfray and company took heart and moved cautiously forward.

Once again they were examined from head to foot, when their hosts invited them into their "holes." At first, the visitors were afraid to follow, sure that, once underground, they would be murdered. But upon realizing that they were in no condition to resist they entered the unusual homes.

However, no sooner had Homfray and Cote entered one of the lodges than the muffled explosion of a musket sent them running outside, Cote yelling that their companions were being slaughtered. Much to their relief it was but another false alarm, their trigger-happy Indian having again fired his musket while excited.

Although the shot terrified their hosts the incident was soon forgotten and Homfray and Cote again followed the chieftain "on our hands and knees into the underground den. It was a place about 10 feet square and about eight feet deep. When we got inside we saw a very old squaw and her daughter. They had a small fire burning."

When the explorers offered them their last piece of bread their hosts refused to touch it until Homfray ate a piece to show that it was not poisonous. The woman, apparently pleased by the gesture, then brought out a wooden bowl, which she held up before the fire to see if it were clean.

Dissatisfied, she spat into the dish several times and wiped it dry with her long, matted hair as an appalled Homfray watched in grim fascination. She then filled the dish with some evil-smelling concoction.

Upon observing his discomfort, Cote whispered that they must eat as the food was undoubtedly intended as the woman's finest offering, and to refuse would not only offend her but, quite likely, insult the whole tribe. Fortunately for the surveyors (who, but hours before, had been afraid of starving to death) the woman was almost blind and they were able to slip the contents of the dish to the dogs lying behind them. Smiling broadly, they rubbed their stomachs as a gesture of appreciation and indicated that they wished to sleep. Their amenable hosts immediately

Alfred Waddington, the man whose dream of a shortcut to the Cariboo was to end in massacre and tragedy. In 1861 Robert Homfray was commissioned by the Hudson's Bay Company to explore the possibility of carving a road to the Interior by way of Bute Inlet. Before the expedition left Victoria all of his friends had warned Homfray that "it was madness to attempt (the expedition) in the middle of such a severe winter." But Homfray and company survived hostile indians and all other hazards to return to Victoria where, in deference to Waddington, who "feared my descriptions of the many dangers encountered would prevent parties joining him in making the road through the Cariboo," he remained silent for 30 years.

turned in, unaware that, throughout the night, at least one of their guests kept watch over the camp.

With morning, Homfray inquired, by sign language, whether there was a trail through the mountains at that point. Much to his disappointment the Indians, by drawing in the snow, explained that the way was blocked for "many suns" by snow and that they should return by the way in which they had come. They could not ask the explorers to remain with them for the winter as they had barely enough provisions to feed themselves.

"So," mourned Homfray, "weary and footsore, with our clothes nearly worn out, we began our homeward journey. We hardly cared what befell us on the way, as it seemed impossible that we could reach the inlet alive…"

But, somehow, they made it downriver to where they had hidden their canoe and supplies. Launching the battered craft, they entered the rapids for a swift descent, time and again being threatened with capsizing before they were swept into the wrong channel and swamped, although without injury.

Despite this near-miss, Homfray's journal notes, the men were not immune to the wonders about them: "We were fortunate enough to witness a grand sight just after sunrise. On the opposite side of the river, nearly half a mile from us, we heard a

From the Cariboo came the golden wealth that attracted tens of thousands of adventurers from around the globe. But the original route, by way of Fraser River, was long and difficult particularly in winter. A shortcut via Bute Inlet would have cut the distance by a full third.

sharp crash followed by loud rumbling sounds high up on the mountain in full view. A large avalanche came thundering down with a frightful noise. The whole side of the mountain for fully a mile in length was in motion.

"Pine trees went down before it like a swath of mawn (sic) grass. It lasted several minutes, the ground sensibly shaking from the violence of the shock which sent enormous masses of rocks crashing down into the valley below. As soon as it was over, dense clouds of steamy vapor arose, caused by the heat from the friction of the immense boulders grinding against each other in their descent."

Minutes later, they swept around a bend in the river—and into a floating tree. Impaled on a branch, their canoe filled rapidly, the men having just enough time to clamber onto the trunk and rescue two tents, some blankets, part of a sack of flour, three iron pots, a musket—Homfray's notebook—their spade, and some matches. Thus marooned on their "raft," they had no choice but to wait until the tree drifted into the riverbank, when they discovered, to their horror, that their axes were still in the bow of the submerged canoe. Fortunately, they succeeded in salvaging the precious tools before the bottom of the craft fell out and plunged the rest of their equipment to the river bottom.

"The Indians were crying and beating rocks together, saying they would never see their children again. We were very thankful our lives were saved, but what was to become of us now, God only knew. It was a very long way to where the Indians lived on Desolation Sound, perhaps 90 miles further, with no other way of reaching them except by water. With our canoe lost, death seemed to stare us in the face…"

Converting their spade into a crude dish, they boiled some water to drink. They had no tea or coffee with which to give it flavor but it had to do. However, even this seemed to taste good, in their loneliness and cold, when, spirits somewhat revived, they decided to build a raft. Chopping down three trees, they tied them together with cedar bark and launched the float. Two of the logs promptly sank, the third being so waterlogged that it would hold only two men.

"Cote and one Indian volunteered to go on the raft; the rest of us had to wade through the deep snow along the riverbank. Cote said that the two on the raft might be lost, and those who walked on the bank might be saved."

Slowly, painfully, they made their way downstream, wading through the frigid water and clambering over deadfalls that were treacherous with ice.

All the while, they worried that Indians had found their last remaining food cache. Four days later, they found it intact, "at which we greatly rejoiced."

"We were now at the head of Bute Inlet, very weak from cold and exposure, our clothes continually freezing as we waded through the many streams. We were in hopes that we might see some Indians who would take us in their canoes, but there were none to be seen. All our hopes of safety had vanished. Our only hope was to cut down a tree, and on it float down the Inlet some 70 miles into Desolation Sound…"

With the wind blowing at hurricane force and constantly threatening to topple trees onto their camp, the worried explorers readied themselves for the final challenge—when they were attacked by 12 wolves. Retreating to their fire, they faced the growling, snapping horde by throwing "fire boards at them." The wolves finally retired to the woods but this assault, coming on top of all the other hardships, was almost too much to bear. Two of the men began to cry, further dampening the spirits of the others, and dinner, such as it was, was consumed in silence. Now "on very short allowance," and having lost all of their cutlery in the canoe, they ate with their fingers, taking turns at drinking from their solitary cup, a baking powder tin.

They then started another raft. The first two trees they cut split in half. "The next one seemed all right. It was 30 feet long. We cut a long hollow in it eight inches wide. It took us 10 days to make it, as we had but two blunt axes to work with. We rolled it the short distance to the water, and then nearly everyone refused to get on it. The men said they would sooner die on land than be drowned. Eventually, however, they were persuaded, and we all got in with our things."

As the log lacked a keel it tended to roll at the slightest motion; each and every man clinging to its side painfully aware that, should it turn over, they had not a chance of regaining a hold on its slippery flanks. Several times, the log attempted to turn turtle and its passengers, "expecting to go down at any moment," rode on without speaking.

By following the shoreline, they came to a safe landing place and prepared for the three-mile crossing of the inlet. Now reduced to half a bag of flour, a musket, some powder and a few bullets, they made camp and debated their next step. After some discussion it was agreed that Cote and three others (as many as could hope to navigate the inlet on a log) would proceed to the other side, Homfray and two others remaining on shore. Then, convinced that they would never see each other again, each man shook hands with his companions, when Cote and crew cast off. After raising their sail, a torn flour sack, they headed to sea. For hours, Homfray and companions watched their comrades make steady progress, until they at last vanished in the distance. Cote's plan was to proceed to Desolation Sound where he would attempt to induce the Indians to return for the others. If all went well he would be back in 10 days.

In the meantime, Homfray's party remained hidden on the beach. Worried that they might be spotted by the piratical natives who had captured them at the start of their expedition, they constructed a screen of bark and kept a constant watch. One morning, the lookout "espied a dark spot on the water a long distance off… As Cote had not had sufficient time to get back, he was greatly distressed. I told him to cheer up and be brave…"

Half an hour passed, the dark form rapidly approaching until they saw that it was a large canoe, paddling hard, with a tall Indian standing in the bow. "Presently we heard a loud war-whoop sounding along the water. Our death seemed now certain; a cold perspiration came over me. Neither of us spoke. A short time later another war-whoop sounded, louder and longer than before. We resigned ourselves to our fate."

Moments later, their agony was ended: it was Cote. After thanking God for their escape, Homfray chided Cote for having frightened them by instructing the chieftain to issue his warcry, when all returned to the village at Desolation Sound. After resting and regaining their strength, they headed for Victoria in two canoes with several of the tribesmen. Days later, they crossed the Gulf (in the midst of a squall which almost swamped them) and landed near Nanaimo. Then it was on to Fort Victoria, their considerate guides being astonished, off Cadboro Bay, by the sight of their first cows; a thrill which was forgotten off Beacon Hill when they caught their first glimpse of riders on horseback!

Upon landing at the HBC wharf all were met by company officials and Alfred Waddington (whose dream of a shortcut to the Cariboo had prompted the expedition), who expressed amazement at their ragged and half-starved condition.

"The Indians were afraid they were going to be separated from us, and would not leave us," Homfray noted "The company put up a tent for them in the lot where I lived. They would not go outside the fence for a week as they were afraid the other Indians would kill them. At last we persuaded them to visit the HBC store where the Company gave them as many blankets, muskets, etc. as their canoes would carry." The natives were then sent part-way home by steamer so as to prevent their being robbed and massacred by southern tribesmen.

And that was that. For 30 years, Robert Homfray withheld publication of his memorable expedition to Bute Inlet in deference to Waddington, who, he said, "feared my descriptions of the many dangers encountered would prevent parties joining him in making the road through the Cariboo."

Finally in 1894, he gave his story to posterity. Today the map honors this heroic adventurer with a channel, two creeks and two lakes. ●

HESQUIAT TRAGEDY

**Father Brabant
Hesquiat Mission
1869**

**Shocking tragedy on the west coast!
A devoted Catholic priest shot and mortally wounded while engaged in performing his holy office!
A first-class medalist the assassin..!**

THESE were the headlines which stunned Victorians on the morning of November 6, 1875. From far up the rugged and isolated coast of Vancouver Island, from the Indian village of Hesquiat, had come word that Father Augustus Joseph Brabant had been fatally wounded by one of his converts.

Ironically, the first man in the provincial capital to receive word of tragedy was Brabant's superior, Archbishop Charles J. Seghers, who himself would be assassinated by a companion in Alaska, several years after.

On November 5, several Hesquiat braves had paddled their dugout into the Inner Harbor, to rush several urgent dispatches to the bishop. Smeared with blood, the letters, written by the gravely injured Brabant with his left hand, were almost illegible. Dated four days earlier, the first missive read: "My Lord.—Sad news, I am shot in the right hand and in the back. Please send a priest at once. I may get well if a doctor comes at once to extract the shot. (Signed) A. BRABANT."

Below, Brabant had added: "My Lord.—Matlahow (sic) the chief of the Hesquiots (sic) has shot me a double shot."

On the reverse, he had painfully scrawled, his blood and ink mingling in grisly pattern: "The chief has run away," and, again: "My Lord.—I am dying, I am shot in the right hand and back by Matlahow the Hesquiot chief. I have been given no reason, Adieu!

Pray for me. A. BRABANT.

"My Lord.—Inflammation is setting in my right hand. The Indians are very kind. The whole tribe is crying, day and night. At least three are taking care of me. Do not blame them. Praise for their kindness, and may another priest be soon here to take my place is the wish of your lordship's dying servant. A. BRABANT."

As so much time had elapsed before Archbishop Seghers received word of Brabant's precarious condition, it was speculated that the priest had likely died in the meantime.

Upon being questioned, the Indian messengers replied that they could "not disclose any motive which could account for such a deed and particularly by one who has on a former occasion been rewarded for his kindness to the whites, this same Matlahow having been presented with a silver medal by the Canadian government for his humane conduct to the shipwrecked crew of the bark *Edwin*, wrecked a year ago near Barclay Sound."

However, if the messengers could not understand Matlahaw's treachery, they did provide enough information to enable the authorities to piece together an outline of the events leading up to the tragedy. Apparently members of a neighboring clan of Hesquiats had recently visited Victoria, only to contract smallpox. Panic-stricken, they had paddled homeward in hopes that a woman "belonging to the Hasquiats (sic) who had some renown on that coast

Victoria, where, on the morning of November 6, 1875, newspaper headlines announced a "Shocking tragedy on the west coast!"

as a doctress" could help them. The villagers, understandably, had greeted them with alarm and hostility, driving the ailing callers away from their campsite.

But one, a woman, driven by desperation, had somehow managed to get into the camp, despite the Hesquiats' every precaution—and the damage was done. Within days, the scourge had broken out among Brabant's parishioners. Among the immediate victims, according to the messengers, had been Chief Matlahaw's wife, sister and two children.

To Father Brabant, and two Indian volunteers, had fallen the unpleasant task of burial, the priest personally dragging the canoe used as a temporary coffin to the cemetery. Then he had returned to Matlahaw's lodge to face a more pressing problem, that of the chieftain's avowed determination to wreak vengeance upon the tribe which had infected his family.

But, no sooner had Brabant entered his lodge "to expostulate," than he "was shot with a double gun, one barrel being loaded with ball which took effect in the back, and a charge of shot from the other (striking) him in the right hand."

With this conjectured scenario of the tragedy at Hesquiat, authorities made ready to rush to the in-

jured priest's aid (assuming that he were still alive) but, owing to heavy weather, neither the government steamer *Sir James Douglas* nor the powerful steam tug *Isabel* could depart immediately for Barkley Sound, the gunboat HMS *Rocket* being pronounced as unfit to go to sea.

Consequently, for all of the emergency consultations held between Bishop Seghers, Superintendent of Indian Affairs Dr. I.W. Powell, and Lieutenant-Governor Joseph Trutch, no help was immediately forthcoming for the wounded Brabant.

In the same issue, the *Colonist* expressed dissatisfaction with the delay, explaining: "We furnish today all the details obtainable of the circumstances attending the shooting of Rev. Father Brabant at Barclay Sound. The information gathered here from the disconnected and somewhat incoherent letters (written while he was writhing in pain and apparently dying) of the revered gentleman, and the statement of the Indian messengers, is meagre; but enough is told to satisfy everyone that the life of a devoted Christian missionary is in great danger, and may be sacrificed if relief be not at once dispatched.

"There will be but one expression—and that of deep regret—wherever our paper is read today at the intelligence. Cut off from communication with the outer world for several months in the year, Father Brabant has devoted himself to his sacred calling with a spirit of self-sacrifice and zeal worthy of emulation. Under any circumstances death by violence is a shocking thing; but it is rendered trebly shocking when the victim is a missionary in performing a sacred office among savages... Father Brabant when he fell by the assassin's hand was endeavoring to bring about a good understanding between two tribes, and the chief by whose hand he fell was the one from whom the fatal blow was least expected—the assassin holding a medal from the Canadian government..."

The *Colonist* (and, quite likely, many of its readers) was less than happy with the halting steps to meet the emergency which had been announced by the authorities, the newspaper suggesting that Ottawa be telegraphed for permission to dispatch the *Sir James Douglas* to Hesquiat. In the meantime, a delegation headed by Rev. Father Kirley, P. McTiernan and T. Burnes met with Lieutenant-Governor Trutch and members of the legislative assembly, to be informed that the government had no intention of ordering a gunboat, "or any boat," to Barkley Sound. When McTiernan testily asked if the government were willing to share the expenses of chartering a private steamer, the answer was in the affirmative, with the result that the tug *Isabel* was formally chartered for the run to Hesquiat.

It was then announced that the tug would sail from Esquimalt, with Bishop Seghers, Dr. W.W. Walkem and Superintendent of Police Todd, the instant the latter returned to Esquimalt. Then it was revealed that the government, which had been reluctant, for reasons unknown, to become involved in the tragedy, had relented and dispatched HMS *Rocket* to the Island's west coast. Clearing Esquimalt at dawn, November 7, the gunboat sailed for Hesquiat, with Bishop Seghers, Dr. Walkem, Father Kirley and Superintendent Todd, some 36 hours after Father Brabant's blood-stained letters had reached Victoria. Retorted the *Colonist*: "It is to be hoped that the aid thus tardily rendered may yet be in time."

The newspaper then proceeded to publish excerpts from Brabant's "diary" which, apparently, had also been delivered to Victoria by the Hesquiat messengers. Although referred to as his diary, the notes actually were in letter form and addressed to Bishop Seghers. The first entry, dated October 14, some three weeks earlier, reported that 15 Mouetsat Indians had died of smallpox, the resulting "immense excitement" in Hesquiat prompting the priest to "write things down as they occur."

The previous day, he reported, the Hesquiat villagers had been alarmed at rumors that the inflicted Mouesats would descend upon their village as an act of revenge, apparently blaming them for the fact that the disease had erupted in the Mouetsat camp. "Speeches about self-defence, about preventing the disease from coming around, are made from morning till night," penned the missionary. "Fright and consternation is general. Towards evening firing of guns in the direction of the lake. Girls and boys uttering wails and shrieks."

The following day, Brabant had faced a crisis when an Indian named Tom tried to return to the village with his wife and child, the villagers, almost blind with fear, warning him not to land. Despite the threats of violence, Tom's father had persuaded the latecomers to come ashore, when Brabant vaccinated each, and a "doctor-woman."

That evening, he recorded, the frightened family had taken shelter in a house, amid "immense excitement and noise. Some Indians are in the bush, howling and growling. Superstitious prayers."

On Friday, October 16, Brabant had determined to visit each house in an attempt to calm the villagers. Upon being informed that Matlahaw's wife had died, he instructed the villagers to abandon the chieftain's longhouse, to clean their own homes, and to put on fresh clothing, upon which he had vaccinated them all.

October 17—All at church. After mass three cases of smallpox. I baptize Charley's...mother and aunt. Touchingly good dispositions of both dying Christians.

By the following day, both were dead, Brabant digging their graves with the help of two Cape Flattery Indians named Dick and Tsoquiet as no others were willing to help. Earlier, there had been a scene at his house, none wanting to assist him. "The Indians stand at a distance, pale with fear and chewing tobacco. Cape Flattery man enters with me. Roll Charley's father in two red blankets and his sister is covered with two black ones. I carry out both with a Cape Flattery man and Charley's father-in-law; we lay them in a canoe. The canoe is pulled by all the men (each struggling to be farthest distant). The rain falls in showers. Leave the canoe under a big tree and cover it with two large cedar boards. R.I.P."

Happily, however, the epidemic appeared to have peaked, only one villager, Matlahaw's sister, remaining ill, and she was reported to be recovering.

But, within 24 hours, she was dead, and there was further excitement among the survivors. As before, only two volunteers were forthcoming to assist the priest in interring the woman. Worse, Brabant had detected another victim, named Peter, and had ordered him to be isolated in a small hut on the village's outskirts.

For all of Brabant's vaccinations, the Hesquiats had virtually no defence against the scourge, the priest outlining the swiftness and ruthlessness with which the disease ravaged an entire village, striking down man, woman and child: "Origin of sickness, Charley's mother a doctor, does the medicine on a Mouetstat Indian woman. Gives the sickness to her husband who dies. The chief's sister does the medicine on Charley's mother, who also dies. The chief's wife lives with the chief's sister who has the small-pox, dies also. Charley's father is taken care of by his sister; she is found dead with him the same morning."

And so it went, Brabant time and time again having to use the canoe as a sled to haul the victims over the sands and into the trees.

Then, by October 22, the epidemic had done its worst, the last victim, Peter, being reported as recovering...

Six days after HMS *Rocket* cleared Esquimalt Harbor, northward bound, anxious Victorians received new word of the Hesquiat tragedy. After having been delayed by a stiff head-wind and fog, the gunboat, Captain Harris commanding, reached its destination the following evening. Immediately, a small boat headed for shore, carrying Bishop Seghers, Superintendent Todd, Dr. Walkem, three heavily armed marines, and Charley, the loyal sub-chief who had brought word of Brabant's condition to Victoria. Upon landing, all had rushed to the patient's house, where they found him "on a bed alive, and with his arm extended over the side, and a piece of lint soaked in cold water lying over the hand."

Dr. Walkem's cursory examination showed that Brabant—remarkably—was fit for travel; at least as far as the gunboat, which afforded better facilities. The next morning, upon his being carried to the water's edge, a large crowd of villagers gathered to express their regret for the affair and to ask when he would return.

Once aboard the *Rocket*, Dr. Walkem completed

Father Augustus Joseph Brabant. On November 5, 1875, word reached Victoria from the rugged and isolated coast of Vancouver Island that he had been fatally wounded by one of his converts.

a thorough examination. He discovered 20 punctures in the priest's back, and 12 in his hand, which he reported as being "in a sloughing state and pretty badly injured," both wounds being infected. Surprisingly, the back injuries were not as serious, although it was feared that Walkem would have to amputate Brabant's hand.

Since the gunboat's arrival, and after a "full dose of medicine"—from a bottle of port—Brabant had remained conscious and able to converse freely with his rescuers. Thus he had been able to recount the events leading up to Matlahaw's treachery. For some time, the chieftain had been a regular sight in Victoria, Matlahaw having, for several weeks prior to the fatal outbreak of smallpox at Hesquiat, made himself comfortable daily before the post office there, resplendent in his "Dominion Militia uniform, wearing a silver medal on his breast and a cap of a glazed peak and red band around it, and the Canadian Beaver in the front (part of his reward for having aided in the rescue of the American bark *Edwin's* shipwrecked company)."

Upon his return to Hesquiat, with his friend Charley (Brabant's faithful messenger), Matlahaw had developed a morbid fear of the evil disease (having already lost his wife and daughter, and aware that Brabant's vaccination had not had its expected effect upon him) and, convinced that the priest possessed holy powers which would protect those about him from infection, he had taken to sleeping, with his father, Charley, and an old chieftain named Omak, in the mission house. For several nights he and the others followed this routine without incident, although, strangely—or so it had seemed to Brabant at the time—Charley had asked to be allowed to sleep upstairs, rather than with the others. Then, on the eve of the shooting, Matlahaw's father had slipped away during the night, not being missed until morning.

With morning, Matlahaw had asked to borrow Brabant's shotgun, saying that he was going to shoot the bluejays which had been ravaging the priest's potato patch. Suspecting nothing, Brabant had handed the chief his unloaded weapon (for which he had no birdshot). With this, Matlahaw had departed for his own lodge to load the weapon, as Brabant completed his breadfast, held service, visited a sick woman, then started back towards his mission. At this point, he had encountered Charley, the latter wearing a glum expression, and warning: "Take care, sir, Matlahaw is sick, and he is afraid he will die."

Charley also had been depressed, and afraid of dying of smallpox, Brabant recounted, and after attempting to cheer him up, he had decided to call upon Matlahaw. Upon entering the chieftain's lodge, he found the man sitting despondently in the twilight. Asked how he felt, Matlahaw had replied either (Brabant wasn't sure of the translation) "I am dying," or "You die," at the same time kneading the slackened flesh of his leg and throat to show that he was not well. The chieftain wore "a peculiar, ghastly grin upon his features," said Brabant and, without warning, grabbed up the shotgun and fired.

Instinctively, Brabant turned his head away from the muzzle, the shot tearing into his raised hand at point-blank range. Stunned by the sudden, searing pain, the priest stumbled outside to a nearby stream where, thinking the attack to have been an accident, he began to wash his injured hand.

At this moment, Matlahaw charged out of the lodge to fire the second charge into Brabant's back. When hit the second time, the stooping priest forced himself to his feet and, reeling with shock, pain and loss of blood, stumbled toward the village centre. Within minutes, his cries for help drew a large crowd when, "feeling himself getting faint, and as a film seemed to be gathering over his eyes, (he) knelt down, as he feared he was about to die, and prayed." This done, his parishioners helped him to his house, where he scrawled the brief messages to Archbishop Seghers and sent them to Victoria in Charley's care.

By this time, the anxious crowd surrounding his mission had turned into a lynch mob and was about to kill Matlahaw and all of his relatives when the injured missionary beseeched them to remain calm. Then had begun the long, agonizing wait for help, Brabant lying in his cot, shivering violently, his hand bathing in a pan of cold water as the hours, then days, ticked by ever so slowly. Although convinced he was dying, help finally came, and he had been removed to the *Rocket*, which proceeded to Victoria. Because the priest had talked his followers out of punishing Matlahaw—even having dissuaded them from tying up the assassin—Superintendent Todd's "bird had flown," and the officer could do no more than offer a reward of $100 and some provisions for the man's capture. Villagers reported that he either had escaped to the mountains or that he was already dead, and with this Todd had to be satisfied.

With Brabant's arrival in Victoria, and with the attention of Dr. Walkem, four colleagues, the Sisters of St. Ann (not to mention a minor miracle) his ulcerated hand was saved and, after five months' recuperation, he returned to Hesquiat to continue his career as missionary among the west coast Indians. A native of Courtray, West Flanders, and graduate of the acclaimed university of Louvain, Augustus Joseph Brabant had been ordained a priest in the Roman Catholic church in 1868, arriving in British Columbia the following year. After five years with the Victoria diocese, he had volunteered to establish the Hesquiat mission, where he remained for an amazing 33 years until 1908, when Archbishop Orth of the see of Victoria appointed him Apostolic Administrator of the diocese.

In 1912, Hesquiat's grand old missionary passed away at the age of 67. ●

Ss MINTO
Lady of the Lake

In 55 years she steamed 2,500,000 miles, and won the affection of all, crewmen and passenger, who boarded her. When she died, thousands, from coast to coast, mourned Kootenay's "Lady of the Lake."

IN 1896 the Canadian Pacific Railway had assumed control of the defunct Columbia and Kootenay Railway's steamboat service, comprising seven steamers, 10 barges, various other assets, and contracts to construct three more vessels for use on the Arrow and Slocan Lakes. The *Kootenay*, *Rossland* and *Nakusp* entered service on schedule, the *Naskusp* being lost by fire at Arrowhead, December 23, 1897.

In the meantime, the CPR had ordered two 830-ton sternwheelers from Toronto for its "All Canadian" Stikine River route to the Klondike goldfields. When this scheme proved unfeasible, and with the sinking of *Nakusp*, the 140-foot sisters *Minto* and *Moyie* were reassigned to Columbia River and Kootenay Lake respectively. Shipped by rail in more than a thousand pieces each, the ladies were assembled, lengthened 20 feet, and launched at their destinations. In following decades, the lovely twins were to write illustrious chapters in provincial maritime lore, and earn warm niches in the hearts of those who sailed in them.

Minto, named after the Earl of Minto, then governor-general, became the pride of the Arrow Lakes. During the next half-century, she faithfully plied the 134-mile "milk run" between Robson, at the southern end of Lower Arrow Lake, and Arrowhead, at the head of Upper Arrow Lake.

"Prior to the completion of the Kettle Valley Railway in 1930," it has been noted, "the Arrow

(Right) The difference in size between the Bonnington and the Minto and Rossland, is clearly evident here. The Bonnington was built especially for the tourist trade. (Below) Ss Minto. Upon her destruction thousands mourned the passing of an old and faithful friend.

Lakes, actually a widening of the Columbia River, formed the only route of travel to the Kootenays and the state of Washington, from the main line of the CPR west of Calgary.

"The sternwheelers on the route, whose scenery is unsurpassed anywhere on this continent, were something like those of the Mississippi—glamorous and well-patronized."

Originally, the Columbia and Kootenay Steam Navigation Company had operated six first-class steamers on the Arrow Lakes route between Revelstoke and Northport, Washington. But with the eclipse of Kootenay mining, dwindling freight and passenger traffic meant the end for half of the romantic fleet and the CPR kept only its three newest steamers, *Minto*, *Rossland* and *Kootenay*.

Rossland and *Kootenay* had been built in Nakusp in 1897 upon the elegant lines of inland Oregon and California steamers, as specified by Captain J.W. Troup. "The *Rossland*," wrote Edward L. Affleck some years ago, "with its sheer lines and powerful engines, was capable of an astonishing turn of speed (and an astonishing fuel consumption), while the *Kootenay* was a broader-beamed, more matronly vessel."

"The *Minto*, having originally been designed for service on the Stikine River route to the Klondike, could not match her sister(s) for speed and appearance, but she could boast the more durable assets of a low fuel consumption, a very shallow draft (5' 1"), and a steel constructed frame."

Speedy *Rossland* retained title of monarch of the inland fleet for a further 10 years, when overshadowed by a newcomer, the shining three-decked, steel-hulled mammoth, Ss. *Bonnington*. With her mighty compound reciprocating engines, the 1,700-ton sternwheeler reigned supreme.

Sadly, she was too late, belonging to another age. Within nine years, she and *Minto* were alone, but for the little tug *Columbia*. Gracious *Rossland* had foundered in 1916, sturdy *Kootenay* had been beached as a houseboat.

Throughout the twenties, *Bonnington* churned the placid waters of the Arrow Lakes, *Minto* in the humble role of relief steamer. But *Minto*'s years in her glittering kin's shadow were about to end. In 1931 her turn finally came when Nelson and Nakusp were linked by road and the *Bonnington* was laid up. For seven years the CPR promised she would be restored to service. But when season traffic did not warrant her return to duty the company began cannibalizing her equipment for other vessels in the B.C. Lakes and River Service.

Interest in the forlorn beauty was revived in 1938 when it was rumored that the provincial government would purchase and remodel her as a car ferry. But it was not to be and, in 1944, she was sold for dismantling.

Throughout these years, *Minto* quietly plied the milk run. The Arrow Lakes' "plain Jane" had

outlived her more glamorous sisters.

More years passed, *Minto* steadily continuing her schedule of two round trips a week, except during winter when the busy dowager confined herself to the run between Arrowhead, Nakusp and Carrols, the tug *Columbia* assuming her duties in Lower Arrow Lake due to low water. Fog and ice were further inconveniences encountered during winter, but her 22-man crew proceeded with few interruptions. "She always manages to get us through," declared an officer.

Striking sandbars became almost routine and a former master praised her shallow draft: "She could run in a heavy dew."

Minto had changed little since the day of launching, so many years before. Although her interior had been renovated, the aging sternwheeler still boasted most of her original fittings and machinery; passengers never failing to marvel at her faded yellow certificate of registry, number 32. Dated 1896, it was displayed in a glass frame in the forward lounge.

Beside *Minto*'s legendary cuisine—"all you can eat for a dollar"—passengers enjoyed the majestic scenery of snow-capped mountain peaks, sparkling water and ruffled greenery. In the narrows between the upper and lower lakes, *Minto* charged through the surging current, almost touching the banks on either side, paddle threshing loudly, tall funnel belching black smoke. Then there were her "ports of call," from government wharf, where she unloaded cargo to clay riverbank where she nudged her bow to pick up a passenger or two.

But more than the scenery, good food and rustic routine, passengers remembered the steamer's warm hospitality. It was like stepping into the past, away from the bustle of everyday modern living. There was little formality on the *Minto*, travellers enjoying dinner with such popular masters as Captain Walter Wright and the reminiscences of pipe-smoking first mate and future master, Bob Manning.

There were exciting times, too, such as the day *Minto*, under command of the new skipper, Captain J. Thompson, collided with her Halcyon dock during a storm. Characteristically, she did not pause for repairs, the crew attending to her injuries while underway.

Other memorable occasions included the Golden Spike Days festivities at Arrowhead in 1948, when the beloved steamer—"symbol of the courage and determination that made B.C. what it is today"—was presented a plaque by Revelstoke Kinsmen, for 50 years' dependable service "through storm and fine weather, through flood and low water." Many recalled the gala excursion of 34 years before, when *Minto* and Ss. *Kootenay* had carried 500 holidayers and two brass bands to St. Leon for a picnic, the last time any of the once-proud fleet had steamed above the Arrow Lakes on the original run.

The historic voyage marked *Minto*'s 7,000th trip.

Minto had been busy during the late forties. In

1947 she carried 12,000 passengers. With construction of the Lower Arrow Lake hydro development, her duties increased as she carried men and materials to the project site. At the other end of the scale, she was still her old self, as illustrated by part of one cargo—a ball of knitting yarn.

The paddlewheeler gained international acclaim in 1949 through an article in the *Saturday Evening Post*, Richard L. Neuberger describing the old lady's working schedule and surroundings in glowing prose: "The *Minto* remains the only courier of mail and freight to those who mine, log and cultivate the shaggy slopes of the Selkirks... Rainbows and Dolly Vardens feel the throb of *Minto*'s paddle and mountain sheep and mule deer watch...from the precipitous shore."

Another passenger, Les Rimes, extolled the breathtaking scenery to be savored from *Minto*'s worn decks: "Willows overhanging the beach, then a rock bluff where pines are bent and gnarled, then a leaning farmhouse with a wisp of smoke lazing out, a field of cattle, an orchard red with fruit, low-lying swamp land where bulrushes grow and the decks make their resting place. More farmhouses and orchards. Then, miles of virgin forest. And, above the passing panorama, the blue mountains."

Of *Minto* herself: "It was dusk; rain began to fall. A flashlight signal blinked from shore as we continued on our way. We altered course for the deep shadows of the beach. The ship's searchlight picked the way as we slowly drifted in. The gangplank went down, but nobody came aboard. A man wanted the skipper to mail a letter!"

During another passage, he witnessed a man waving from a deserted beach. Dutifully nosing her into shore, *Minto*'s master fulfilled the man's request —he wanted to know the time—and calmly proceeded on his way.

1954 brought the inevitable. On April 23, 93 passengers from every corner of the continent who had reserved cabins for the occasion, boarded *Minto* for her last official voyage. H.W. Herridge, MP for Kootenay West, had fought a valiant battle in Ottawa for a reprieve, as had Kaslo-Slocan MLA Randolph Harding in Victoria, but to no avail. *Minto* was too old, she no longer paid her way and, despite vehement public protest, the federal government refused a subsidy.

That afternoon, 200 persons crowded the little dock at Nakusp to wave fond farewell, as aircraft pilot Dave Duncan flew over twice, dipping his wings in salute, and the motor vessel *Beaton* whistled goodbye. At Arrowhead, 73-year-old John Nelson had erected two signs: "Let us honor the brave pioneers of navigation on scenic Arrow Lakes by making it possible to continue the Ss *Minto*'s services," and, "Au revoir, *Minto*." At Edgewood, Charles Maynard had erected a sign which read, "Goodbye, old girl—gone but not forgotten— though absent ever dear."

Off lonely Blondin's Point, *Minto* whistled salute to the grave of Mrs. Blondin who, until her death, had never missed waving to the ship from the rocky point.

The Nakusp *taking on wood.*

When Captain Manning brought *Minto* alongside for the last time, passengers headed ashore with their memories and souvenirs—including a lifebuoy and fire axes—as hundreds lined the wharf solemnly. Then they were gone. The next day, work crews began the final cleanup.

Months later, it appeared *Minto* was to have a new lease on life when the CPR donated her, for a dollar and five cents (provincial sales tax), to the Nakusp Chamber of Commerce. At a public

With the sinking of the Ss. Nakusp, the Minto and the Moyie, shown here, were shipped by rail in more than a thousand pieces each, assembled, lengthened 20 feet and launched on the Columbia River and Kootenay Lake respectively.

meeting, a committee was formed to consider possible uses for the old ship. Among suggestions put forward were a bowling alley, museum and community centre. The following spring, bulldozers cleared a sand foundation on the lakeshore above high water at Nakusp.

But, despite the dedicated attempts of history conscious organizations, Ss. *Minto* had fallen upon hard times. Finally, when funds to preserve her were not forthcoming, she was sold for scrap.

And scrapped she would have been, but for her old friend John Nelson of Galena Bay. He it was who had painted the signs for her farewell. He had seen her for the first time in 1904, and for 50 years had watched her ply her rounds. In anguish, he had watched the ill-fated attempts at preservation. But her sale to the wreckers had been the last straw. For $840, he bought her on the basis of where is, as is, then paid to have her towed to Galena Bay.

Unfortunately, the wreckers had already ravaged her paddle, engines, funnel and brass, but this did not deter Nelson, who set to work with hammer, saw and love. From the bones of old *Bonnington* he salvaged door and window frames and lovingly reproduced *Minto's* nameplate—lost to the wreckers—in his workshop.

"It's a pleasure to do it," the old man in the officer's cap with the "Ss. *Minto*" badge told a reporter, adding mournfully, "I'm the only one in the world to do it."

He had been blessed with nothing less than a miracle in 1960. When floods floated *Minto* to the very field he had in mind from the beginning, the receding waters left his prospective museum high and dry. Over the years, the gallant old man invested his savings and devotion in restoring *Minto* to her former glory, repairing her rusted equipment, clearing away debris, drying her out. In winter, he patiently shovelled snow from her weakening decks.

By 1966, 87-year-old John Nelson was battling yet another foe: The High Arrow Dam meant Galena Bay would be flooded.

MLA Randolph Harding then took up the defence, urging the provincial government to save the *Minto* and appoint Mr. Nelson curator.

Alas, his dream was to be denied. John Nelson died, and his beloved ship was left to son Walter. Walter tried to interest the provincial and federal governments in saving the ancient steamer, but it was too late. Despite his father's loving attention, the years had taken their toll. B.C. Hydro offered to move the hulk to higher ground and commissioned a marine surveyor to estimate the costs of transfer and restoration to a museum. His estimate: $95,000.

"While I appreciated the hydro company's offer I had to decline it," sighed Nelson. "As an individual I simply can't look after her. Snow removal in the winter and vandalsim in the summer are just two of the problems I can't cope with."

The end came at last for Ss. *Minto* in August of 1968, when hydro workers pumped her dry, then towed her into midstream. There, in the waters she had known for over half a century, for 2,500,000 miles, Walter Nelson set her ablaze. Minutes later a plume of smoke rose 2,000 feet over the Columbia River. Then the old sternwheeler's skeleton, hissing violently, settled beneath the blue waters.

As Captain Bob Manning had said upon her retirement in 1954, "That's the way an old ship should die—gloriously!"

(Opposite page) The Skuzzy battling the strong current of the Fraser River. (Above) Andrew Onderdonk (1848-1905) and his home in Yale. Onderdonk's home was later converted to a girl's school.

If ever British Columbia has known the right man for the job, that giant was Andrew Onderdonk, unsung hero of the rails. He built a railroad where few — man or beast — dared set foot, along Fraser River's precipitous canyons, and, in so doing, wrote a unique chapter in provincial marine lore.

Andrew Onderdonk Tamed Mountain Horror

THIS apparent anomalism dates back to March of 1880, when the building Canadian Pacific faced seemingly insurmountable obstacles. Beset by financial crises, political scandal, unbelievable construction difficulties, and the impatient clamoring of British Columbia, the transcontinental had fallen far behind schedule and faced a complete halt.

One of the more formidable problems facing harried director William Van Horne was but a tiny line drawn upon a map. On paper, this vital link in the continental chain looked anything but complicated. In reality, it was an engineering nightmare. For, rearing its ugly head between Port Moody and Savona Ferry, at Kamloops, lay some of the grimmest terrain ever challenged by human ingenuity — and guts. Through the awesome rocky fortresses of

Fraser River, the Coast Mountain Range, and the Thompson River, 213 miles of track had to be laid.

Yet there was one who did not hesitate to attempt the impossible: Andy Onderdonk, an enigmatic 32-year-old engineer from New York. A direct descendant of the first Dutch settlers in America, he had graduated from Troy Institute of Technology with honors. In following years, he supervised the construction of vast projects throughout the United States, including the building of ferry slips and a mammoth sea wall in San Francisco. This was the man who won the multi-million dollar contract for the controversial Port Moody-Kamloops section.

And having decided to accomplish the impossible, Onderdonk calmly proceeded to do just that.

(Above) The Onderdonk sawmill at Texas Lake. (Right) Sarah Delia Onderdonk, the wife who launched the Skuzzy on May 4th.

On horseback, he inspected the notorious Fraser River Canyon, following a precarious goat track blasted from solid rock, high above the boiling river. In places, frail wooden trestles seemed to hang over eternity, suspended from invisible supports. With dynamite, his men would have to gouge a railway along the canyon's very edge. Where sheer, thousand-foot cliffs barred the way, men with explosives would have to be lowered by ropes.

Making Yale his headquarters, Onderdonk began by constructing a hospital, and established work camps with generous cooking and boarding facilities. Years after, former employees would hail him as "the best boss we ever had." Upriver, he built a dynamite plant. He then faced his first obstacle, a shortage of labor.

Manpower was at a premium in British Columbia, a century ago, and, despite the attractive offer of two dollars per day and all found, Onderdonk could not recruit a sufficient force. In typical manner, the engineer's answer was nothing less than a continental advertising program. Within months, a ragtag army of inexperienced laborers formed at San Francisco and was ferried north to Fraser River. Farm boys, adventurers, misfits and thieves, they undertook to tame a mountain horror.

On the morning of May 14, 1880, the first blast was detonated. With a mighty roar which echoed throughout the canyons and started a thunderstorm, the vast project was begun.

"It was difficult to get men willing to drill and blast, suspended by ropes over the chasm walls," one historian has noted. "Slides kept hampering the work, and the road below, lifeline to the Interior, had to be kept clear. Accidents kept mounting, attended by difficulty in conveying the injured down to Yale, where Mrs. Onderdonk, a capable and un-

pretentious woman, did a big job in superintending the hospital and being hostess to visiting dignitaries.

"The blasting, which continually reverberated along the canyon, caused a lot of rainfall. In spots the work cost $300,000 a mile, with the Macdonald government in Ottawa hard-pressed to raise the funds."

Despite constant complaints from a worried Ottawa, Onderdonk forged ahead. But he was already losing his race against time. By summer he realized he could continue no longer without thousands of additional workers.

In desperation, he informed the federal government of his intention to import 2,000 Chinese coolies. Without waiting for a reply, he put his plan into action, chartering two steamers to rush the Oriental laborers to British Columbia. Their sudden arrival took the province by storm, but effectively skirted vehement public outcry.

Immigration of the industrious Chinese was for many years a bitter issue and ignited violence more than once. Onderdonk knew this as well as the next man, but, acting with his usual daring, his gamble paid off.

It was then that he faced the problem which was to make history. Hindered by the exhorbitant tolls (10 dollars a ton) on materials freighted over the Cariboo Road, he determined to send a steamboat to Boston Bar. The fact this manoevre meant navigating Hell's Gate Canyon, the worst series of white water in Fraser River, meant little to the engineer.

"You're crazy!" cried veterans of the northwest swiftwater fraternity upon the announcement of Onderdonk's plan. All agreed that it was impossible—all but Andrew Onderdonk.

Early on May 4, 1882, pretty Sarah Onderdonk

formally christened her husband's 127-foot stern-wheeler *Skuzzy* at the little settlement of Spuzzum. Minutes later, the 254-ton craft, named after a nearby stream, was launched into the Fraser. Some ridiculed the engineer, many pleaded with him to change his mind, warning the *Skuzzy* would be lost. But Onderdonk would not be swayed.

He had already found the man to tackle the raging waters of Hell's Gate, Captain Nat Lane Jr., and even his detractors agreed he had made the right choice. However, when Lane saw the maelstrom of rapid and rock which was Hell's Gate, he promptly returned to the lesser hazards of the Stikine.

When, finally, Onderdonk located Captain Isbury Insley, the unnerving dangers facing gallant *Skuzzy* had increased immeasurably. From high in the mountains, melting snows poured millions of gallons of water into the swelling Fraser. Within days, the river was a rampaging monster, overflowing its banks and flooding thousands of acres.

By May 17, the day of the immortal contest, the Fraser was roaring seaward at its highest level in 40 years.

Undaunted, Captain Insley, acknowledged as the best Fraser River pilot of the day, swung *Skuzzy's* spoon-like bow into the surging current. Tall funnel belching black smoke, the courageous steamer charged upstream, an angry white froth sweeping past her bluff nose. Again and again, Insley forced his bucking command to the attack, exhausting his vast store of experience. He tried every trick he had ever learned or heard of. But it was no use. Hell's Gate had beaten him.

But if Onderdonk was disappointed, he did not let it show. Rumors swept the northwest that he had given up, that *Skuzzy* would be dismantled and shipped overland. Weeks later, Onderdonk quietly announced it was Boston Bar or bust—through Hell's Gate.

In the meantime, he had replaced Insley with three Columbia River veterans. From Lewiston, Idaho, came Captain S.R. Smith, the only man ever to navigate the treacherous Shoshone River through the Blue Mountains. He was accompanied by W.H. Patterson and engineer J.W. Burse.

On the fateful day of September 7, 1882, hundreds of eager spectators lined the rugged banks to watch the herculean struggle. News of the one-sided duel had excited mariners and landlubbers alike, and bets were placed from Spuzzum to Seattle. Few backed the *Skuzzy*.

To the cheers of those ashore, Captain Smith forged into battle. Boiler almost bursting, paddles threshing frantically, *Skuzzy* inched ahead. The little steamer bucked in terror, her bow plunging beneath the foaming current time and again, as, in the wheelhouse, Smith and Patterson fought her wildly spinning helm and shouted orders to the seventeen-man crew.

Hours passed, *Skuzzy* gaining ever so slowly. then the first day was followed by a second. Still, the straining steamer moved forward. Three days. Four. By then, the exhausted crew realized they had achieved little headway. Worse, it was becoming increasingly apparent that they were losing. *Skuzzy* could not maintain the agonizing battle much longer. Soon she would be spent, and the triumphant Fraser would hurtle her downstream.

And so she would have been, but for Onderdonk's eleventh-hour inspiration: 150 Chinese workers placed at strategic points along the canyon rim. Heavy ringbolts had been hastily driven into solid rock, through which were passed stout hawsers, secured to *Skuzzy's* capstan and steam winch.

As *Skuzzy's* puny 30-horsepower engines thumped loudly, above the thundering roar of the river, the shore gangs heaved on the lines and 15 crewmen worked her capstan, pitting muscle against the might of the Fraser. Inching along the cliffs, where a false step meant instant death, the Chinese pulled with every ounce of strength.

Once, twice, they strained at the ropes, the steamer seeming to be held fast in the rapids' grip. Then—*Skuzzy* moved ahead. One foot, two...over the infamous China Riffle, she struggled.

Finally it was ended. *Skuzzy* rested in the calmer waters above Hell's Gate, crew slumped in exhaustion, hull scraped and gouged almost beyond recognition. Andrew Onderdonk, mad genius of the CPR, had won, his remarkable achievement being hailed the length of the west coast and across Canada, as one and all praised his determination and the courage of his river men.

Skuzzy still faced over 20 miles of rough water and rock before she reached Boston Bar, but the battered lady limped into town without further incident. Captain Smith then braved the current once more, battling his way to Lytton, after a further 20 miles of terror, before returning to Boston Bar, where *Skuzzy* enjoyed a well-earned rest, made necessary by a large rip in her side, when she grounded below Siska. Her 20 watertight compartments, an innovation in ship design, had saved her from destruction.

Repaired, she began regular service between Boston Bar and Lytton with Onderdonk's vital supplies, under command of Captain James Wilson. Sadly, the harrowing run was to prove victorious within two years. *Skuzzy* had beaten Hell's Gate, but she could not sustain the daily hammering of raging river and continual collisions with submerged rock. In 1884, her hull strained and worn almost paper thin, she was hauled up on a sandbar, where her crumbling bones remained for years after as a sad reminder to passersby of one of the greatest days in British Columbia marine history.

The spirit of Ss. *Skuzzy*, long remembered as the "White-water Boat," was to continue, however,

(Top) The Acid and Powder Works, Yale. The powder slid down a chute to awaiting wagons, a dangerous practice which resulted in the entire shed being destroyed. The blasts shattered every window in Yale. (Center) Onderdonk's car and machine shops, Yale. (Bottom) Old Curly. Originally used in the construction of the Panama Canal, it was later used by Onderdonk in San Francisco. The third man from the right appears to be Onderdonk.

Onderdonk having salvaged her valiant engines and machinery and installed them in a new steamer, the 140-foot *Skuzzy II*. For 13 years, the second steamer of this famous name plied the Thompson River, when she, too, was retired. Remarkably, her engines again went to work; this time in the steamer *Lytton*, on the upper Columbia.

The saga of the *Skuzzy* was but a single achievement of the amazing Mr. Onderdonk in his construction of the infamous Port Moody-Kamloops line. No less an accomplishment had been his building of 16 tunnels, one a quarter of a mile in length. Finishing on schedule, Onderdonk contracted for the extension to Eagle Pass, and completed this section September 30, 1885. A week later, he paid off his men. As 1,200 Chinese laborers quietly marked the historic occasion by setting up camp in the woods, 1,000 white construction workers embarked upon a monumental drunk at Yale by taking possession of the town. Several "lunatics," according to one newspaper, even "attempted to force their way into private homes."

In the summer of 1969, a 34-foot aluminum boat powered by a 475-horsepower V-7 engine coupled with a twelve-inch jet, rather than a propeller, braved Hell's Gate Canyon. Designed and operated by Prince George residents Howard Witt and Gary Reinelt, little *Scuzzi II* (named, although misspelled, after valiant *Skuzzy I*) was forced to turn back before the incredible onslaught.

"It was like hitting a solid brick wall," Witt said.

Twice, *Scuzzi II* had grappled with the overpowering current. At one point, the daring duo were but 10 feet from victory when forced to turn back.

Engineer Andy Onderdonk went on to other challenges in South America, the United States and eastern Canada. Some historians have considered his building of the first subway tunnel under New York's East River his greatest achievement. But old-timers in British Columbia remember that long-ago day when little *Skuzzy* dared the swirling rapids of Hell's Gate Canyon.

This, they proudly maintain, was Andrew Onderdonk's finest hour. ●

JAMES MOORE OF CARIBOO

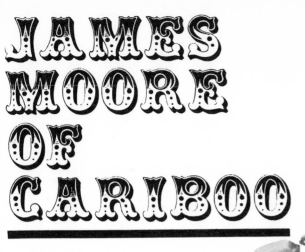

When the whisky seller refused to stop peddling tanglefoot whisky to the Indians, the miners confiscated his load, knocked the head off each barrel with an axe, and poured the contents onto the ground. The bootlegger was then given the choice of leaving camp or accepting "a present of a hempen necktie." He left camp.

THE oldest pioneer miner in British Columbia, they said of James Moore "of Cariboo" in the winter of 1909.

It was a claim that the wizened prospector made with justifiable pride. For his had been a life of adventure and history-making; a record of earlyday mining and exploration with which he enthralled a Victoria audience late in 1909.

Addressing the Young People's Society at St. Andrew's Presbyterian Church, Moore said that he welcomed the opportunity to address "this young generation...and those old pioneers, the bone and sinew of this great province."

For it was the prospector of old, he said, who "made this province what it is today, the greatest province in the Dominion of Canada." He then reached half a century into the past to paint a vivid portrait of the British Columbia of the mid and late 1800s; this, despite the fact that, as he admitted, 50 years was a long time and he had to rely upon memory.

"It may be interesting to know," he began, "what led up to the first discoveries of miners in the province. The question is still in doubt (as to) when the first gold was found in the province. But, sir, I am speaking now from my own recollections. In speaking with Donald McLean, chief trader of the Hudson's Bay Company at Fort Kamloops in 1861, he told me the first gold he received was in 1856 and 1857, from Indians on the Thompson River.

"This gold he sent down to Fort Victoria, and in February, 1858, the H.B. Co. steamer *Otter* left Victoria for San Francisco. The purser, having this gold dust, took it to the U.S. mint in San Francisco, and had it coined as the first gold found in New Caledonia..."

It was in the Bay City, as a result of this incident, that British Columbia's gold rush began. For, in those days, it was incumbent upon good citizens to belong to their volunteer fire department. Shortly after, the superintendent of the mint was attending a drill, when the conversation drifted to "gold excitements." With great foresight that worthy exclaimed: "Boys, the next excitement will be on Fraser River."

Upon his explaining the first, small shipment of dust from "New Caledonia," a small party of adventurers including James Moore resolved to "explore and report" on the distant Fraser.

Sailing from San Francisco on March 12, 1858, the prospectors reached the mouth of the Fraser on March 20. Three days later, they "discovered and located the first mines on the mainland of British Columbia..." And the rush was on!

The significance of their discovery did not escape Moore, particularly some 50 years after, when he beamed: "When we located this mine we laid the foundation stone of mining in British Columbia, as this was practically the commencement of mining in the province.

"I may go a little further, and say we laid the foundation stone of British Columbia, and I am proud to have the honor of stating here tonight that I helped to lay that foundation stone. But, sir, I am sorry to say I am the only one left of that little party that discovered those mines on Hill's Bar, as all my

(Left) In 1859 one of James Moore's colleagues, Charley Snider, led a three-man expedition to Quesnel River. On one bar alone they earned $1,700 a day for almost a week.

In 1861 Moore and comrades made some of the richest strikes in the Cariboo, including that of Williams Creek. "Some of the claims on those creeks were fabulously rich," he told a Vancouver audience half a century after. "For example, I will state (that) the Diller claim on William(s) Creek, where two men were working in the face of the drift with picks, took out in 24 hours' work 202 pounds of gold, the day-shift recovering 102 pounds and the night-shift 100 pounds." (The picture on the opposite page is Barkerville in 1868.

associates have crossed the great divide. I trust they have struck it rich and have a claim staked for their old partner..."

The historic discovery was made purely by chance. While working their way upriver, they camped on a sandbar for lunch, when an eagle-eyed member of the expedition spotted the winking of yellow in moss growing on the rocks. Intrigued, he washed a pan of the moss and "got a prospect," when all traded their dinner plates for gold pans. Minutes later, it was apparent to all that they had struck it rich, Hill's Bar, as they named it after their observant partner, yielding the richest treasure on the Fraser and its tributaries. Over the years, Hill's Bar was to produce an astounding $2 million—and change the course of Western Canadian history.

When their small stock of supplies ran low, the prospectors dispatched several men to Fort Langley to restock. The Hudson's Bay Company trading post had little to offer in the way of provisions but relayed word of the activity on Hill's Bar, "the news of which soon spread across the Sound," Moore continued. "We were not left long in possession, as the whole tribe of Yale Indians, about 300 men, women and children, moved down the river and camped on our bar. They soon tumbled to our game of mining, and they also commenced washing for gold."

Next to arrive at the bustling camp was a Captain Taylor, with a boatload of tanglefoot whisky (Moore marvelling that "the first supplies most always to arrive in a new mining camp take the form of liquor.") With an unerring instinct for easy riches, Taylor landed on the bar almost immediately after the Yale tribesmen, selling his rotgut whisky for $5 a bottle which was payable in gold dust. As the Indians were not aware of the mineral's true worth, his actual charge must have been considerably higher. Whatever, the natives purchased enough to have an all-night celebration, when Moore and his partners collared Taylor and offered to buy out his remaining stock. Worried that the Indians might become hostile, the miners planned to destroy the captain's inventory.

But Taylor, convinced that this was the chance of a lifetime to get rich—by robbing his customers of their gold when incapacitated—refused to sell. The miners then confiscated his load, knocking the head off each and every barrel with an axe and pouring the contents onto the ground. Chuckled Moore: "We had christened the baby Hill's Bar a few days before. We now baptized the infant." As for Captain Taylor, he was cordially invited to move on or the prospectors would "make him a present of a hempen necktie. He would not accept our present, but left the bar and went downstream."

Despite their action (or, perhaps, because of it) the attitude of the Indians cooled considerably, the miners of both races continuing to work alongside each other in sullen silence. Matters became sticky when an Indian borrowed a pick from one of the whites, then refused to return it—at which its owner expressed his resentment by breaking a shovel over the offender's head. This act, as Moore drily noted, was not conducive to good relations, the natives taking up their muskets and grouping together. The outnumbered whites, 20 in all, also armed and grouped and waited for the attack which

they were sure was coming.

They were still waiting when the Yale chieftain decided to give his men a pep-talk. Mounting a stump, he addressed his followers at length when suddenly (and much to the miners' joy), a barge of the gunboat HMS *Satellite* appeared around a bend in the river. Aboard were Governor James Douglas, the captain of the gunboat and a dozen armed blue-jackets.

"If ever visitors were welcome," grinned Moore, "Governor Douglas and his bargeload of marines were welcome to this little party of ours, whom they saved from annihilation. When the governor landed on the bar we fired a salute in his honor. We then stated our grievances to him, and he persuaded the Indians to leave the bar and go to Fort Yale, where a small Hudson Bay trading post was established, and pacified the Indians by giving them a 'blow out' of hardtack and molasses. We had no trouble with the Indians after that on Hill's Bar. About six weeks later Governor Douglas appointed the first justice of the peace on the mainland, George Perrier."

Their next visitor on the bar was the fabled Billy Ballou, of express fame, the miners loading him down with letters and samples of gold dust for their relatives and friends in the outside world. This was in April of 1858. Word of their fabulous strike on the Fraser electrified the entire West Coast, particularly California. By the following month, eager prospectors lined the riverbanks from its mouth to Fort Yale, a distance of 100 miles.

Yet, curiously, the fabulous diggings could not hold many of the diehard prospectors for long. Unable to remain long in one spot regardless of reward many of them soon moved on in search of fresh strikes. For the miners of old, as Moore explained, were fickle and gypsies at heart. "In those days, no matter how rich a camp we discovered, we could not remain long in it. As we were of a roving disposition we had to explore. I am still of the same disposition, sir, and will not remain long in one camp tonight, but will proceed to the interior.

"But before I do so I would like to say in those days we had no railroads, wagon roads, or pack trails. We had only an Indian trail along the great canyon of the Fraser, and the large chasms were spanned by poles tied with twisted willows from which we could look down several hundred feet to the mighty Fraser rushing below. We had to cross these bridges with our packs or turn back, but I assure you, sir, we did not know what that word meant. Our motto was 'onwards and upwards'."

In the fall and early spring, when the river was at its lowest stage, they were able to take heavily-laden boats through the canyons of the Fraser from Yale

to Lytton. Once beyond Lytton the original party split up, some sticking to the river and discovering new bars. Moore and several others obtained horses and headed inland to locate, in due course, the celebrated Blue Lead mine on the Horsefly River in Cariboo.

Forty years after, Moore revisited the old Discovery claim of 1859 and was surprised to find it still in operation. He was even more amazed when the foreman allowed him to wash a pan of gravel. "It looked to me to be as much gold as gravel in that pan!"

He was further intrigued by the method by which these latter-day miners did their work. Instead of the gold pans and sluiceboxes of old, they employed hydraulic monitors, the camp being illuminated by electricity. Four decades before, only the miners' campfires had braved the wilderness night, although Moore smugly noted that he and his partners had enjoyed the satisfaction of "declar(ing) a dividend every night of $100 per man."

It was back in 1859 that one of Moore's compatriots, Charley Snider, led a three-man expedition to the Quesnel River. On one bar alone they earned $1,700 a day for almost a week!

With 1860, Moore and others worked further inland, to discover Duck, Keithly, Goose, Harvey and Snowshoe Creeks. The following year they made the richest strikes in Cariboo: Antler,

Williams, Lightning, Lowbee and Grouse Creeks. "Some of the claims on those creeks were fabulously rich," Moore recalled. "For example, I will state (that) the Diller claim on William(s) Creek, where two men were working in the face of the drift with picks, took out in 24 hours' work 202 pounds of gold, the dayshift recovering 102 pounds and the nightshift 100 pounds.

"Other claims on the creek paid in the following order: 50 feet of the Diller claim paid $240,000, or $4,800 per foot of channel; 50 feet of the Moffatt claim paid $90,000, or $1,800 per foot; 80 feet of the Burns claim paid $140,000, or $1,750 per foot; 80 feet of the Steele paid $120,000, or $1,500 per foot; 120 feet of the Canadian claim paid $180,000, or $1,500 per foot; 100 feet of the Watty claim paid $130,000, or $1,300 per foot of channel.

"Those are only some of the claims on Williams Creek that paid. There were a number of other claims that paid equally as well. As regards pan prospects on Williams Creek, the biggest prospect I now remember was $1,650 to one pan. I also remember $6,500 to five pans on the same creek."

The treasure yielded by Lightning Creek was every bit as staggering to the mind, nine companies reaping a total windfall of $2 million.

Williams Creek, during those palmy days of 1862 and 1863, was a lively place. There were (in order of Moore's recollection) theatres, dance halls, hurdy-gurdy girls, saloonkeepers and gamblers. All lived off the hard-working, hard-drinking miner

(Opposite page) A gold nugget from the Cariboo, shown actual size. The Neversweat claim on Williams Creek in 1868. It yielded $250,000 from 120 feet of ground.

(Right) The Davis claim on Williams Creek, one of the most productive creeks in the Cariboo. It yielded $350,000.

who, having struck it rich, was sure that his supply of gold would never fail him. One miner, named Long Abbott, gathered $40,000 in gold, only to squander it on champagne and girls. His most memorable feat of this period was the time he smashed a bar-room mirror by using it as a target for $20 nuggets. Then he was broke.

"Others who deserved a better fate, and were instrumental through their discoveries in making large fortunes, died poorer than the very latest arrivals in the diggings. Witness Jim Loring, who had a third interest in the Diller claim that paid $500,000 in 300 feet of ground. He died in Victoria without a dollar. I may mention here the fate of two other explorers, John Rose and his partner Johnson, who was (sic) murdered for their grub by Indians on Bear River. Their flesh was burned from their bones, and their bones buried under the camp fire... The fate of another prospector, whose name I cannot recall, is tragic. He wrote his name and scratched a few broken words on his tin cup, being afterwards found by Sam Kyes and party, dead, in his blankets, at the head of Bear River. They buried him where they found him, and brought the tin cup to Richfield and gave it to Judge O'Riley (O'Reilly)."

Moore particularly recalled some of the more memorable characters who made their way to the wilds of Fraser River in search of fame and fortune. Some, such as the notorious Ned McGowan, found it easier by far to "mine" the miners. Others such as the eccentric Gold Commissioner Cox brought law and order—of sorts—to the diggings. Although few argued with his decisions, they must have marvelled at the way in which he arrived at his verdicts. Usually Cox preferred those involved in civil suits to

settle out of his courtroom. Once, when they insisted upon his hearing their case, involving a claim-jumping suit, he ordered both plaintiff and defendants to settle the issue by racing each other the two miles to the disputed claim. Starting point was the courthouse and first to drive in his stake was the winner.

Such had been the beginning of mining in British Columbia. As for the future, James Moore, veteran of 51 years' active prospecting in the province, was sure that British Columbia, particularly its Cassiar region, remained an as yet untapped treasure-house of valuable minerals: "If capital once gets interested in this northern section of B.C. and opens up this section with railroad communication, they will open up the richest mineral district known in the province. There are millions here to be made by the first enterprising financiers who will stretch out their hand to receive it..."

The remarkable pioneer concluded his lecture with a plea for all oldtime prospectors to hold a reunion, that their reminiscences might be gathered in book form: "There are a great many instances occurred in those days which has slipped our memory, but one speaking may then refresh the memory of the other; by that way, and having a shorthand reporter present to take down notes, we may then get some very interesting reading. If this is not done soon there will be no one left to tell the tale."

His fear, alas, was all too soon realized. Fortunately, however, a reporter, adept at shorthand, was present at that Young People's Society meeting, back in the winter of 1909, and James Moore's remarkable recollections of British Columbia's second gold rush were recorded for posterity. ●

"SALE of the Burrard's Inlet mill—the sawmill owned by Mr. J.O. Smith was sold on Thursday by his creditor's assignees. It was purchased by Mr. Moody for the sum of $6,900."

This brief business notice of 1865 announced the start of a remarkable career in pioneer provincial commerce, that of the far-sighted American financier Sewell Prescott Moody. Sadly, this highly respected pioneer's career was cut short by disaster: a tragedy made all the more piognant by Moody's message from the dead.

If nothing else, Moody left a legacy of foresight. For he had been among the first—and among the few—to recognize the future of "Burrard's Inlet" when it was no more than a rain forest. In those days, when New Westminster was capital of the mainland **colony of British Columbia,** and Victoria the capital of Vancouver Island, as well as the commercial leader of the entire Pacific Northwest, the brash young Yankee's predictions were greeted with open contempt.

Yet, within 20 years, the future became apparent even 'to the scoffers and, although Moody did not live to see his dream come true, today his faith in the future is recognized by historians.

When Captain George Vancouver had poked about Burrard's Channel in the late 18th century, he learned to his disappointment that the Spanish had arrived first. Notwithstanding this, he proceeded to name many of the predominating geographical features and described the inlet: "From Point Grey we proceeded first up the eastern branch of the sound where, about a league from its entrance, we passed to the northward of an island which nearly terminated its extent, forming a passage from 10 to seven fathoms deep, not more than a cable's length in width. The island lying exactly across the channel, appeared to form a similar passage to the south of it, with a smaller island lying before it. From these islands, the channel, in width about half a mile, continued its direction about east. Here we were met by about 50 Indians, in their canoes, who conducted themselves with the greatest decorum and civility, presenting us with several fish cooked, and undressed, of the sort already mentioned as resembling smelt."

With HMS *Discovery's* departure the inlet returned to normal, its only inhabitants the Squamish and Musqueam tribesmen. Not until the mad rush up the Fraser River in search of gold, almost a century after, did this forest attract the fleeting attention of passersby. Even the Yorkshire potter, John Morton, who became its first settler, tried his luck in the gold fields before becoming interested in reports of clay deposits near Coal Harbor. Upon discovering that the clay was actually sandstone, the undaunted Morton decided to homestead and, with partners Bill Hailstone and Sam Brighouse, fellow Forty-

The Moody sawmill at Moodyville. Today the Moodyville of long ago is known as North Vancouver and is a suburb of the third largest metropolis in Canada. Each January 30, residents honor Moodyville Day and recall the area's former glory as well as Sewell Prescott Moody, the timber prophet who showed the way.

Upon his untimely death at sea, all mourned the passing of the founder of Burrard Inlet's lumber industry. When his funeral service was held in the reading room of the Mechanics' Institute at Moodyville, one of those attending reported, "Never on any occasion, religious or otherwise, have we seen the room so well filled. . . ."

SEWELL MOODY'S LEGACY OF FORESIGHT

Niners who had accompanied him up the Fraser, Morton pre-empted 550 acres in what is now Vancouver's highly-priced West End.

Alas, their struggle against the wilderness was doomed to failure, the partners having to move on in search of wages. For a time they were able to rent their rancherie—until local Indians took exception to its presence and burned it down.

It remained for two entrepreneurs named Hicks and Baker to point the way in 1862, when they salvaged the power plant from a wrecked steamer and set up a tiny mill on the North Shore. When, finally, the laboring lumbermen got going, they cut an impressive 10,000 feet of lumber in their first day of operation. Unfortunately, their first day of operation was also their last as their creditors foreclosed.

Such was the price of prophecy for, although few realized it at the time, Hicks and Baker had attempted to harvest one of the richest stands of timber in the world: a seemingly-limitless jungle of fir, cedar, hemlock and pine which would sire a metropolis.

The same year, T.W. Graham and Company of New Westminster gambled that they would succeed where Hicks and Baker failed and took a lease of 500 acres on the North Shore. Graham's company obviously enjoyed greater operating capital than had the partners as the newcomers soon erected a water-powered sawmill and named their little set-tlement Pioneer Mills. Within months, the sternwheeler *Flying Dutchman* loaded the first cargo of 500,000 board feet, and the great logging boom was on.

However, Graham and associates (although they were cutting 40,000 feet of lumber daily) also failed, and sold out to New Westminster grocer John Smith. He in turn sold out to a Victoria businessman from Maine named "Sue" Moody, who had become involved in the young logging industry by hauling rafts of timber from Burrard Inlet to Victoria. Ironically, Smith had succeeded, before bankruptcy, in setting a record when he shipped an amazing 278,000 feet of lumber and 16,000 pickets in a single cargo to Australia. With his failure, S. P. Moody and Company became the fourth venture to try for the golden ring on Burrard Inlet's North Shore.

But Moody also got off to a rocky start (literally) when his scow, the *Matilda*, stranded off Victoria and, with cargo, became a total loss. Declared the *Colonist*: "Much sympathy is expressed for Mr. Moody, who has only recently built the mills, and was about to commence operations."

Despite this setback, and with buyers in Victoria, Nanaimo and the Royal City only, Moody, Nelson and Company (as it was now known) proceeded with plans to build a worldwide network of markets. Moody visualized a steady stream of ships calling at

Burrard Inlet to load British Columbia lumber for ports of all nations. And, almost immediately, he succeeded where his predecessors had failed—and Burrard Inlet was on the map.

Another pioneer to see the potential of this region was Captain Edward Stamp, founder of Vancouver Island's first sawmill at Alberni. Upon personally examining the south shore of Burrard Inlet, Stamp returned to England to raise the necessary capital to form his British Columbia and Vancouver Island Spar, Lumber and Sawmill Company. Stamp apparently experienced little difficulty in convincing British backers of his project for, in 1865, he returned with the tidy sum of 100,000 pounds.

Interestingly enough, Stamp's first choice for beginning operations was what is now Stanley Park. But he changed his mind and his millsite to eastward when he learned of the riptides there which would wreak havoc with his log rafts. His British backers' confidence in his business ability became readily apparent when Stamp renegotiated with Governor Frederick Seymour for a timber lease of 30,000

John "Gassy Jack" Deighton, the Falstaffian saloon-keeper who was the undisputed king of the wild and woolly settlement of Stamp's Mill. Unlike Moody's Mill, Captain Stamp's sawmill town was wide-open. Today Vancouver's Gastown honors the popular Gassy Jack who arrived in the settlement with his in-laws, a barrel of whisky and six dollars in his pocket. Nevertheless, and almost overnight, Jack's Globe Saloon opened its swinging doors to the thirsty lumbermen.

Gastown about 1870, showing, on the left, the verandah of Gassy Jack's hotel and saloon.

acres (for 21 years at one cent per acre!) and permission to import all of his equipment duty-free.

Thus, on opposite shores of Burrard Inlet, Stamp's Mill and Moody's Mill came into being, the former consisting of the sawmill, one store and a four-acre clearing of shacks and saloons. A later visitor was unimpressed with the new townsite, terming it an "aggregation of filth" and "a running sore!"

Unlike Captain Stamp, who seems to have run a less-than-tight ship, Sue Moody was one of the province's first conscientious businessmen. Not only was his renamed Moodyville reasonably neat but it boasted a library, school and electric lighting—luxuries as yet unknown to Victoria, New Westminster or, for that matter, any settlement north of San Francisco—and no saloon. Stamp's Mill, on the other hand, continued to grow topsy-turvy and was wide-open, its population of Indian and Kanaka loggers, with a sprinkling of Scandinavian ship deserters, enjoying their choice of saloons which outnumbered all other business establishments. Consequently, when residents enthusiastically changed the settlement's name to Hastings Mill, in honor of Rear-Admiral George Hastings, the Esquimalt Commander-in-Chief must have been something less than flattered.

Undisputed king of this wild and woolly congregation was Gassy Jack Dieghton, after whom today's Gastown is affectionately named. Jack had descended upon the settlement with nothing more than his Indian wife, his in-laws, a native servant, a barrel of whisky and six dollars in his pocket. Despite this modest wealth, and almost overnight, Jack's Globe Saloon opened its swinging doors to the thirsty loggers. A contemporary (and competitor) later described Jack as having been of "broad, ready humor, spicy and crisp and everglowing, of grotesque, Falstaffian dimensions, with a green, muddy, deep purple complexion that told its own story. He had the gift of grouping words, which he flung from him with the volubility of a fake doctor. These words, shot at random, always hit a mark; unlucky would be the man whom Jack would nickname, for he would carry it as long as he lived."

Across the inlet, under the stern eye of Sue Moody, residents displayed considerably more decorum, the timber magnate preferring married employees and favoring their building their own homes. Instead of spending their free hours exercising their elbows, Moodyville residents enjoyed the library and reading room of the Mechanics' Institute. On Sundays there was Reverend Ebenezer Robson's service.

Regardless of the loggers' pleasure, business grew on both sides of the inlet, with ships from as far distant as Australia dropping anchor off the towns to load spars of Douglas fir and cedar.

Although force of business kept Moody in Moodyville much of the time he continued to call Victoria home and married Janet Watson there in 1869.

As early as mid-1868, Moody's mill (now steam-powered) had shipped almost 6,000,000 feet of lumber and 800,000 shingles (all cut by hand) in a year, compared to Stamp's 4,000,000 feet of lumber and 100,000 shingles. Another difference in figures was more noteworthy: Stamp had bellied up, whereas Moody continued to prosper. As evidence of his financial health, he ventured farther afield by building a telegraph line between Hastings Mill and the Royal City. Moody had become so comfortable that, when his mill burned down, he was merely inconvenienced and soon back in production.

But November of 1875 brought tragedy when Moody sailed for San Francisco aboard the ill-fated steamer *Pacific*. Within hours, the *Pacific* met disaster off Cape Flattery when rammed by the sailing vessel *Orpheus*. In a matter of minutes *Pacific* was gone, only two surviving of a company of more than 250. Among the dead was Sue Moody, beloved timberman of Victoria and Burrard Inlet.

Mourned the New Westminster *Herald*: "A gloom was cast over the community by the receipt of the sad intelligence of the loss of the *Pacific*, many of the victims being known and esteemed here, and one of them, Mr. S.P. Moody was among the foremost men in the New Westminster district, and whose loss will be at once sincerely regretted and widely felt. Always ready to hold forth a helping hand to those who needed it, genial in manner, enterprising and energetic in business and the head of a large and wealthy firm—he was one whose place will not easily be filled."

Many mourned the Maine businessman whose humor, honesty and regard for his workers had made him universally popular. Few were prepared for the shock of learning that, in death, Moody was to have a last word. This macabre twist occurred in Victoria when a resident walking along the Beacon Hill Park shore came upon a length of beam, later determined to be a piece of wreckage from the infamous *Pacific*. What caught the beachcomber's eye was the brief message which had been pencilled on its paint surface: "S.P. Moody, all is lost."

Immediate reaction to the discovery was that a "heartless hoax" had been perpetrated by someone with a perverted humor who, upon finding the board on the beach, had written the message, then launched the plank again. But when friends identified the writing as being unquestionably that of Sewell Moody, it was "supposed that when the vessel was going down he wrote the inscription on one of the beams of his stateroom with the faint hope that the board would be found and his friends informed of his fate.

"If such were his purpose it has been attained by the casting up of the fragment after it had floated nearly 100 miles on the breast of the hungry sea, and reached the shore within sight of the deceased

(Left) Victoria's Clover Point where, a century ago, heartbroken Victorians searched the beaches for bodies and wreckage from the Ss. Pacific. Although his body was never recovered "Sue" Moody sent a message from the grave.

(Below) The tragic steamer Pacific. Among her victims was Sewell Prescott Moody who, as he calmly waited for death, pencilled a brief message on a length of beam. Days later, his message from the dead drifted ashore in Victoria, 100 miles from the scene of the Pacific's foundering, and "within sight of the deceased gentleman's home."

(Right) Rear Admiral George F. Hastings, Commander-in-Chief at Esquimalt, must have been something less than flattered when the rowdy residents of Captain Stamp's sawmill settlement christened their community in his honor. One visitor called the four-acre collection of shacks and saloons an "aggregation of filth" and "a running sore," whereas Moddy's Mill was a model community complete with library, school and electric lighting.

gentleman's home. The feelings of a man taking leave of life under such circumstances can neither be imagined nor described."

In Moodyville, all mourned the founder of Burrard Inlet's lumber industry, the Mechanics' Institute being filled to overflowing for the service conducted by Reverend Dinnick. "Never on any occasion, religious or otherwise," reported a witness, "have we seen the (reading) room so well filled and the number there was a sufficient indication of the kindly feelings of the community toward the deceased."

Today Moodyville is a suburb of Canada's third largest metropolis and continues to prosper under the name North Shore. Each January 30, residents honor Moodyville Day, recalling the area's former glory—and Sewell Prescott Moody, the timber prophet who showed the way. The coming of the railway in the 1880s may have been Vancouver's guarantee of maturity, but lumber had rocked the cradle.

For years Moody's family kept the piece of weathered stanchion bearing his final farewell before presenting it to the Vancouver Maritime Museum. It is a sad memento of that sad day when Ss. *Pacific* foundered with her hapless hundreds and Sue Moody hastily pencilled a last goodbye on a broken plank. ●

Minnie, Grace Darling

THE San Francisco bark *Coloma* drifted a helpless punching bag before the sou'easter, each 80-mile-an-hour gust jarring her to the keel and pounding the 850-ton ship beneath the waves. Caught in the deadly reaches off the west coast of Vancouver Island, whose thick fogs, treacherous currents and sudden storms have claimed ships of many flags over the years, the 168-foot *Coloma* was awash, her lifeboats gone, a spider web of collapsed rigging spilled over her sides.

Clutching the stump of mizzenmast were 10 frightened men.

Captain J. Allison had long given up hope. In the raging dawn of December 6, 1906, the sea and sky met in a ragged grey line, offering little chance that the tattered ensign flying upside down in the international distress signal would be spotted.

Then, poking through the murk like an eerie yellow finger was Cape Beale light. Allison knew what that meant. Soon the gale would hurl them against jagged reefs when, unknown to the lightkeeper, *Coloma*'s crew would be drowned almost at his feet. Ten men eyed the slim tower hungrily, praying for some sign of recognition, of salvation. "Oh God, why doesn't he see us?" someone groaned. That was all: no panic, just a desperate plea for a miracle. Then they could hear the rocks gnawing at the bow, and old *Coloma* groaned violently…

Lightkeeper Thomas Paterson was worried. He had spent the wild night in the lantern room, 170 feet above the sea, drinking hot, strong tea and chewing his pipe pensively. His eyes followed the red flash, then the white beacon as Cape Beale light stabbed outward 19 miles over the black ocean. Above the banshee wailing of the wind he could not even hear his own fog horn, and the tower shivered under the onslaught of breakers booming in from a thousand miles at sea to shake the very land.

When a timid dawn broke at 3 a.m., Mrs. Paterson brought him fresh tea. She was restless too. As their five children slept soundly below, the couple stared into the gloom, expecting they knew not what.

Suddenly Tom rubbed his eyes and pointed. "Minnie, look. A dismasted ship and there's men aboard!"

A single thought flashed through their minds: the

British Columbia's own "Grace Darling," Minnie Paterson, who risked life and limb to bring aid to the men of the Coloma. *Unlike the British heroine, however, Mrs. Paterson never fully recovered from her ordeal. (Opposite) The lighthouse tender* Quadra *which hastened to the rescue of* Coloma's *crew when alerted of her peril by the combined efforts of Minnie Paterson, "Grace Darling of the Northwest," and Annie McKay.*

Sacrifice was no stranger to Minnie Paterson. Upon her epic hike overland to bring help to the company of the foundering Coloma, the Sailor's Union of the Pacific recognized "her sterling worth as the highest type of womanhood."

Paterson: Of The Northwest

derelict's only chance was the lighthouse tender *Quadra*, then sheltering in Bamfield Inlet, six miles away. But the telegraph key in the living room was dead. So was the telephone. And Tom could not leave his post.

Even as Minnie said, "I'll go, Tom," she was pulling on his heavy clothing. His slippers would offer better footing on the trail that ran along the shore and through wilderness, and she put them on. With a quick farewell kiss she grabbed a lantern and, accompanied by faithful collie Yarrow, she began her immortal race against time.

Tom readied a lifeboat in case the *Quadra* could not arrive.

The trail, a series of blazes on trees supporting the telegraph line, was difficult to follow at best of times. At the height of a gale it was hell. Pressed by urgency, Mrs. Paterson moved as fast as she dared. The wind lashed her with broken branches. Rain, driven

horizontally, blocked her vision and threatened to snuff out her small lantern. Every few feet, she had to feel her way about severed telegraph wire that snaked across the path, trying to trip her.

Exertion and frustration racked her body. Breathing was painful, swallowing difficult.

Frightened and bewildered Yarrow remained close to his mistress, both receiving slight comfort from the flickering lamp.

The trail became a succession of windfalls, icy water traps and knee-deep mud. Slipping and sinking in the mire, she pushed onward, ever onward, clambering over stumps and rocks and through thick underbrush.

Swelled by torrential rains, Bamfield Creek had washed out part of the trail and, moving downstream, she started to wade. The muddied, surging waters climbed her legs until waist-high, then crept higher when, murmuring a short prayer, she took a tentative step forward. A second. A third. Slowly the water receded. She was across. Turning to the unbroken bush, she cut cross-country.

Four hours after leaving the lighthouse, her clothing in rags, soaked through and exhausted, she reached the Bamfield home of Mrs. James McKay. With waning strength she pounded on the door and prayed that she would be heard above the storm. At last Mrs. McKay answered.

"Why...why, Minnie Paterson! Look at you!

What's wrong? For heaven's sake, come inside before you catch—"

"No, Annie, we haven't time. Where's your Jim? A ship's coming ashore off the light and we've got to warn the *Quadra!*"

"Oh, no! Jim's been out all night. They're trying to repair the telegraph—look, if we try finding someone it'll be too late. Come on, we'll take our boat and warn the *Quadra* ourselves!"

Mrs. McKay grabbed a jacket and both women raced to the beach.

They were in luck. Smoke trailing above the *Quadra's* tall funnel showed that Captain Hackett had maintained a head of steam during the night in case his anchors dragged. He would be able to cast off immediately.

The storm was abating but heavy swells buffetted their small rowboat like a tennis ball, battling them first one way, then another. The women's progress was slow as they had to take turns at bailing their slight craft. Then they saw the *Quadra's* longboat coming toward them. Aboard were Captain Hackett and two seamen. As the boats neared, Mrs. Paterson shouted: "Close in to Cape Beale there's a ship coming ashore with the crew in the rigging. She's not more than half a mile from shore!"

Captain Hackett needed no prompting. Hurrying back to his ship, he ordered her underway as the two women made their way back to shore and to the McKay home.

"Minnie, you're bushed. Come in, get on some dry clothes and have some hot tea."

"Thank you, Annie, but my baby needs me." With that, Mrs. Paterson turned and began her tortuous way homeward. Mrs. McKay watched the beaten figure until out of sight, then went inside. Everything depended upon Captain Hackett and his crew now.

Quadra butted her way around Cape Beale. Before her lay the shattered hulk of the *Coloma.* Those aboard the lighthouse tender later described the dramatic scene:

"The crew members were clustered on the poop, huddled under the shelter of a little deckhouse. The bow was open, the seams split so wide that lumber from the cargo was floating out stick after stick. Bulwarks were gone, and the deck, from which the cargo had been washed away in the night, was flush with the high-running seas which surged over it and battered against the poop, throwing clouds of spray over the crew. The vessel was as helpless a derelict as any of the *Quadra's* crew had ever seen. Her masts, held by the wire rigging, floated from the vessel like a huge sea-anchor and she swung around and around as the big seas swept against her."

The heavy swell prevented the *Quadra* from getting too near. While she hove to, Second Officer McDonald and a picked crew were lowered over the side when, with great difficulty, they brought their small boat under the bark's counter. Time and

again, McDonald attempted to heave a line aboard, only to have the bucking waves spoil his aim.

At last he had it secured and, one by one, at the crest of each wave, *Coloma's* crew members leaped to safety or slid down the line. After narrowly escaping being crushed against the wreck, the small boat made its way back to the *Quadra.* The rescued seamen were then taken to Victoria and placed in care of the United States Consul.

The *Coloma* was left derelict and drifted for weeks, a navigational hazard, before she finally drove ashore on a small island, a total loss.

In Victoria Captain Allison, who had survived no fewer than four shipwrecks, told of the last, terrifying 12 hours aboard the *Coloma,* which had cleared Port Townsend with lumber for Australia: "All hands took to what was left of the mizzen rigging towards 3 a.m., when the vessel had settled so that the decks were completely awash. At 3:15 we saw Cape Beale light and were no more than a mile off the rocks of the Island coast. We could see the breakers right under the bow and all thought we were going to be dashed on the rocks at any time. However, the tide swept us off again...

"Soon after daylight we dragged a spanker boom and some other wreckage to the poop, and with difficulty constructed a raft. The boats had all been carried away in the night."

Before the raft could be secured a large sea had washed it over the side.

Unknown to his men, Allison had kept his pistol ready, "for no one knows what will happen, and I only had the crew on board two days. I didn't know them. But they were brave men. They looked death in the face. At one time when we didn't expect to live another 15 seconds, the men were deliberately and calmly contemplating the end."

Although there had been only one lifebelt among the 10 men, "There was no clamor for it," continued Allison. "The man who found it kept it, and none struggled to take it from him, even though they thought the vessel must break to pieces against the rocks.

"It seemed as if the forward part of the vessel had broken loose. We were practically exhausted when the *Quadra* came."

Because of poor visibility the rescue had not been seen from the lighthouse. It was not until a week later when the telegraph line to Victoria, broken in more than a hundred places, had been repaired, that Mrs. Paterson learned that her mission had not been in vain.

Sacrifice was no stranger to Minnie Paterson. Earlier in the year she had spent 36 hours at her telegraph key, and fed and comforted the pitifully few survivors of the San Francisco steamer *Valencia.* The passenger liner had overshot her course in fog and run up on nearby Pachena Point with the loss of 117 lives, one of the worst marine disasters on the West Coast. Years before, Mrs. Paterson's

*The dying bark **Coloma** off Cape Beale. When the **Quadra** attempted to approach the wreck one of those aboard the government steamer noted that the sailing vessel's "bow was open, the seams split so wide that lumber from the cargo was floating out stick after stick... The vessel was as helpless a derelict as any of the **Quadra's** crew had ever seen."*

mother, also the wife of a lightkeeper, had saved two men on the Atlantic shore.

Like the original Grace Darling, Minnie Paterson captured the public's imagination. The American and Canadian governments paid her homage as, all over the Pacific Northwest, the public contributed to a fund to give her a Christmas present as a "more tangible reward."

But, unlike her prototype, Mrs. Paterson was to pay a heavier cost for her courage. After four years of poor health, the result of exposure and over-exertion, she died. Both nations mourned the loss of a great woman.

Thomas Paterson died on his way overseas with the army during the First World War. Mrs. James McKay died at Bamfield in 1956. The *Quadra*, after years of government service, was sunk in a collision in 1917. Salvaged, she passed into private hands. Eighteen years later, she again made headlines when she was captured while rum-running and towed into San Francisco. During the lengthy court proceedings that followed, she rotted at her moorings and subsequently was sold for scrap.

One of the Paterson family treasures is a citation awarded their mother by the Sailor's Union of the Pacific, which reads:

"Whereas, Mrs. Thomas Paterson of Cape Beale, Vancouver Island, has repeatedly, at the risk of her health and life, proven herself a heroine by assisting in saving the lives of unfortunate castaways on the rocky shores of her chosen home, or adrift in the nearby ocean, therefore, be it, by the Seattle Branch of the Sailor's Union of the Pacific in the meeting assembled RESOLVED that we, the seamen of America fully recognize her sterling worth as the highest type of womanhood, deeply appreciating her unselfish sacrifices in behalf of those 'who go down to the sea in ships' and assure her and hers of our undying gratitude."

Minnie Paterson was not likened to history's Grace Darling without reason. Grace's well-earned claim to fame dates back to September 7, 1838, when the *Forfarshire* wrecked in a gale near her father's Longstone Light, in the Farne Islands. Forty-three drowned immediately but, by "a combination of daring, strength and skill," Grace and her father then returned to the splintered hulk with two of the survivors and saved the four still aboard. ●

(Far left) Colonel Richard Clement Moody who, as well as being in command of the Royal Engineers, served as Chief Commissioner of Lands and Works, supported Moberly's proposal for a road by way of the Fraser River — the great Cariboo Wagon Road. (Left) Sir Matthew Baillie Begbie, British Columbia's so-called "Hanging Judge," whom Moberly met at a dinner at Governor James Douglas' home. With several other guests and the governor's family, the young engineer "spent a most enjoyable evening and on my leaving received their best wishes for the success of my undertaking." (Below) Fort Langley. It was on a "cold, stormy, dreary and dismal day" that Moberly boarded the steamer Otter to cross the Gulf of Georgia and ascend the Fraser River as far as the palisaded trading post where, after meeting Chief Factor Yale, he continued upstream to the north of the Harrison River, thence on to Port Douglas.

He was true to his beliefs, loyal to his friends; he killed bears with pistols and swung an axe (even at the age of 70) with the best of them. He was. . .

WALTER MOBERLY
Explorer and Engineer

TODAY, more than half a century after his death, Moberly's vital role in the founding of British Columbia is virtually unrecognized.

This, despite the fact that he participated in the surveying of New Westminster, worked on the historic Cariboo wagon road and Dewdney Trail, and discovered Eagle Pass—"the true northwest passage to the Pacific," and a vital link in the transcontinental railway route linking eastern and western Canada.

In March of 1907 Moberly delivered a speech to the Canadian Club in Vancouver in which he recalled his early career as an engineer in the vast wilderness which was to become Canada's western-most province. Then a resident of Vancouver (a residency which preceded the birth of Gastown by a generation), Moberly had been asked to give a brief outline of "matters connected with the development of British Columbia," from its inception as a crown colony and the discovery of gold in the Fraser River. Humbly acknowledging the fact that he had taken "a very prominent part in the explorations, works, etc.," that led to Vancouver's founding as a city, Moberly began his story.

"When I was a very young man, I took great interest in all the voyages made by vessels of different nations for the purpose of making discoveries in various parts of the world, and also in expeditions by

For centuries, Europeans dreamed of a fabled Northwest Passage to the Orient. Thousands tried— and hundreds died— in the search for this route across the top of North America. Explorer and engineer Walter Moberly believed that the true Northwest Passage lay not in the frozen wastes of the Arctic but overland to British Columbia. Only in this way, he argued, would Canada and the British Empire at large develop its potential by forging a commercial link with the Orient: at the same time developing "the immense extent of almost unknown British territory extending westerly from Lake Simcoe to the North Pacific Ocean."

land for the same purposes. Those made in connection with the continent of North America were carefully studied by me, more especially those relating to British North America and the waters of the different oceans that wash its northern, its eastern and its western shores."

These "many and noble efforts" in search of the legendary Northwest Passage convinced the young engineering student that such a northern sea route through the Arctic ice, even should it exist and be charted, would never amount to any value as a commercial lifeline for the British Empire. Whatever, his interests in exploration were temporarily set aside in 1855, when, at the age of 23, he became the owner of a large timber limit between Lake Simcoe and the Michipicotin River, which empties into Lake Superior. But it was not long before his eye was again fixed upon the horizon and a new dream: the construction of a transcontinental railroad.

For the next three summers, he explored the little-known country west of Lake Simcoe and north of Lakes Huron and Superior. During winter months, he became intimately acquainted with the great Canadian artist, Paul Kane, who had recently returned from his cross-country tour on behalf of Sir George Simpson of the Hudson's Bay Company. Travelling westward, Kane had worked his way via Lake Superior, Fort Garry, Edmonton, Jasper House, the Athabasca Pass and, by way of the Columbia River, to Washington and Oregon Territories, before proceeding to Victoria. He returned by the same route and, said Moberly, "being of a very observant nature had collected a great deal of information regarding the vast extent of territory traversed by him, and which, during the many days and evenings we spent together, he kindly imparted to me..."

It was in the course of these discussions that Moberly became convinced that the "true Northwest Passage" lay not in the frozen Arctic wastes, but overland to British Columbia. Only in this way, he argued, would Canada and the British Empire at large develop its potential by forging a commercial link with the Orient: at the same time developing "the immense extent of almost unknown British Territory extending westerly from Lake Simcoe to the North Pacific Ocean."

Coincidentally upon his return to Toronto, late in 1857, he heard that the Palliser expedition had been commissioned by the imperial government to explore this very wilderness. About the same time he learned of the discovery of gold in distant British Columbia: "Here now was the opportunity to push forward my idea of a northwest passage by land, and I immediately sold all my interests in Ontario to raise money to get to British Columbia, where I proposed to meet Captain Palliser and find out from him if a route for a railway through British territory could be obtained and to have money to enable me to push forward my proposed explorations in British Columbia."

Through Kane he was introduced to Sir George Simpson who, upon hearing the young adventurer's scheme for a transcontinental railway, wrote him a letter of introduction to James Douglas, governor of the crown colony of Vancouver Island. Thus armed, he left Toronto early in the summer of 1858, sailing from New York and around the Horn, and arriving at Esquimalt late the same year. More than half a century after, he vividly recalled the muddy hike from Esquimalt to Victoria, and his colorful introduction to the "Songish" Indians.

His first view of Victoria, circa 1858, was no less memorable: "a small town with muddy streets." After finding indifferent accommodation in a little clapboard hotel known as Bailey's, he had his first encounters with the vanguard of goldseekers bound for the Interior diggings. They were, he said, "an openhearted and interesting community, but their language was very forcible."

The next day, he called upon Governor Douglas, presented his letter of introduction, and received both a hearty welcome and the offer of a job. The latter, he politely declined, explaining to Douglas that he was eager to meet Captain Palliser. When the governor explained to him that it would be at least a year before the Palliser party could reach the coast, and that "exploring through the mountains of British Columbia was a most formidable undertaking, more especially so as the winter had just set in and supplies were very scarce, and in fact almost impossible to obtain in the interior," Moberly was undaunted. He was determined to begin his explorations on the mainland and thanked Douglas for his concern and the tendered appointment.

After further stressing the difficulties of the British Columbia mainland topography, particularly in relation to Moberly's proposed railway—and in dead of winter—Douglas gave him a letter of introduction to Hudson's Bay Company officials and invited him to dinner that evening. At the appointed hour Moberly presented himself at the Douglas residence, where he was introduced to several other guests: Judge Begbie, Captain Richards, RN, then in charge of coastal surveys for the Admiralty, Colonial Secretary Young, Justice Cameron, Dr. Helmcken, Donald Fraser and Alexander Dallas, as well as "all the members of the Governor's kind and interesting family with whom I spent a most enjoyable evening and on my leaving received their best wishes for the success of my undertaking."

For all of his doubts as to the practicability of building a railway, Douglas was interested in wagon roads—particularly over the portages between Port Douglas and Lillooet—and he asked Moberly to report to him upon the feasibility of building roads between those points. So long afterward, Moberly noted with justifiable pride that as the Royal Engineers had not yet arrived in the colony his reports, as duly forwarded to Douglas, were "the first ever made regarding public works on the mainland of British Columbia." When the engineers did arrive, Colonel Richard Moody endorsed Moberly's recommendations and the projects were carried out "forthwith."

It was on a "cold, stormy, dreary and dismal day," that he boarded the Hudson's Bay Company steamer *Otter* to cross the Gulf of Georgia and ascend the Fraser River as far as palisaded Fort Langley where, after meeting Chief Factor Yale, he continued upstream to the mouth of the Harrison River in the sternwheel steamer *Enterprise*, owned and commanded by "that prince of good fellows," Captain Tom Wright. He then proceeded up the Harrison by canoe, reaching Port Douglas after a "miserable journey" of cold, storm, rain and snow.

Port Douglas, he found, was small, new and crowded with miners, packers, traders and Indians. After hiring an Indian packer, he made a hasty departure. His destination was Lillooet Lake, 29 miles distant by way of a narrow, winding trail through dense forest and, at that time of year, snow. Travelling was "most fatiguing," and, three or four miles from town, his assistant deserted him: "As I could not make any progress through the deep snow with my blankets on my back, I abandoned them and experienced many a cold and miserable night during this, my first, and never-to-be-forgotten journey through the mountains of British Columbia." Nevertheless, he pushed onward as far as Pavilion Mountain, when, weak from hunger, he returned to Fort Langley content with the knowledge that country so inhospitable to a man on foot was no place for a railway.

Turning to the mountainous region of Pitt River and Pitt Lake, he was again forced to concede defeat although, on this survey, he noted the ideal site for a city on the north side of the Fraser. He returned to Victoria before trying a third route: this time, the formidable canyons of the Fraser between Yale and Lytton. As before, he was doomed to disappointment and, upon his return to Victoria, he was engaged by Colonel Moody to "proceed to the locality I had previously visited and there 'found' the new capital of British Columbia, as the site at first adopted for the capital city, which was on the south

The famous Cariboo Road is considered to be the greatest single achievement of Governor James Douglas. But it was engineer Walter Moberly who convinced Douglas that the best route lay through the forbidding canyons of the Fraser and Thompson Rivers, "which latter route I strongly advised in lieu of the Harrison-Lillooet route which was a mixed and broken land and water route necessitating much handling of freight."

(Above) When Moberly's third quest for a route for a transcontinental railway failed, he was engaged by Colonel Richard Moody to "found" the new capital city, Queenborough. The result, after a change of name, was New Westminster.
(Right) Esquimalt. More than half a century afterward, Moberly vividly recalled the muddy hike from this naval base and port to Fort Victoria.

bank of the Fraser River, about two miles below Fort Langley, and which had been named Derby, was abandoned. The new city I was sent to found was called Queenborough, but the name was subsequently changed to that of New Westminster which was given to it by her late Most Gracious Majesty, Queen Victoria..."

This historic assignment completed, he and Robert Burnaby went to Burrard Inlet in search of coal deposits near what is today the north end of Bute Steet. Although their test-shafts did not prove successful, they did leave their mark on the map, Captain G.H. Richards of the survey ship *Plumper* entering the harbor at this time and duly christening their little cove, Coal Harbor. But even as his crews were mining for coal, Moberly was thinking about his elusive railroad, and he made a brief survey up the Squamish River to see if this region presented a more favorable route for a railway or wagon road. As ever, he was frustrated—but far from being beaten. Turning to real estate, he pre-empted "the land on which the City of Vancouver now stands, as I saw the many and great natural advantages it possessed for a future large city and I then made up

my mind to do my utmost to get such a city built and I feel very much gratified and somewhat proud to stand here today. . ." This accomplished, he again wintered in Victoria where, finally, he met the man for whom he had travelled so far and waited for so long to meet: Captain John Palliser. Curiously, Moberly makes no further mention of his meeting with the famous Palliser, for that officer was not impressed with his grandiose ideas of a transcontinental railway through the Rockies. Although disappointed, he was determined to prove such a route existed and turned to Governor Douglas in hopes that the colony would underwrite the costs of his investigating "unfavorable reports regarding the building of a transcontinental railway exclusively through British Territory, and which was of such vital importance for British Columbia and British interests generally."

When Douglas did not grant him funds he was

unable to continue his "much desired explorations" and, instead, decided to "develop" British Columbia. To this end, he spent the years 1860-61 carving a trail and constructing a section of wagon road over Hope Mountain (also finding time to further examine the Fraser and Thompson Valleys). The result of his surveys to date convinced him that the best route for a wagon road and, ultimately, for a railway was along the Fraser River and through the formidable canyons between Yale and Lytton—provided a pass could be found through the Gold Range, giving access to the valley of the Columbia River.

This in mind, he "went to work to accomplish the building of this great wagon road and the finding of a pass, through the Gold Range, for a railway that I intended should have its western terminus at Burrard Inlet, or, rather, I may say in this City of Vancouver.

"During the years 1860 and 1861 Governor Douglas had caused to be undertaken the building of a wagon road from Port Douglas at the head of Harrison Lake via the valley of the Lillooet River to Clinton, over the route I had explored and reported upon in the winter of 1858-9, with the intention of making it the great thoroughfare for the development of British Columbia as he then considered it impracticable to construct a wagon road through the forbidding canyons of the Fraser and Thompson Rivers, which latter route I had strongly advised in lieu of the Harrison-Lillooet route which was a mixed and broken land and water route necessitating much handling of freight."

But, late in 1861, fate conspired on his behalf when the "wonderful deposits of gold" in the Cariboo were confirmed, and Moberly was presented with an opportunity to make another, desperate effort for a road by way of the Fraser River—the Cariboo Wagon Road. Previously, he had discussed this project with Colonel Moody who, as well as being in command of the engineers, served as Chief Commissioner of Lands and Works. After hearing Moberly's idea, Moody suggested that they examine "those obstructive canyons of the Fraser." Upon completing their survey, Moody was "as convinced as I was before we parted, after we had made a careful examination of (the canyons) that the great wagon road should be built through them. We arranged to meet in Victoria the following winter and press our views on Governor Douglas."

In due course Douglas agreed to build a road to Cariboo, Moberly spending the next three years at work on this project, the last in the capacity of government engineer and superintendent of works in Cariboo. He modestly admitted that the Cariboo wagon road was "mainly instrumental" in developing British Columbia. When British Columbia and Vancouver Island became colonies, Moberly recognized another opportunity to "push...forward my wishes to get assistance from the government to enable me to find the remaining portion of the much desired

route, if it existed, for a railway through the mountains of British Columbia." He resigned from government service and ran for the legislative council. After a hot and expensive campaign he carried Cariboo West by a large majority, when newly-appointed Governor Frederick Seymour made him minister of lands and works.

As such, Moberly drew up the Land Act and, with Peter O'Reilly, drafted the Mining Act. He then persuaded Governor Seymour to finance exploratory surveys of the country east of Kamloops. As soon as the council adjourned he resigned his seat and accepted Seymour's appointment as Assistant Surveyor General of the Crown Colony of British Columbia, and set out to "undertake the explorations I had so much desired."

Handing over the reins to his department to Joseph Trutch, he returned to his first love. It was during this survey that he finally found the key for which he had been seeking for so long—Eagle Pass—the doorway through the Gold Range "which hitherto had been considered to be an unbroken chain of mountains presenting an impassable barrier for a railway; at the same time I also reported the discovery of the valley of the Illecillewaet River, penetrating far into the Selkirk Range of mountains, and that it would probably afford a direct passage through that range in the desired direction.

"As soon as I had discovered the Eagle Pass I then knew that an imperial highway—the true Northwest Passage—of the greatest value to the British Empire and especially to the Dominion of Canada and to British Columbia was a certainty; and that my discovery, made in the year 1865, would result in paving the way for Britain's sway in British North America, and across the North and South Pacific Oceans, and thus consolidate the Empire, and that its western terminus would be at Vancouver, and I felt gratified that the years of toil, of hardship, of privation and expense I had gone through and incurred, would be of great and lasting benefit to my native and adopted countries—England and Canada."

The rest—the exploration east from Revelstoke, through the Selkirk Range via the valley of the Illecillewaet River and the valley of the Columbia, around and through the Big Bend to connect Eagle Pass with the passes discovered by other explorers, "only required detailed surveys to decide upon the best route to adopt," he concluded.

Unfortunately, since his passing, in 1915 at the age of 83, Walter Moberly has been allowed to drift into obscurity. Little recognition other than the naming of a school in Vancouver and a monument in Revelstoke has been paid this great explorer (the Peace River country's Moberly Lake being named after brother Harry) who gave much of his life and his personal wealth for his country—one country unified by an "imperial highway" through the mountains and canyons of British Columbia. ●

On Chilkoot Pass

(Opposite page) Over the notorious Chilkoot Pass. Among the thousands of adventurers who risked life and limb to reach Dawson City was Nellie Cashman. (Inset) Nellie Cashman. Upon her death, thousands of husky, bearded men wept unashamedly. (Above) St. Joseph's Hospital, Victoria. When a dying Nellie Cashman entered the hospital she had helped to establish so many years before, she "scorned to be carried in, but walked 'on her own two legs' into the ward." Days later, her amazing career was ended.

The Miner's Angel

Though records differ as to the date of her birth, her arrival in the New World, even to the color of her hair, on one fact all heartily concur: That her heart was as large as the great American and Canadian West she conquered with her ever-cheerful smile, her indomitable courage, her hand outstretched to any man down on his luck.

A Florence Nightingale to miners from Tombstone to the Klondike, when she died in the Victoria hospital she helped to establish, thousands of husky, bearded men wept unashamedly for their tiny saint of half a century. . .Nellie Cashman.

According to one account, "The Miner's Angel" landed in Boston in 1847, at the age of three, sent by her mother in Ireland to be raised by an aunt. Young Nell learned to look out for herself—and others—early. Twelve years later, she was raising her four orphaned cousins. For the rest of her active life, in some way or other, loved one and stranger, Nell would care for anyone in need.

Nell began setting records early, when she became a bellhop, at 16, in a Boston hotel to support her family. Some claim she was the first lady to enter that profession. Unlike later feats of kindness and courage, this honor is unconfirmed.

Besides tending her aunt's children, Nell was able to save enough to bring her mother from the Emerald Isle. It was then she decided to answer the call of adventure, a call she would heed for almost 50 amazing years.

Across the Isthmus of Panama to San Francisco trekked the daring company. Finally reaching the Bay city, 28-year-old Nell struck out on her own, heading for the rip-roaring boom town of Virginia City, Nevada, to open a restaurant. Charging a dollar for her soon-to-be-famous meals, her establishment was immediately popular with the Comstock kings and miners. The bearded, ever-hopeful clientele struck an unknown chord in Nell. Now she realized that these rough miners were of her own: always seeking that pot of gold at the end of the rainbow.

Saving enough to buy a grubstake, Nell trudged into the wilds with pick, shovel and pan. At first her husky neighbors laughed at the determined young woman. But laughter soon gave way to respect and Nell was accepted into the fraternity of eternal hope. She would follow this elusive trail of wealth—sometimes with success—to the end of her days.

It was back in San Francisco that Nell decided upon British Columbia. Actually, her decision was made by the flip of a coin. With six other disheartened prospectors, she flipped to see whether they would try their luck in the gold fields of South Africa or B.C. Heads—they went to South Africa. Tales—it was British Columbia.

The 20-dollar gold piece winked tails: It was north to Cassiar.

That summer of 1874, the noisy troop of six bearded, brawling miners and five-foot, three-inch redhead landed in Victoria, enroute to the diggings at Dease Lake.

While in Victoria, Nell heard that the Cassiar miners were suffering from scurvy. Hiring six men to haul her supplies to open a hotel, she included in her cluttered inventory lime juice and fresh vegetables. Boarding a steamer, the expedition headed north to Wrangell, to follow the frozen Stikine River to Dease Creek. From the blazing heat of southwest deserts, the hardy company struck upriver through snowdrifts and sub-zero temperatures—Nell gamely towing a sled with 200 pounds

The Dease Lake country of British Columbia, where Nellie Cashman hauled lime juice and fresh vegetables for 160 miles to relieve miners dying of scurvy. It was but a single act of kindness in a lifelong career of caring for those in need.
Heading for the Klondike the hard way. Scenes such as this were all too familiar to the indomitable Nellie Cashman, who had hiked to the scene of many a gold rush.

of supplies. Nell, in snowshoes, hauled the load every inch of the way—160 miles—for 77 days!

Asked many years after whether she had been afraid of being the only woman on that hazardous journey, Nell had chuckled:

"Bless your soul, no, I have never carried a pistol or gun in all my life. I wouldn't know how to shoot one. At one time for two years I was the only white woman in camp. I never have had a word said to me out of the way.

"The 'boys' would sure see to it that anyone who ever offered to insult me could never be able to repeat the offence. The farther you go away from civilization, the bigger-hearted and more courteous you find the men. Every man I met up north was my protector, and any man I ever met, if he needed my help, got it, whether it was a hot meal, nursing, mothering, or whatever else he needed. After all, we pass this way only once, and it's up to us to help our fellows when they need our help."

One of the adventures on the trail had been the night her companions erected her tent on "a steep hill where the snow was 10 feet deep.

"The next morning one of my men made a cup of hot coffee and came to where my tent was to bring me the coffee. It had snowed heavily in the night, and, to his surprise, he couldn't find the tent. Finally they discovered me a quarter of a mile down the hill, where my tent, my bed and myself and all the rest of my belongings had been carried by a snowslide. No, they didn't dig me out; by the time they got there I had dug myself out.

"We finally reached our destination, and I put off running my hotel until I had nursed a lot of the sick miners back to health. Word went out to the nearest military post (Wrangell) that I had cashed in my checks. The commanding officer sent a detail of soldiers in to get my body and bring it out to the post. It was a mighty nice thing for them to send clear in there to get my body so I could have Christian burial. I appreciated it, and got those soldiers the best feed they ever had!"

Actually, the officer's concern had been for Miss Cashman's mental health, not her physical condition! Any woman who would hike 200 miles through wilderness in the dead of winter had to be insane, he reasoned. But when the rescue party found Nell "cooking her evening meal by the heat of a wood fire, and humming a lively air, so happy, contented and comfortable did she appear that the 'boys in blue' sat down and took tea at her invitation, and returned without her." Nell hiked out that fall to spend winter in Victoria. While there, she learned St. Joseph's Hospital was being built. Back at Dease Lake with the spring thaw, she canvassed the miners for contributions and collected a respectable sum.

The following autumn, she again hiked down to Wrangell, intending to spend winter at Victoria. But in the Alaskan port she heard a group of prospectors also heading downriver had been strucken by scurvy. With medicines and spruce bark, the indomitable colleen raced back up the Stikine to nurse the laboring party. When all finally reached Wrangell, the miners said Nell had saved their lives.

In 1876 Nell heard wild, tantalizing rumors concerning a fabulously rich strike in Arizona. It was all the prompting she needed. Packing up her few possessions and what money she had saved, she headed for Tucson, to open the Delmonico Restaurant. In her free time, she tried her hand at prospecting, but with little success.

Within a year she headed for the beckoning bonanza of Tombstone; the famous camp which was to be her home, off and on, for 20 historic, exciting years.

She started in Tombstone nearly penniless, all her savings having gone to help the needy. "Her principal business was to feed the hungry and shelter the homeless, and her chief divertisement was to relieve those in distress and to care for the sick and afflicted," praised John Clum, editor and friend.

She was not long in the lawless camp when she heard that a miner had broken both legs. Hands ex-tended, she canvassed the town, visiting every establishment, respectable and notorious, until she had raised $500 for the ailing man.

Once her restaurant and general store were established, Nell sent for her family. Over the following years, Nell stole time from home and business to investigate the surrounding region. Gold, silver and copper interested her and whenever she found a likely camp she would open a restaurant. When the local mines petered our or she considered them to be of little potential, she would move on to the next camp or back to Tombstone for a while.

Among her famous clientele were the Earps, the Clantons, Doc Holliday, Johnny Ringo and Pat Garrett.

Nell's attention had early been drawn to the fact Tombstone boasted 50 saloons and "nary a church." Result of this observation was a one-woman campaign which saw the Sacred Heart Catholic Church open its doors February 1, 1881.

Then she noticed Tombstone lacked a hospital. Her answer to this problem was to journey to Tucson and return with three nuns to act as nurses. And Tombstone had its hospital.

When miners struck the town's three leading mines, in 1884, Nell heard a terrifying rumor: The outraged miners were going to lynch the superintendent of the Grand Central Mine, Edward B. Gage. Nell had an answer to that problem, too. Hiring a horse and buggy, she smuggled the frightened Gage to a nearby town. When the lynch mob called on its intended victim, to find he was safely enroute to Tucson, they dispersed and the crisis passed.

By the mid-eighties, Nell and her family were following the rainbows again: Montana, Wyoming, back to Arizona, then Oregon and Washington, then back to Arizona once more. In 1889, she was talking of diamonds in Africa, but ended up in the promising gold fields of California. The years passed, Nell ever on the move. Idaho and even Mexico hosted the indomitable Irish lady. Sometimes she was lucky, finding enough to keep her family going. Any extra money was spent on anyone who needed nursing, a hot meal or a grubstake.

February of 1898 saw Nell back in Victoria, staying at the Burns House. The fabled Trail of '98 was in full swing and Nell was to be part of it. She was in her 50s, but this fact mattered little to Nell. Somehow, she joined the mad rush through killing snows and untold hardships through famous Chilkoot Pass to Dawson. Once again she opened a restaurant, again calling it the Delmonico. Her fare was as popular as ever. Because provisions were almost impossible to obtain, she recalled, "meals ran anywhere from two or three to five or six dollars.

"At that, I didn't make any fortune. Part of the reason, though, was because if a young fellow was broke and hungry I would give him a meal for

A busy street scene in Dawson City. Nellie had known many such boomtowns. In most she operated a restaurant, her food being universally popular among the miners. For those down on their luck, the generous restauranteur was always a soft touch for a free meal.

nothing."

More hectic years came and went, Nell sneaking survey trips into her crowded schedule and always hoping for that lucky strike. When Dawson began to slow, she settled in Fairbanks. Then it was off to the distant wilds of Tanana and Koyukuk, to claim the most northerly mining property on the continent.

Before leaving Dawson, Nell made the best strike of her career, No. 19. Years later she recalled: "It proved to be a rich claim. I took out over $100,000 from that claim. What did I do with it? I spent every red cent of it buying other claims and prospecting the country. I went out with my dog team or on snowshoes all over that district looking for rich claims.

"After spending seven years in Dawson I went to Fairbanks. That was in 1904. I stayed there three years. I was in the grocery business and made $4,000 the first winter.

"In 1907 I went to the Koyukuk district. I had a funny experience going down the river on a raft. I went with an old sourdough. If you know anything about that river you know how many rocks there are in the channel and how swift the rapids are. In any event, coming down through some swift water we struck a submerged rock that wrecked our craft. It knocked all the middle logs out.

"All we had left were the two cross pieces and the two outside logs. Sure, we got to shore all right, and fixed up the raft and went on. There is always

something interesting happening. You never quite know what's going to happen next, or when your time will come to cash in your chips.

"It all adds interest and variety to life."

But the end was nearing at last for the amazing colleen whose name had become synonymous with warmth and generosity in every mining camp from Mexico to Alaska. In 1924, at the age of 80, "Miss Alaska" mushed 750 miles to Seward! Said the local newspaper: "From the farthest north mining camp to New York City is her trail trip this time, and any obstacles that surmount the trail between here and New York might just as well get out of the way for she's hit the trail and is going through!"

But this time Nell faced a tougher enemy than snow and wilderness: pneumonia. Upon reaching Victoria, she entered St. Joseph's, the hospital she had helped establish so many years before; newspapers noting that she "scorned to be carried in, but walked 'on her own two legs' " into the ward.

Days later, Nellie Cashman "cashed in her chips," as she would have put it. The trail that had spanned half a century and half a continent had finally come to an end.

Just before the last, Nell had been asked if she wished her body sent to relatives.

No, she replied, the old determined fire in her eyes. She wanted to be buried in Victoria, that her tiny estate might be used in aiding the poor.   ●

Even miners such as these were subject to McLaughlin's wrath. Half a century after, one of the butcher's many victims marvelled: "How we submitted patiently to the tyrannous conduct of the ruffian, even at the risk of losing our meat supply, I cannot imagine now. He led us captives to the block and decapitated us morally, if not physically...."

Terrible Jim McLaughlin:
Terror Of The Tenderloins

Prospector, packer and painted lady, merchant, gambler and thief, they all called rip-roaring Fort Yale home, more than a century ago. Here, on Fraser River's western flat, bonded in restless union by their quest for gold, 9,000 men, women and children from every quarter of the globe toiled, fought and died for the elusive metal.

OF this motley populace, one man towered above his fellows. The proudest grew humble before his command, brave men faltered, women fainted, dogs and children flew terror-stricken from his rage. Undisputed monarch of all he surveyed through eyes bloodshot red, he was Big Jim McLaughlin— terror of the tenderloins.

"He was a most desperate blackguard, both in appearance and action," one pioneer recalled 50 years later. "He was a huge, bloated specimen of humanity and was generally filled to the throat with drink."

He was, in fact, the town butcher.

In the whole of teeming Fort Yale there was but one meat market. A state of affairs which tickled the perverted fancy of jaundiced Jim no end, for every man, woman and child in the community, regardless of fortune or fame, relied upon him for a steady source of fresh meat. Until someone dared set up shop in competition, McLaughlin reigned supreme.

From his throne, a carving block, McLaughlin regarded each and every customer with open contempt. Every order was served with insults and curses. When suffering from a hangover, as often was the case, he even threatened assault, his ravaged face glowing redder as his temper flared ever higher.

For those foolhardy enough to express indignation, Jim had two favorite tricks: Firstly, he would fill the order with obviously inferior cuts and wait belligerently, yellow fangs bared in sadistic smile, for complaint. It seldom came. Then, adding final insult to injury, he would openly lean a ham-like fist on the scales when weighing the purchase.

"He insulted and bullied everyone..." wrote one of Jim's victims in 1904. "He could cut off the supply of meat at any moment.... The language he used was fearful to listen to. He browbeat women as well as men. He hated children and would often turn them crying away without the food they had been sent by their parents to buy."

Foraging dogs, he sighed, afforded McLaughlin his "greatest joy and satisfaction." Every canine was greeted with a heavy foot, a string of curses and, once or twice with deadly effect, a flying meat cleaver.

"How we submitted patiently to the tyrannous conduct of the ruffian, even at the risk of losing our meat supply, I cannot imagine now. He led us captives to the block and decapitated us morally, if not physically... I had two or three tilts with the fellow and every time was worsted because he held the key to my stomach."

Jim's crimes were legion. Like the hapless morning a Scottish prospector's terrior wandered into the shop to beg for scraps. With a roar of outrage, Jim seized his carving knife and slashed at the dog's back. The maimed terrier then dragged itself, bleeding profusely, from the shop and collapsed in the street.

Immediately informed of what had happened to his little companion, McDermott grabbed a revolver and charged to the meat market, friends at his heels vainly imploring him to surrender the gun. But the enraged miner ignored their pleas and marched into the shop, pistol at the ready.

Fortunately for McLaughlin, McDermott had begun to calm down somewhat and contented himself with aiming the muzzle at the butcher's face with the warning: "If I ever catch you on the other side of the line I'll kill you—kill you."

Instantly, Jim's confidence returned. Realizing that the Scotchman would not fire, he laughed, "Go on out of this or I'll serve you as I did the dog!"

Frustrated by his own impotence and McLaughlin's sneer, McDermott stomped out, with the promise: "Remember, you will be my meat if I ever catch you on the American side."

The butcher spat, motioned suggestively, and the incident was closed.

But big Jim's time was running out, his Waterloo fast approaching. As has happened so often in history, the worm was to turn. And, as has often been the case in times old and new, the mighty was to fall before the feet of a tiny woman.

Which makes this a good time to introduce the other members of our cast: Journalist David W.

Higgins was 24 when he joined the rush for gold on the Fraser River. Previously, he had spent six years recording the hectic affairs of rough-and-tumble San Francisco. Forty-Niners, the famous Vigilante Committee, he knew them all. In July of 1858 he had traded pen for pick and pan in a short-lived and unsuccessful attempt at mining in Fort Yale. It was there he encountered the loathesome Jim McLaughlin.

At least two others of his acquaintance shared this dubious distinction. The first was an Irishman, Captain William Power, who later made his fortune in Vancouver real estate. A "splendid specimen of mankind and...an accomplished athlete" (according to Higgins) Power had met the stocky writer aboard the steamer bringing them upriver, when looking for a steward.

The refined captain had been in search of hot water for shaving. "I've travelled all over Europe and the Holy Land and have been on the Nile, but this is the first time I have found it impossible to get a cup of hot water to shave with," he had sighed.

Soon Power had introduced Higgins to his lovely wife and, by the time they reached Yale, the three were fast friends. Upon landing at the booming gold town, they had pitched their tents on the river flats, Higgins securing employment as manager of an express office, the Powers opening a hotel which was immediately successful. It was through Power's buying food-stuff for his establishment that he frequently endured the abuse of vitriolic Jim McLaughlin. Much to Power's disgust, his "restraint was at the mercy of the bloated butcher. He (Jim) could cut off the supply of meat at any moment and put Power out of business."

The third character of our melodrama is a frail English lady, Mrs. Burroughs. With her young son and daughter, she lived in a small tent on the river bar. Some time before, her husband had ventured upriver in search of his fortune, leaving them a meagre supply of groceries and money. Soon all had been exhausted and Mrs. Burroughs was reduced to "great straits." Her neighbors, most of whom were in grim circumstances themselves, did what they could to help. Despite her situation, the heroic mother refused to seek aid. But with winter approaching, her future was fast becoming desperate.

Remarkably, McLaughlin had allowed her several purchases on credit. But, one autumn morning, the fateful encounter came to pass. Mrs. Burroughs had taken her place in the line awaiting Jim's pleasure. Service was slow as the evil monarch was recovering from a double hangover—too much rotgut whisky and a bad night at the faro table.

When, finally, it was Mrs. Burroughs' turn before the carving block, wretched McLaughlin stared through bloodshot eyes then bellowed: "What do you want!?"

Timidly, the woman whispered, "I should like to

Yale, 1858, where Jim McLaughlin "Terror of the Tenderloins," held court before his frightened clientele— until a tiny woman led to his downfall.

get a little more meat on credit for a few days. Mr. Burroughs will be here soon and he will pay you."

With a leer, Jim leaned on his knife and smirked, "Is there a Mr. Burroughs? Was there ever a Mr. Burroughs? I doubt it!"

According to Higgins, who witnessed the affair, "The hot blood mounted to the woman's face and painted it crimson. She fixed her eyes in a terrified stare on McLaughlin and her lips moved as if in remonstrance; but no words came from them. She leant forward on the block and then sank to the floor. She had fainted dead away. Strong hands raised the thin, wasted figure (for it turned out afterwards that for some weeks she had systematically lived on the shortest of short rations so that her children might have enough to sustain them), and a low murmur of indignation ran through McLaughlin's subjects who awaited their turn to be served."

Unmoved by his victim's collapse, the monster then turned to the next customer and barked, "Come on, now, and give your orders quick. I can't stand here all day. What do you want?"

The customer, "white as a corpse," did not answer immediately. For Captain William Power stood in stunned disbelief of the tragedy he had witnessed. When at last he spoke, he said in slow, measured tone: "McLaughlin, every time that I come to your shop I am insulted. This thing has got to stop."

Pointing to Mrs. Burroughs, who was being led gently away in the arms of two miners, he continued: "I don't care so much for myself and I could have stood it, but I do care for that little woman."

The captain's rebuke ignited Jim's demoniac fury.

Roaring like a wounded beast, he threw down his carving knife, ripped off his bloodied apron and charged Power. But the latter stepped neatly aside, delivering a smashing blow to the puffed face as it reeled past.

The "fight" ended in moments, as Power rained blow after blow "with smashing effect upon his antagonist's face and body until the latter sank insensible to the floor and stayed there, the bad blood and bad whiskey flowing from numerous wounds."

Without so much as a glance at the fallen monarch, Captain Power sauntered behind the infamous block, selected a cut of meat, weighed it, threw down 60 cents and walked leisurely toward his hotel, as a spectator called after him: "I think the man's dead, Power."

"Well, if he is dead you know where to find me," replied the captain without turning.

However, much to Yale's regret, Jim lived. For hours he lay in the dirt where Power had left him, not a soul moving to help him. When at last he regained consciousness, the battered butcher pulled himself painfully erect. Then, although "groggy on his pins," as he expressed it, he resumed his duties, viewing his customers hazily through eyes swollen and almost closed.

But the Jim McLaughlin who now waited upon a quavering clientele was a changed man. Not an insult escaped his crushed lips. Where, before, his fist had accounted for half the weight registered on his scales, he now carved generous cuts with scarcely a glance at the weight.

"Every trace of ruffianism had oozed out through his wounds," marvelled Higgins, "and in place of

Yale in 1868. By this time Terrible Jim McLaughlin had moved on to fresher fields.

the bully whom everyone feared and hated there stood a polite and decent man whose manners were almost obsequious and who never again was known to browbeat or insult a customer."

Once women, children and dogs had been the favorite targets of his invective—and worse. Now he could not do enough for one and all. Sending for McDermott, the Scottish miner, he pleaded with him to send his dog to the shop, that he might feed him daily. As word of his magnificent reformation circulated, the beaming butcher's popularity soared. Those who had fearfully addressed him as "Mr. McLaughlin" soon began calling him "Jim" and "Mac."

Almost as extraordinary as McLaughlin's change of disposition was his change of evil pursuits. Swearing, gambling and drinking were now sins of the past. "Boys," said he to his former drinking partners, "I've drunk my last drink and I'm going to save my money from this time on forevermore till Kingdom Come—so don't tempt me, for I won't go."

When a Methodist missionary paddled into town a year later, it was big Jim McLaughlin who greeted him with open hand and heart, and attended the first sermon. He even joined in singing the hymns. "You know," he blushed, awkwardly crushing his hat in calloused hands, "I used to belong to a choir when I was a young fellow back in Maine."

"But the strangest part of the affair," marvelled Higgins many years afterward, was that Jim never by any chance referred to the pounding that he had received at the hands of William Power. Asked as to how he received the injuries to his face he would attribute them to having run against a side of beef in the dark. His memory of that event ever seemed a blank.

"All that he knew was that he had been hurt, he believed, by accident, and that was all there was to be said."

For Mrs. Burroughs, her sad story was not ended. Months after, a miner rushed into town with word

that a companion had shot himself in the leg while climbing over a fallen tree, down the trail. By the time a doctor could reach the scene, the man had bled to death. A search of his clothes revealed $700 in gold dust and letters, bearing the Yale postmark, addressed to "Charles Burroughs, Lytton."

Inquiry failed to locate a single person who had known the deceased, until Jim McLaughlin suggested asking Mrs. Burroughs. Sadly, as some had come to fear, Charles Burroughs had been her husband. He had been returning with his purse of hard-won gold when the accident occurred. One of his companions on the trail later told Mr. Higgins that Burroughs had been in gay spirits, whistling and singing, "The Girl I Left Behind Me."

When Burroughs was interred in Yale's little cemetery, Higgins and McLaughlin led the pallbearers. After the ceremony it was Jim who humbly stepped forward to take a child in each arm as Power gently offered his arm to the grieving widow. A week later, Mrs. Burroughs and family left Yale for friends in California, never to return.

In 1860 journalist Higgins moved to Victoria, which was to be his home for the remainder of his life. Over the years he lost touch with his former friends in Yale. Among this vanished company was Jim McLaughlin. Fifty years after, Higgins wondered: "Was the regeneration of Jim McLaughlin permanent? I do not know. I hope that it was, for at the bottom he was a good sort and was capable of noble actions.

"Let us trust that he never relapsed into evil courses, and that as he must have long since gone the way of all flesh he continued to grow in grace until when the end came he won a starry crown."

Unknown to the retired journalist, in 1872 the *Colonist* had published a summary of the activities of the province's more successful citizens who had gone on to bigger and better things. Among the list was the name James McLaughlin, of Yale. He was in San Francisco, and doing well. ●

From every corner of the western hemisphere, from every walk of life, by land and by sea, thousands followed the magical lure of gold to British Columbia a century ago. For many it would mean a new, fuller life, for a very few, even fortune and fame. Others, sadly, were to find only disappointment, hardship. . . and death.

THE OVERLANDERS

SUCH was the fate of a small band of "Overlanders" in 1863.

The ill-fated expedition, consisting of Englishmen John Helstone and John R. Wright, and Canadians William, Thomas and Gilbert Rennie, struck out for distant Cariboo on May 15. The trek which began with such high hopes was to end in horror and death.

A "melancholy diary," one newspaper was to term Gilbert Rennie's heartrending account of the tragedy, months after.

From London, Ontario, he, his brothers and the Britons had made their way to St. Paul, Minnesota, up the Mississippi to St. Cloud, on to Red River, through North Dakota, finally reaching Fort Garry (Winnipeg) on July 7. The first half of their journey had been by railroad, riverboat and stagecoach. From there to the Fraser River, they would have to hike.

Then it was on to Fort Ellice. Touchwood Hill House, Fort Carlton, Fort Pitts, Fort Edmonton fell behind as they struggled slowly westward. St. Albert, St. Ann, Mission Lake, Pembina River... ever onward toward the Rocky Mountain Foothills, through a September "open and pleasant." The party observed rich veins of anthracite coal, using it for their camp fires, then proceeded through swampy McLeod Valley to mighty Athabasca River which they crossed on a flimsy log raft at Jasper.

Westward through the Rockies they continued to the abandoned Hudson's Bay Company post at Tete Jaune Cache, arriving October 4. The weary foot-party had encountered some snow, but here the "weather was very fine and blackflies caused great annoyance." It was so mild, in fact, some of their precious dried meat spoiled. Eleven days were

spent in building a canoe to navigate the Fraser.

Apparently they purchased or traded a second from Indians, as Rennie's next entry mentions them beginning the descent in two canoes lashed side by side, "recommended as the safest plan to avoid upsetting."

By now the season was far advanced, the men becoming so anxious they did not even pause to dip their gold pans in the swirling stream. They had just enough provisions to see them to Fort (Prince) George and would be in serious trouble if snow or mishap altered their schedule.

Then. . .their first delay. After miles of braving fierce rapids, submerged rocks and cold, they encountered a canyon too swift to navigate. This meant a three-day portage—three days of painfully fighting their way over and around sheer cliffs, ice-smooth with spray and moss, and straining to keep their balance and footing as they shouldered canoes and supplies.

Then it was back to battling the malevolent Fraser. They made fairly good time until October 29, "when their troubles truly commenced.

"The large canoe, while running a swift rapid from eight to 10 miles long, about 100 miles above Fort George, struck a sunken rock. On both sides of the canoes was a boiling rapid, rendering it impossible to reach the banks. Every effort was made to get them off but without success, and they remained there for three days and two nights during heavy falls of snow with nothing but dried meat to eat."

This meant 60 hours of below-freezing temperatures on their bobbing island for Gilbert and Thomas Rennie. The others fared considerably worse. Helstone, Wright and William Rennie had attempted, on the second day of their stranding, to make shore in the smaller canoe. They had hardly taken their seats when "she capsized," flinging the brave trio into the swollen river. Somehow Helstone and Rennie were hauled into the other canoe by the brothers.

Poor Wright was swept downstream astraddle the bucking runaway. About a mile and a half downriver, he managed to land on the opposite bank. Drenched to the skin, teeth chattering violently, he slipped and rolled along the icy rocks until across from his marooned companions. They succeeded in throwing him a box of matches on a stick, but to no avail.

Fingers wooden with cold, Wright could not manipulate the slivers which promised warmth and a chance to dry his clothing. Without a fire, he "was compelled to walk about to keep his blood in circulation." By morning his feet were severely frostbitten. Again, his comrades threw him matches. Again, they were useless. His fingers were now almost frozen.

Desperately, his comrades shredded a mooseskin, braiding the strips together to form a rope. Weighting a light cord with a piece of driftwood, they finally landed an end within his reach. Unable to use his hands, Wright folded the line in his arms, then drew in the rope. In the same awkward manner he wound the lifeline around a tree trunk, somehow securing it.

Helstone "passed the other end round his body, and jumped into the current, in an instant swinging himself ashore. The rope was pulled back by means of the cord, and the rest of the party succeeded in getting ashore; everything having been first got out of the canoe.

"By capsizing of the small canoe the party lost nearly all their money, a lot of clothing, bedding, and most of their provisions."

The five who had so gaily departed from Ontario months before, buoyant with the optimism of youth, now faced a grim future: long, dangerous miles above Fort George, only a fraction of their irreplaceable food remained, winter was fast setting in. It meant a frantic overland race against death through deepening snow unless they could retrieve their canoe.

Even on its banks, the vindictive Fraser was mistress, as now all five were too frozen to light a fire to dry their clothes. Night came with a vengeance. Finding a cleft in the rocks, they bundled together in buffalo robes and blankets, trying vainly to warm themselves. It was a long, agonizing night. By dawn, Helstone and Thomas Rennie were complaining of frostbitten feet.

With daylight, the others painfully kindled a fire by igniting gunpowder in a dry handkerchief, which enabled them to dry out and cook a meal. Somewhat revived, they set about cutting brush to make a crude shelter.

The next few days were spent in constructing a bridge of rocks and timber to their stranded canoe. It took thousands of stones and branches to reach the craft, with frostbitten hands, bodies that were ever cold, and bellies that growled from hunger. But they worked on and eventually rocked the craft loose of its perch.

November 4, the desperate band clambered into the canoe and headed downstream. Hours later, they struggled back to camp, heartbroken. The calmer stretches of river had frozen solid, winter had trapped them.

It was a grim discussion they held that night, huddled about their little fire.

Finally "all parties agreed that William and Gilbert Rennie should proceed to Fort George, which they thought was not more than five days' journey there and back. Accordingly, on the morning of the 5th, the two brothers started out with only one meal, and a rifle and ammunition, having left about 10 days' provisions with the other three."

It was a lonely march through hell. Snow began falling the moment they left camp. The ordeal the brothers experienced defies description: day after day, night after night of freezing temperatures, their clothing never drying out, often frozen hard on their backs. Through terrain which is hazardous at best of times, in mid-winter, snow up to their waists…trying to exist on the few scrawny birds and squirrels they could shoot. Now William reeled forward on frozen feet. But each agonizing day brought them a shade closer to the fort.

Often they were near surrender, able to force themselves on only with the knowledge that their companions' lives depended upon their reaching help.

The brothers had early realized their estimate of the distance to have been unduly optimistic, even had they been well provisioned and in good health. Instead of a five-day roundtrip, as hoped, their race for help took 28 days. When they staggered out of the bush, across the river from the fort, William had to be lifted into the canoe.

The day after their arrival, post manager Thomas Charles reluctantly surrendered to their pleas for a relief party. Although the anxious brothers were to bitterly denounce his apparent lack of concern for the missing men, it it likely the trader believed it to be hopeless at such a late date. He dispatched two Indians to the scene but "they returned after a few hours, stating that the snow was too deep and the river not sufficiently frozen to walk on.

"The Rennies were therefore compelled to abandon all hopes of sending succor to their brother and comrades."

According to the brothers, Charles even urged their departure, claiming the fort was critically short of supplies. But it was six weeks before William was ready for travel.

Hiking to Quesnel River, the grieving brothers

learned Indians had visited their campsite and found brother Thomas and the others dead.

William sadly penned the news to a friend in Victoria: "We arrived here a few days ago, in a desperate condition, after one of the very roughest journeys that ever any poor mortals had almost in this world.

"Poor Thomas is starved and frozen to death, and all that is left of the party is Gilbert and I. We got stuck on a rock in a rapid in the Fraser River 100 miles above Fort George, and we could not get off it for three days and two nights, and it snowed and froze most desperately. Thomas, Mr. Wright and Mr. Elston (sic) had their feet and hands frozen, and we were dispatched to Fort George for provisions and assistance.

"The snow was so deep and travelling through the woods so difficult that it took us 28 days to accomplish the task. We had only one meal of provisions, I got my feet badly frozen, and for 15 (nights) and days we had nothing to eat—so that when we reached the opposite side of the river to the Fort I had to be carried to the boat, I was so weak. We could get no one at the Fort to go to their assistance, and I was so reduced by starvation that I could not walk. I have no more time to write you, as the man is starting. Yours, Wm. Rennie."

It was not until a year after Gilbert and William Rennie staggered into Fort George that the full, appalling details of their comrades' fate were learned.

Prospector John Giscome had been wintering at Fort George. During the Rennies' long recuperation, they visited his cabin and while there, four Indians called at the post. One of the brothers, who spoke

Fort Garry (Winnipeg). Upon leaving their homes in London, Ontario, the ill-fated Rennie brothers and their two companions headed for the prairie settlement by railroad, riverboat and stagecoach. From Fort Garry they struggled slowly westward until overtaken by starvation and exposure in the British Columbia wilderness.

In Red River carts such as these, on horseback, afoot, and on flimsy rafts, parties of "Overlanders" battled 1,000 miles of prairie, swamp, mountain and murderous river rapids to reach the gold fields of British Columbia.

Prince George (Fort George), for which the tragic Overlanders were headed. When finally, William and Gilbert Rennie reached the fort, post manager Thomas Charles was reluctant to organize a relief party for their comrades.

French, asked the party if they had seen or heard of the missing men. The braves replied they came by a shorter route and they left the next day, "professing to return to the lake they had come from."

Giscome learned later, however, that two of the Indians had left the others to check the overlanders' camp. According to the report, "Two of them (believed to be Helstone and Wright) were still alive but had killed William (sic) Rennie and had eaten all but his legs, which they held in their hands when found, and were tearing the raw flesh from the bones. The Indians were going to light a fire for them when the two men drew their pistols and the Indians fled, but did not return to give information to the Fort."

By the time Giscome heard the horrifying tale, it was March. At manager Charles' request, he altered his planned prospecting trip to visit the camp. Charles had since learned only one man had survived, but had been murdered by Indians. Giscome's expedition found travelling in April to be rough going, the rivers swollen with melting snow, but finally located the camp, "with the remains of two men, but the third was missing.

"Their canoe was still lying close by but blankets, and everything else worth removing had been carried off by the Indians. Inside the camp, in one corner, there lay a small pile of bones, carefully packed together; among them was the skull of a young man (supposed to be that of William Rennie) with the whole of the lower jaw and a row of good teeth still perfect.

"He also found the skull of an older man which had eight prints of an axe upon it where it had evidently been chopped open. Some of the bones were still bloody and half-chewed at the ends."

Burying the gruesome remains, Giscome left a written notice "in case the spot should be visited by any other persons."

As he jotted down the grim details in a note to Charles, Giscome noticed his Indians to be agitated. Asked the reason for their concern, the natives accused him of writing that they had murdered the man still unaccounted for. The prospector assured them this was incorrect; whereupon a relieved guide admitted he knew where the missing body was to be found. The hapless overlander was "lying 300 or 400 yards from the camp, over a rise, stripped of his clothes, and several cuts from a hatchet on his head and body." The informant promised to bury him upon his return trip.

Giscome's probing eye uncovered further evidence of the tragedy at a nearby Indian encampment, spotting several articles he knew to have belonged to the overlanders. They knew nothing of the slaying of the last survivor, the Indians swore, only looting the camp after all three were dead. All other effects had been taken earlier by another band, camped four days away.

One of the salvaged effects was particularly gruesome. This was young Thomas Rennie's jacket, "which had nine holes in the back and one under the right arm, apparently made with a knife." The natives swore they found it in that condition. Giscome also recovered three letters addressed to the Rennies and shoemaker's tools.

"From the statements of the Indians and personal inspection by Mr. Giscome and his companions," the record concludes, "he came to the painful conclusion that the poor men had been reduced by starvation and cold to the last extremities, and had actually killed and eaten one another.

"There were no signs of fires having been lit, or wood cut, and yet they must have existed for about 10 weeks, the longest liver having to all appearances suffered a cruel death at the hands of the Indians for the sake of plunder." ●

Pioneer Adventurer Faced Shipwreck And Hostile Indians.

Few men could boast of having experienced a more adventurous career than did earlyday British Columbia trader, customs officer, sealer and miner, Morris Moss. In fact, one leading historian has credited the handsome Jewish pioneer with having been "one of the most colorful figures this coast has ever seen."

Adventurer, pioneer, law officer, sealer, miner and synagogue president: Morris Moss was quite a man.

HANDSOME and rich, the London-born Moss was drawn halfway round the world to British Columbia by glowing reports of the gold strikes at Barkerville, to begin a career more colorful than many leading characters of fiction.

Twenty-year-old Moss immediately gave evidence of his passion for mining of all types, when he led an expedition to "Dean's Channel to explore a copper lead discovered some time since by myself & party..." Then, switching roles from that of miner to merchant, he opened shop in Bella Coola, where he first became involved in law enforcement, in July of 1863, when he wrote Governor James Douglas of reports that several murders had been committed by Indians. Upon reminding the governor that he had written earlier upon the same subject, Moss conceded that "I am fully aware that it is not from any indifference on the part of your Excellency, well knowing how you have been similarly employed in the more immediate neighborhood of Victoria.

"Yet being a resident merchant here, I think it my duty to inform you there is every likelihood of a large number of men wintering here this coming season, there being many inducements for miners to stay in this place which other localities do not present. I need not inform your Excellency of the character of a mining crowd & I fear unless some person be invested with authority there will be daily disputes with the Indians which may lead to more bloodshed. The natives here, as a body, are well

disposed towards the whites & wish them to settle here. I have never had any trouble with them myself, but there are black sheep in every fold & if I might presume to advise your Excellency I should suggest your sending a gunboat here before the winter sets in as the knowledge that you would revenge any white man's murder would restrain them in a greater course from committing any further violence."

Then, apparently feeling that he had presumed too much, and noting that he was "unknown to your Excellency," Moss suggested that Douglas might check his references with Wharf Street (Victoria) merchant Henry Nathan, "to whom I am well known."

Moss then told of an incident of a week before when he had freed a miner from several Indians "after some trouble," stressing the incident to the governor so that the man's companions, who had escaped previously, did not report in Victoria that their comrade had been murdered.

"My thanks to Mr. Moss for much valuable information," acknowledged Douglas to his secretary, A.G. Young, who duly informed Moss that "A ship of war will be sent to Bentinck Arm in course of the season and a magistrate will be appointed when necessary."

Ironically, but months after, Moss had more on his mind than murder, his trading schooner, the *Rose Newman*, having been wrecked during a snowstorm in Queen Charlotte Sound. According to the first reports which reached Victoria, Moss, Captain Walter and crew had escaped without casualty, although the schooner and cargo were a total loss. The following day, it was learned that the *Newman*, fully loaded, had been heading for Bentinck Arm when the storm carried away her mainsail and drove her onto the rocks where she soon broke up. Almost $500 worth of cargo apparently had been salvaged.

The reports of the *Newman's* loss were not only brief but erroneous. For Morris Moss and companions had endured one of the more remarkable ordeals of shipwreck in provincial history. Curiously, although historians have paid tributes to Moss' other adventures, few have recounted his miraculous escape from the foundering *Rose Newman*...

Almost from the beginning, Moss had encountered one obstacle after another as a trader. According to one historian, he had first noted Bella Coola as a potential trading post when passing through on his way to the Cariboo diggings as a prospector, going by way of Bentinck Arm. When next he headed for the gold fields, it was as a merchant, with a large stock of goods to sell at Williams Creek. However, upon reaching Quesnel Forks, the Moss party was turned back by one of the worst blizzards in memory, Moss having no choice but to sell his goods on the spot and return to the coast.

Undaunted by this initial setback, he purchased a second stock of goods and proceeded to Bella Coola aboard the Hudson's Bay Company steamer *Labouchere*—to find that the prospective customers he had seen during his earlier visit had been decimated by smallpox. Although convinced that the Bentinck Arm route, specifically Bella Coola, could be developed into a thriving venture, Moss returned to Victoria to organize several further pack trains to Cariboo. In the meantime, he continued to push Bella Coola as a strategic winter quarters for those bound for the Interior. When a number of miners agreed to wait there for the spring thaw, Moss chartered the schooner *Rose Newman* from the well-known West Coast traders, Captains Mackay and Spring, and loaded her with provisions to open a trading post at Bella Coola.

But, once again, his cherished ambition was foiled when Robertson Stewart, agent for the Koshuma coal mines, situated on the west coast of Vancouver Island, pleaded with him to land his stores at the company mine, which was critically short of supplies. "It was a dangerous trip, and quite out of Moss' way," this acount continues. "He refused it at first, but Mr. Stewart begged it as a favor to himself and insisted it was the only way of bringing food for the stranded miners there, and Moss weakened."

Before Moss sailed from Victoria, he was appointed government agent for the Northwest Coast by Governor Douglas and named a justice of the peace (no doubt the result of his letters of concern to the governor).

Heavily-laden with supplies, the little schooner *Rose Newman* cleared Victoria on the first leg of her voyage, reaching Koshuma after a savage beating by gale force winds, late in November, 1864. The weather did not ease and, upon beating her way from Koshuma, bound for Quatsino, at the northwestern end of the Island, the schooner had to battle mountainous waves as winter storms continued to wreak havoc along the exposed west coast. But, once again, the staunch *Newman* landed her cargo safely, although she was forced to shelter at Quatsino for a week.

By this time Moss was beside himself with impatience and determined to reach Bella Coola as quickly as possible despite the weather which, he knew, offered little enough chance of clearing in the immediate future. Thus he informed his crew, consisting of Captain Walters, mate Ben Spain, and three Indian seamen, that he was pushing on to Bella Coola. At this, his native crewmen deserted ship, convinced that it was suicide to continue. Walters and Spain, however, remained faithful to Moss and, confident that the *Newman* would continue to withstand the worst that nature could throw at her, Moss and company sailed northward.

"The inevitable happened. Three men (of whom one was captain and another an amateur) could not keep the schooner afloat in the dangerous, storm-swept waters, and they had not proceeded far when with a crash the mainsail and the jib were blown away. To complete the picture, a dense fog closed in about them, so that they could barely see the length of the schooner.

"For three days they drifted at the mercy of the waves before they struck a rock. The waves dashed over the weakening vessel, and they clung to the rigging for their lives. Through the wind and waves they thought they heard some breakers and they jumped overboard. After a difficult struggle with the waves, weakened though they were by fatigue and exposure, they miraculously reached land..."

According to another source, Moss and his two companions had clutched the rigging for some time, unable to see ahead through the fog and waves dashing over the schooner. Finally Moss had yelled, "Every man for himself; I'm going to breast the breakers!" and plunged into the surf. Somehow he reached the beach, the others following his example. Unable to see where they were, they sought shelter in the rocks and huddled together for warmth above the waterline, their lonely vigil made all the more unpleasant by the first snowfall of the season.

With daylight, they were surprised to find that their schooner had crashed ashore upon a small islet connected at low tide to "Lochaboo Island," northwest of Safety Cove. "They were without matches or water," the old record continues, "but during the day managed to drag in two or three sacks of flour which had floated off the schooner. The following day, with a lucky low tide, they managed to salvage several other articles of foodstuffs which had drifted to the beach. Among other things was a keg of gunpowder which the water had penetrated only about a-quarter of an inch. They also found a flint-lock gun. With these they managed to start a fire by shooting into dry moss and blowing the sparks into flame. They kept the fire burning continuously for three months, during which time they were compelled to remain on the island..."

Other recovered foodstuffs included more sacks of flour, some canned goods, molasses and liquor. Saved from immediate starvation, the castaways turned to building a shelter. Using rocks, driftwood and the schooner's foresail, they managed to erect a reasonably comfortable hut.

The days began to pass with increasing monotony, Moss, Walters and Spain subsisting upon clams and their salvaged provisions. During their explorations of the island, they learned that it had not always been uninhabited; numerous skeletons attesting to the fact that an Indian village had been situated there until devastated by smallpox.

Day in, day out, from December through January, and well into February of 1865, they paced the beach and gazed anxiously to seaward. But no friendly sail came into view, no native canoes passed them by, the signal poles they had erected about the island bringing no response. They were alone.

The months passed, their supplies, despite careful rationing, diminishing steadily. By late February, but for the clam beds, their food was almost gone, the men disheartened. They were eating a spartan breakfast in grim silence, when, unbelievably, they heard a shout from the beach. Rushing outside, the traders saw a canoe containing three Indians. As the ecstatic whites rushed forward, shouting, the strangers approached the beach but remained at a healthy distance, obviously unwilling to land.

Despite the entreaties of the castaways, the natives hesitated further, when Moss recognized one as being a half-breed named Yellow Charlie, from Bella Bella. Upon Moss' identifying himself, Charlie, fears dispelled, landed immediately and, after some negotiation, agreed to take them to the village, 40 miles distant. However, as the canoe was too small to carry all six, Moss volunteered to go ahead with the Indians, a second canoe to be dispatched for Walters and Spain.

Not long after they reached the village, a sloop owned by an old prospector named Sebastopol called at the camp, its owner graciously offering to take the three to Fort Simpson, his next port-of-call. Moss' captain and mate agreed but the trader was still determined to reach Bella Coola. When the Indians assured him that he was a welcome guest in their camp until a northbound vessel called, the three parted company, Walters and Spain accom-

Pioneer highway builder Alfred Waddington denounced Moss as a profiteer during the Indian uprising known as the "Chilcotin War." The colonial government thought that "Mr. Moss behaved uncommonly well."

panying Sebastopol, Moss remaining with his hosts.

But he soon learned that his ordeal was not yet over. For the Indians, rather than treating him as a guest, acted more and more as if he were a prisoner, keeping him under close watch, "though not confined... and slowly reliev(ed) him of the little wealth he had left."

For a month, Moss was forced to cool his heels among the Bella Bella tribesmen. Although allowed the run of the village, and treated civilly by his hosts, he became more and more determined to make good his escape at the first opportunity. But escape was impossible as the village was situated upon a small island "on which there was neither wood nor water," the natives having selected the barren rock for its protection against marauding Haidas. Hundreds of dogs which roamed the island at will as guardians against surprise attack by the Queen Charlotte Islands' pirates insured that Moss would not slip away in a canoe during the night.

Once again, Moss waited for rescue. The days passed without incident, although he was fast being reduced to a pauper, having to pay for his accommodation with the few effects he had salvaged from the *Rose Newman*. Even his ragged clothes were bartered for scraps of food.

Salvation finally came in the form of some visiting Indians who agreed to carry a message from Moss to Bella Coola. A week later, his urgent appeal for assistance was answered in the form of 40 canoes of friendly Bella Coola Indians and eight whites who demanded his release. Moss' captors, terrified by the sight of the rescue fleet, whose occupants gave every sign of meaning business, readily turned him loose. This time, Moss' rescue was official.

But the greatest blow of the entire disastrous voyage awaited Moss in Bella Coola. For, upon landing, and expecting to find his affairs there in order, his stock of supplies intact, he was heartbroken to find his clerk bedridden, half of his original stock missing. Combined with the loss of the cargo aboard the *Newman*, Moss' setback amounted to 2,000 pounds.

Almost ruined, and disgusted, he made arrangements with a packer to have his remaining goods freighted to the mines in the spring and returned to Victoria, where he astonished his friends who had long since given him up for dead.

The final straw came when, during the excitement immediately following the infamous "Bute Inlet massacre," or so-called Chilcotin War, the packer's train was attacked and captured by Indians. Earlier, Moss and a hundred volunteers had offered their services to Governor Frederick Seymour at a stormy public meeting, each and every man vowing to avenge those who had been murdered. Seymour publicly thanked the volunteers but declined their proffered services. He did write Morris Moss, however, to privately request that the trader "assist and advise" the government during the crisis. Moss jumped at the opportunity and attended several sessions of the Legislative Council, "at which it finally was decided to send 50 men from New

(Left) Governor Frederick Seymour accepted Moss' offer of assistance during the Bute Inlet "massacre" emergency.
(Below) Bella Coola, where adventurer-trader Morris Moss risked shipwreck and hostile Indians to open a trading post.

Westminster and 50 more from Cariboo. Mr. Moss was attached to the Westminster corps, under Judge (Chief Inspector Chartres) Brew, and proceeded with them to Bella Coola."

On the trail, Moss met the very man to whom he had entrusted the last of his stores, to be told of the Indian attack. Three of the packer's men had been killed, Moss' stores carried off.

Although the exact role Moss played in this historic affair is somewhat confusing (he was bitterly attacked by contractor Alfred Waddington, whose road gang had been massacred, for allegedly profiteering and having neglected his duty in arresting an Indian ringleader) the colonial government was more than pleased with his service. In recognition of his having negotiated the return of a number of stolen horses, the government awarded him $380 for expenses. Earlier, Chartres Brew had written the colonial secretary on Moss' behalf, stating that he could not afford to lose the money involved:

"He was of great service to us on the expedition as your Excellency is well aware, and I should be sorry if he came out of the business so large a loser which I know he can scarcely afford. I would

therefore ask your Excellency's permission to return to him the $380 which he paid for the horses. It may set him on his legs though he will still be out of pocket and the sum will only be a drop in the bucket of expenses. It is quite certain that if Mr. Moss had not gone for the horses they would be by this time food for the wolves; as it was seven of them up to this time are dead.

"I trust your Excellency will pardon me for making this suggestion but I am encouraged to do so from feeling that your Excellency is generously disposed towards all concerned in the campaign and would not willingly let anyone be a sufferer by it."

In due course the colonial secretary endorsed Brew's request for the rebate and remarked that "Mr. Moss behaved uncommonly well."

Despite his initial near-disastrous attempts at trading, Morris Moss eventually recouped his losses, and continued to serve the government as a justice of the peace and as a customs officer after the murder of Bella Coola customs officer Jack Ogilvie. For all of his distractions in the form of whisky smugglers and Indian murderers, Moss found time to continue searching for the copper lead which first had drawn him to Bella Coola, reporting that it has "proved itself equal to my anticipations... Although I could not spend much time in prospecting it, I can safely say that it is the richest thing yet discovered on the coast. I have specimens of other minerals which I think will turn out equally as good..."

Even when the government, in February of 1867, abolished his post in a cutback of services, Moss could not easily ignore his sense of duty; drawing Governor Seymour's attention to the fact that several Indians taken to Victoria as witnesses in a trial had been left stranded there and were anxious to return home. In June of 1868, then a "civilian" for all of a year, Moss felt compelled to report that he suspected three Indians at Bella Bella of having murdered two Scottish traders.

Married in 1883, Moss went on to bigger and better things after his civil service. The experience he had gained along the rugged northern coast standing him in good stead as a fur dealer and investor, he later turned his attention to the booming Cassiar mining region, then Denver. Thirteen years after, he was the centre of a mystery, having vanished after leaving Rock Creek, B.C, with "a considerable sum in gold dust and bank bills," and inspiring fears that he had been robbed and murdered. Private detectives were called in by his alarmed friends, but they, too, were unsuccessful. The mystery was finally solved when it was learned that Moss had simply moved to Denver, apparently without having announced his intentions locally.

Three years after, in February of 1896, word reached Victoria that the pioneer prospector, trader and adventurer "well known and much respected for his mild and gentlemanly manners and kind disposition" had died in that Colorado city. ●

A Sea Monster Guarded ISLANDER'S GOLD

Three-quarters of a century has passed since the frigid waters of Alaska's Lynn Canal engulfed the dying liner Islander and her company. Yet the story of her tragic sinking and of her lost treasure remains one of the most colorful in the history of the Pacific Northwest.

(Below) Ss. Islander sailing out of Victoria Harbor.
(Opposite page) The steamship Islander in drydock at Esquimalt.

PERHAPS the most startling aspect of this early-day disaster is the speed with which the *Islander*, rated as a "fast, commodious and handsome craft," sank with a loss of 42 lives. For it is a matter of record that she foundered within 17 minutes of striking an iceberg in Lynn Canal.

The tragedy began with the southbound flagship of the Canadian Pacific Navigation Company racing through the canal's fog-shrouded narrows, early on the morning of August 15, 1901. Despite the gloom, Captain Hamilton Foote was not on the bridge, being in the luxurious main saloon where he presided over a merry group of miners who, with their pokes, moneybelts and luggage packed with nuggets and dust, were celebrating their return from the Klondike. The officer actually in command during those final minutes was the *Islander*'s pilot, Captain Edmund LeBlanc, who, equipped with night glasses, was on the bridge.

Time and again he squinted into the darkness, attempting to see beyond the steamer's rapier-like bow. Despite Lynn Canal's notoriety for floating ice,

and the poor visibility, no attempt was made to reduce speed. And Ss. *Islander* raced to her destruction in blissful ignorance.

At the helm was Captain George Ferry, a veteran mariner who had boarded as a passenger and had assumed the role of quartermaster as a personal favor to Captain Foote. But for an occasional correction of course, when the *Islander* responded smartly to his caress, Captain Ferry found himself with little more to do than to daydream and wait to be relieved of his watch as, up forward, LeBlanc continued his vigil.

When, momentarily, the mist parted off the starboard bow and LeBlanc caught a glimpse of a small iceberg through his glasses, he made sure that it was well out of harm's way before returning to a 180-degree sweep of the canal. And so it went, as the *Islander*, both screws churning through the night at full speed, proceeded toward Victoria. A 10-year veteran of the Alaskan run, she had navigated Lynn Canal's moody weather, sudden fogs and icebergs many times without difficulty and had earned a reputation for speed, reliability and comfort.

Captain LeBlanc was the first to realize that the CPN flagship's luck had run out when he suddenly spotted the iceberg, towering directly ahead. Even as he shouted the order to alter course and reduce speed he knew that it was too late, the *Islander* charging its floating nemesis with almost suicidal glee. Seconds later, with a heartrending crash and tearing of steel, the liner shuddered to a stop, her bows ripped open by the rock-hard ice.

The *Islander*, and many of her terrified company, were doomed.

Immediately upon impact the ship's wildly spinning helm was torn from Captain Ferry's grip. As he battled to regain control he instinctively forced the wheel toward the nearest shore in the hope that the ship retained sufficient headway to drive her onto the beach. But the *Islander* had been ruptured by the force of the collision and the seas rushed into her wounds with overwhelming speed. Within seconds, the steamer was down by the head and sinking rapidly. When her screws rose out of the water she lost her last chance of manoeuvrability.

Just as Captain Foote, his face an ashen mask of disbelief, reached Ferry's side, a deckhand rushed into the wheel-house to ask whether the crew should lower the boats. But the master, unaware or unwilling to believe that his ship had only minutes to live, replied, "There is no need to lower them yet," and merely instructed the man to have them swung over the side.

Then time seemed to stand still, the *Islander* poised at a crazy angle, her bows awash. As Captains Foote and Ferry stood side by side on her sagging bridge, they could hear the cries of terror as the liner's panic-stricken passengers milled about her tilted decks in confusion. For several moments the ship remained suspended, neither officer daring to

contemplate the result should her bulkheads give way before the force of the sea. The *Islander*'s Scottish builders had done their work well but it was an unfair contest and, minutes after striking, there came a blood-curdling groan from deep within. As she began her death plunge Captain Ferry looked at his old friend and sighed, "Captain, I guess we will have to go."

Together they fought their way through swaying passageways to the boat deck and ran for the rail when, with a deafening explosion, the ship's boilers burst, hurtling both officers into the sea. Afterwards, Ferry described his life-or-death race to the rail, recalling how he had overheard the *Islander*'s barber, George Miles, say to a companion as both prepared to jump over the side: "I don't know what may happen to me but if I go down and you are saved, bid goodbye to my wife for me."

Days after the tragedy the friend reached Victoria to carry out his lost friend's last request.

But seconds before the boilers blew, Ferry recounted, he had noticed an old woman of about

Four views showing the luxurious fittings of the Ss. Islander, flagship of the Canadian Pacific Navigation Company until she struck an iceberg on the morning of August 15, 1901.

70. Bent with rheumatism and wearing a life preserver, she had been sitting on deck. She had caught his attention by the calm with which she had obviously been waiting for the end.

The stories told by other survivors of their miraculous escapes were many and, in several cases, heartbreaking. That recited by Dr. W.S. Phillips was one of unparallelled horror, the Seattle medic graphically describing the loss of his wife and four-year-old daughter. They had been asleep in their stateroom when the *Islander* crashed into the iceberg and threw them from their bunks. Upon rushing from the cabin and battling their way towards the upper deck, they found the passageways at an almost impossible angle and awash, as the ship's nose was already under. But, somehow, Dr. Phillips and his family made it to the main deck—where their agony began.

Deep within the dying steamer the flooding seas created tremendous suction and, as the terrified trio passed a large ventilator, the draft from below drew them, slowly and inexorably, to its gaping mouth. Phillips was able to grasp the ventilator lip but his wife and little girl were not as strong. As he watched in wide-eyed horror, both were sucked below and the monstrous vacuum drew him steadily into the

ventilator's jaws. Then his chin struck the lip. The next he knew, he was at the rail and preparing to jump. Then the *Islander* slid under, drawing him down with her. When he came to he was sharing a door as a raft with two other survivors. Hours afterward they were taken ashore where, overcome by shock and exposure as he huddled on the cold beach, he became delirious and began to call aloud for his family. When, suddenly, he heard a child crying, he rushed to her side. But the little girl was a total stranger.

Poor Dr. Phillips' ordeal was by no means ended as, upon regaining his composure, he joined in the task of recovering the bodies which had been washed in with the tide. But fate dealt him one more blow when, upon his dragging a body from the surf, he found it to be that of his daughter. This final shock proved to be too much for the hapless doctor and he fell to his knees on the rocky shore of Lynn Canal, clutching his little girl and sobbing hysterically until sympathetic hands separated them.

One of the heroes of the *Islander* was her second officer who, immediately upon her striking the 'berg, had assumed charge of lowering the lifeboats. Calmly and methodically, Powell had led frightened passengers to the boats and operated the davits until the ship began her plunge, when he shouted to those remaining to jump, and ran for the rail—just as a teenaged girl threw her arms about his neck and begged him to save her. Seconds later, still embraced, they hit the icy waters of the canal. But when Powell surfaced his unidentified companion was gone.

Upon swimming alongside a nearby raft he found the float occupied by several survivors, including Captains Foote and LeBlanc. But, as Powell later testified at the inquiry, as he reached for a lifeline another of the passengers ordered him away. When he persisted in attempting to board the raft the man drew a revolver and threatened to "blow his brains out." Even this drastic rebuff failed to deter Powell, who retorted, "Shoot away, for I guess you'll soon follow me. Anyhow, I believe your cartridges are wet."

Several other members of the *Islander*'s crew who had reacted heroically to the emergency made the supreme sacrifice. When the liner had slammed into the ice two of her firemen had instantly volunteered to attempt to close the valve connecting the forward compartments and the engine room—only to be drowned before the eyes of their comrades. At this, the remainder of the black gang had joined in a human chain to make a run for the deck. Just as they began their mad dash for safety Second Engineer Allan had yelled, "If we meet (we meet), and if we don't we don't. We'll make a bold dash for it anyway!"

When survivors were finally brought together it was learned that all of the engine room crew who had formed the chain had escaped—all but Allan,

who had been married for only five months.

A second, grimmer tragedy had been enacted deep within the *Islander*. Shortly after clearing Skagway 12 stowaways had been found and put to work in the hold, passing coal to pay for their fares. Unknown to the chief engineer the men were still in the bunkers when the steamer struck. He had immediately ordered the holds sealed so as to delay the flooding, an act which undoubtedly saved lives by delaying the *Islander*'s plunge by several minutes. For 11 of the stowaways the engineer's order had meant death, the twelfth having run from the bunkers the instant of the crash.

Sixty years after that fateful morning one of the *Islander*'s survivors recalled his narrow escape from her sloping decks. Ex-Mounted Policeman Edmund Waller of Nanaimo had been en route to Victoria with two other constables after two years' duty in the Yukon and was in their cabin when the ship struck. "We were just settling down," he said, "when we felt a jar. Then the engines stopped. A strange silence settled over the ship. There was no outcry. No shouting. We lay in our bunks and listened and wondered what had happened."

He and his companions soon realized the gravity of the situation when the *Islander* began to list forward. By the time they rushed topside the saloon was awash, the main deck empty, the lifeboats gone. Just then they heard voices and made their way around "the housework to the other side of the ship. It was black dark. We could see a boat pulling away from the ship. It was the last one."

Faced with no other choice but to swim, the three leaped over the side and struck out for the departing craft, to be pulled aboard. The overcrowded boat was just 150 yards from the ship when her boilers exploded. The ear-splitting roar, said Waller, was followed by screaming, then silence.

Few of those in the glacier-fed waters of Lynn Canal survived for long and by morning the shores were littered with dead. Once the survivors were rushed to Juneau the grim task of recovering the bodies of 42 men, women and children was begun.

At the inquiry in Victoria, Second Officer Powell accused the man who had threatened him with a gun with having been responsible for the death of Captain Foote. The passenger, he said, had accused Foote of incompetency and made the dazed master leave the raft. This the unidentified passenger denied, saying that he had not a gun but a pipe, which he had used to bluff those with lifejackets from forcing their way aboard the dangerously overloaded float.

Captain Foote, he said, left the raft of his own accord. Overcome by cold, Foote began to babble deliriously and bade them farewell several times.

A black and white reproduction of a full-color oil painting by Joe Adams depicting the sinking of the **Islander.**

Then, with a final "Goodbye, boys!" Foote raised his arms, allowing his lifebelt to slip up over his shoulder, and "sank like a stone."

For Mrs. Foote the news of the *Islander*'s sinking and of her husband's death had come with cruel suddenness, it being reported that she was "walking along the street on Sunday evening towards her home when a small boy stopped her and said, 'Mrs. Foote, the *Islander* is wrecked and your husband is drowned.'

"Dazed by the sudden shock, she went home, where soon afterward she learned that it was all too true, for a former shipmate of the dead mariner had come to break as best he could the sad news, only to find that his sorrowful tale was already known..."

After due deliberation the inquiry ruled that the *Islander*'s company had, as a whole, acted bravely and unselfishly; that Captain Edmund LeBlanc, pilot, was censurable for having failed to reduce speed upon seeing ice in the canal; that Captain Foote had been negligent in leaving the bridge without giving his officers special instructions. As a special rider to their verdict, and in response to rumors which had been circulating, the members of the inquiry ruled that there was no evidence of intoxication upon the part of any of the *Islander*'s officers.

For Captain Hamilton Foote the tragedy meant not only the loss of his life and ship but, with the ruling of negligence, his reputation as well. It was an ironic turn of events for the veteran master who had encountered ice in Lynn Canal once before. Not two years earlier, when in command of the Ss. *Danube*, he had been holed—just a few miles south of where the *Islander* foundered. But on that occasion the *Danube*'s bulkheads had saved her, Foote eventually coaxing his ship into Juneau with her bow flooded. It was thought that he had been confident that the larger, newer *Islander*'s bulkheads would save her that foggy morning of August 15, 1901. But the *Islander* had been mortally wounded and 42 persons died with her in the fog-bound reaches of Lynn Canal.

* * *

No sooner had the *Islander* vanished than rumors began to fly thick and fast as to the actual amount of raw Yukon gold that had gone down with her, many voicing the opinion that her lost treasure amounted to as much as $3 million. Despite the repeated denials, as late as 30 years after, by Purser Harry F. Bishop, the rumors persisted. As far as Bishop was concerned, "There was only $1,000 in the safe of the *Islander* when she went down. I would have known if there had been more because I would have had to sign for it."

He also refuted stories that many of the ill-fated steamer's passengers had been carrying millions in gold in their luggage, saying: "Miners could get as good a price for their gold in Dawson as the outside. They sold in Dawson and got their money when they reached a bank on the outside."

Bishop's denials were forgotten when other survivors estimated the actual amount of lost treasure to be $275,000. This tempting figure was based upon reports that several passengers had been carrying large amounts of gold in their baggage. One, identified as H. Hart, was said to have had $35,000 in his satchel, which he had been forced to leave on the liner's deck. A second rich passenger had not been as sensible or as fortunate. Believed to have been carrying $40,000 in his portmanteau, he had refused to abandon it. Instead he had carried the heavy case to the railing and jumped overside, only to miss the lifeboat for which he was aiming, when the weight of his gold dragged him under.

Three more claims amounted to $68,000 and other, smaller ones brought the total figure of gold lost with the *Islander* to $275,000, although this figure could well be inaccurate either way. Whatever the case, the lost treasure attracted several corporations bent on salvage. Initial attempts, however, were defeated by the icy depths of Lynn Canal and primitive equipment.

One of the earliest salvors to tackle the *Islander* was Frank Walters, "the international diver," who planned to reach the wreck by means of a "diving suit of newly invented pattern" which, he hoped in the spring of 1921, would enable him to "turn the trick" on the canal's rocky bottom. Confident that the *Islander* contained at least $200,000 when she sank, Walters announced his plan to dive on the wreck that summer. Besides the precarious depth of 140 feet he said that the greatest obstacle facing him was the fact that he would have to break his way into the ship—no easy task, 23 fathoms down. But, he said, the *Islander's* iron hull likely would have deteriorated to the point that he would be able to "hammer his way through the sections which had not been penetrated by rust."

Aside from the $200,000 in gold Walters was after the ship's safe which he believed contained "a large quantity of money deposited...by passengers."

A veteran of salvage operations in Australian and New Zealand waters, Walters was the man who had successfully removed the safe of the *Princess Sophia*, also wrecked in Lynn Canal, with a loss of 343 lives in 1918. Unlike the *Islander*, however, the *Sophia* had been in shallower waters and it remained for Walters to test his new suit at 140 feet. Whether or not Walters did dive on the *Islander* is not recorded. It is a matter of record, however, that it was in 1931, when a diving bell was employed, that salvors first met with any success. Curiously, even this novel approach was not without its hazards, one of its observers reporting that he had spotted a "monster" in the wreck.

According to this fascinating report there were "huge foot tracks on the bottom about two feet apart and the mark where a great tail had been dragged along... Something was lurking in the gloom but

A view of the stern and twin screws of the tragic Islander *after she was raised in 1934. Although it has been estimated that the cost of salvaging her was in excess of $200,000, the actual amount of treasure recovered is not known.*

suddenly vanished in a flash of phosphorescence." Further investigation disclosed that the "brute was living inside the wreck, but we never got a good look at it. It's something like a sea crocodile."

The expedition then turned its attention to salvaging the *Islander's* cargo and valuables by operating a dredge with which they sucked debris from the wreck to the surface, where it was run through a riffle to recover any treasures that it might contain. Almost $6,000 worth of nuggets and a diamond ring were recovered in this manner before the operation was stalled by the great depth.

For the very fact that the *Islander* rested in 23 fathoms made her an almost impossible target for treasure hunters as no diving suit of that period was able to withstand the pressure at this depth. Not until 1934 and the designing of a new diving dress was the *Islander* refloated from her watery grave in Lynn Canal after one of the greatest salvage feats of the era.

The most vivid account of this achievement is that of the diver responsible, Charles W. Huckins: "On first descending to the *Islander* on November 1 (1932), I found the ship easily and stood in bewilderment to see her decks caved in. Tons upon tons of sea growth, shells and silt which had settled upon the decks had caved them in and carried them down into the holds in an awful mess of twisted beams and steel plates as sharp as knives—a terrific place to venture in a suit whose puncture at that depth meant instant death. The steel was encrusted with live barnacles to a depth of two feet.

"I made my surveys of the wreck and hunted among the debris for the treasure for 10 days—diving four times a day for a stay of an hour at a time. I found nothing because of the tremendous depth and the shells and the silt. It was late in the year and the work was abandoned for the winter.

"When I made my first dive in May, 1934, I found the *Islander* had slid offshore 60 feet and shoved up a mud bank. Her shattered bow was in 140 feet of water, her stern in 95. And she was listed 40 degrees to starboard. In all the history of diving, I know of no other commercial job in 140 feet of water. And the water was horribly chilled by the glacier. (There were several near the site of the wreck). The glacier also gave off silt which rolled along the bottom in black clouds, like some awful fog.

"I found that the cables we laid had fouled so badly where the ship had slid over them that we had to pull 17 of them back out from under the ship and saw them back into place. That was my job, down there on the bottom—to guide them into place in utter darkness.

"That ship was bad to work on. The deck plates were so rusted you could stick your helmet through what had been three-eighths-inch steel plates to look inside the cabins. But the hull plates were in perfect condition—we had to cut holes in the hull with a torch to let the water out when we finally had her beached.

"There were bones of the drowned scattered all through the shells and silt.

"The *Islander* was finally beached. The hull broke above the water at 7:20 a.m., July 25, for the first time in 33 years. We all cheered as the barnacle-encrusted thrust of jagged steel came above the surface... We lugged her up on the beach between the two teamed ships, and on July 26 I walked around that hull in ordinary shoes without getting my feet damp. It was strange to walk in ordinary clothes across those decks where I had labored in darkness at the bottom of the sea...."

Thus diver Huckins described his months-long ordeal at the bottom of Lynn Canal, in total darkness, benumbed to the bone by cold, and in constant danger of having his air line cut, or his suit punctured, by the ship's jagged plates. On July 25, 1934, two ships were moored on either side of the wreck's site and secured to the sunken steamer by cables passing under her hull. At a signal the vessels' powerful winches went to work. When the *Islander* finally broke the surface she was hauled ashore at Green's Cove, Admiralty Island, where her bones were picked clean.

Ironically, for all of their perseverance, heroism and ingenuity, the pickings were—reputedly—slim. By literally digging the ship apart with shovels and sluicing the debris for any valuables hidden within the treasure hunters "prospected" for the *Islander*'s legendary wealth. It is known that their efforts were not without some reward, two salvagers finding a poke of gold in what had been a washroom, and the ship's safe yielding Canadian currency amounting to more than $8,000. Also found intact were 25 bottles of expensive champagne.

Whether or not the operation made a profit

(Above) The sinking of the **Islander** *in Lynn Canal with great loss of life was an ironic turn for Captain Hamilton Foote who had encountered ice in this waterway two years earlier. Then in command of the Ss.* **Danube**, *shown here, he had been holed just a few miles south of where the* **Islander** *was to founder. But on that occasion the* **Danube's** *bulkheads had saved her.*
(Below) Floral tributes to victims of the Ss. **Islander**, *in Victoria's Ross Bay Cemetery.*

remains unrecorded as the company refused to disclose the amounts spent and recovered on the project. Their salvaging of the *Islander* is estimated to have cost $200,000, it being thought in some quarters that they recovered only a quarter of that amount.

As for the poor Ss. *Islander*, her ravaged hulk was left on the beach until 1952 when a Seattle salvage firm cut her up for scrap. However, her name remains fresh in the annals of British Columbia marine lore as her gold—wherever it may be—continues to intrigue armchair treasure hunters to this day. ●

ROBERT SMITH
TRIUMPH
AND TRAGEDY

None could accuse Robert T. Smith, pioneer, of having led an inactive or uninteresting life. As customs officer, packer, miner, banker and Member of the Legislative Assembly, he had left his mark on a young province. But Smith's career also seems to have been plagued by misfortune. When he died, tragically and violently, he had been thwarted by success almost to the very end.

Mr. and Mrs. A.D. Macdonald. *Handsome, bearded Alexander Macdonald landed in Victoria in 1859 to open the colony's first banking house. Before long, Macdonald's Bank offered a complete list of services and issued its own banknotes. But, on the night of September 22, 1864, thieves broke into the bank and escaped with more than $30,000 in gold coins, dust, currency and silver.*

A century and some after, Smith appears to have been something of a quixotic figure. Big, bluff and quick to take exception, his temper more than once got him into serious difficulty. But to those who knew him he was honest, reliable and a loyal friend; as quick to lend a helping hand as he was to take offence, and a staunch supporter when the chips were down.

Perhaps the most famous example of his volatile temperament was the time he let his objections be known to a newspaper editor—with the blunt end of his walking stick. For the unfortunate editor the incident resulted in hospitalization—for Smith a day in court.

The story behind this assault began with the rivalry between Victoria and New Westminster, then respective capitals of the crown colonies of Vancouver Island and mainland British Columbia, for the honor of being named the single capital of the united colony of British Columbia. Victoria, of course, won the contest and that was that. But Royal City residents did not take the loss lightly. Rather, they resented the move to the point of holding mass rallies and burning in effigy the members of the legislative assembly who had in their wisdom voted against the Royal City.

One of those who had voted in favor of Victoria was Robert T. Smith, member for Cariboo. When the *British Columbian*, for the edification of those of its readers who did not know who betrayed them, published something of a blacklist in its columns, the name SMITH appeared in capitals, between the drawing of two hands. Smith, who had shrugged off public ridicule and laughed at a threat made against his life, was outraged by the editor's cheek. He had, he said, agreed that Victoria was more suitable as capital after due consideration and after reviewing all of the facts. He had voted fairly and honestly, to the best of his ability. That New Westminster citizens would be upset he could understand. But when the *Columbian* "held him up to scorn and contempt" that was going too far.

When, a week after, the vote was made official and Victoria chosen the one and only capital of British Columbia, the *Columbian* struck again, SMITH appearing between two hands. Thus Smith's fateful encounter with the fourth estate when he waylaid the *Columbian*'s editor and, without so much as an introduction, proceeded to beat the newsman to a pulp.

Curiously, in an age when journalism was not only golden but downright yellow at times, and when libel laws were next to non-existent, the *Columbian* had shown rather admirable restraint in its treatment of a man for whom it had little regard. It, as had every other paper of its day, had used stronger language in dealing with its editorial antagonists, to say the least. Whatever, the use of Smith's name in vain struck that gentleman as being the most despicable of behavior, for which there was only one cure—the heavy end of his cane. The court, unsympathetic, found for the plaintiff and fined Smith for his unsportsmanlike conduct.

R.T. Smith's second claim to fame in provincial history is his involvement with Victoria's "perfect crime," the robbery of Macdonald's Bank. Briefly told, the stage for this drama was set back in 1859, when handsome, bearded Alexander Macdonald arrived in Victoria and opened the colony's first banking house. Setting up shop at Yates and Wharf, Macdonald and company offered a complete list of services, issued its own banknotes, and even boasted a general store on the side. When business prospered Macdonald branched out, building a sawmill at Port Douglas and erecting a beautiful mansion in Victoria.

Although the arrival of more established banks cut into Macdonald's profits towards the end of 1862 he appears to have survived in comfort. Two years later, in 1864, new government legislation gave Macdonald until March 31, 1865, to obtain a royal charter or to petition the legislative assembly for authority to continue business after that date.

But Macdonald failed to meet either requirement when, on the night of September 22, 1864, thieves broke into his bank and escaped with more than $30,000.

Victorians were astounded by the robbery which, to this day, remains unsolved. Suffice it to say that, although several persons — particularly Macdonald, who fled the country when the bank immediately foundered — were suspected of having committed the deed, no one was formally charged.

The night before the burglary, three men had been hard at work in the bank: John Waddell, acting as manager while Macdonald attended to business at the Cariboo branch; clerk and bookkeeper Josiah Barnett; and the bank's agent, Robert T. Smith. Until 10 o'clock that evening the men prepared a shipment of coin and notes which Smith was to take to the Richfield branch on the morning steamer. Upon completion of the shipment, amounting to more than $30,000 in gold coins, dust, currency and silver, the treasure was placed in the heavy safe inside the fireproof vault. As investigating police officers later pieced together the night's events:

"The safe and vault were then locked by Mr. Barnett, who brought the vault key to Mr. Waddell, stating that he had not taken out the metal slide or plug which prevents the safe lock from being picked as, although Mr. Macdonald had once shown him how to take it out and put it in, he had forgotten how to do it."

Strangely, Waddell did not know the secret of operating the lock guard either, with the result that, when Waddell, Barnett and Smith left the premises at 10 o'clock, the safe was locked but its protective slide had not been positioned.

Early the next morning a janitor found that the office had been ransacked, the safe opened "without difficulty" thanks to the key guard not being in place. After a major scandal and an ineffective police investigation the great Macdonald bank robbery was history.

For many of the bank's depositors and Macdonald's personal creditors the robbery and subsequent bankruptcy of Macdonald's financial empire meant heavy losses. For agent R.T. Smith the disaster meant not only that he was unemployed but that he was out the sum of $13,000 which he apparently had invested in the firm. Thus, as far as he was concerned, Victoria's "perfect crime" was a doubly bitter pill.

Four years after, Smith embarked on the little screw steamer *George S. Wright* for Portland. Among his fellow passengers was journalist D.W. Higgins, whom he had met before. Almost half a century after, Higgins recalled the southbound voyage. Upon meeting Smith at the ticket counter the two remained together until Portland, when they boarded the San Francisco bound steamer *Continental*. During their five-day stop-over at Portland both came to the conclusion that the *Continental* was anything but safe. But, as she was the only ship available, they had no choice but to board her.

Their fears as to the *Continental*'s seaworthiness soon proved to be well-founded. Once over the Columbia River Bar, the vessel encountered heavy weather and lumbered sluggishly, her "aged timbers cracking and shaking as if with fright." As the *Continental* wallowed in the waves, her decks awash, Smith and Higgins huddled abaft her smokestack. Unable to carry on a conversation due to the screeching of the wind, they cowered in the comparative shelter of the funnel, where they witnessed a scene which would remain with Higgins for the rest of his life:

"The noise and confusion caused by the storm were so great that we could scarcely hear each other speak; but high above the tumult rose the voice of the captain," he recounted. "He was the greatest brute and most profane man I ever met. His treatment of his sailors was infamous; for the slightest infraction he would strike or kick an unfortunate man in a brutal manner. To his passengers he was curt, insulting and overbearing. No one could get a simple answer to a simple question. The simplest request for something that would add to the comfort or relief of a sick person was refused with an oath which for ingenuity of construction and manner of expression surpassed any profanity I ever heard..."

This was the evil mariner whose roar was to be heard above that of the storm, as he stalked the *Continental*'s deck and barked orders to his seamen. Once the storm had passed and the steamer continued southward it was found that her seams had parted in the gale, causing her to answer reluctantly to her helm. With her increasing recalcitrance the captain's impatience grew and he cursed his crewmen steadily. Upon sighting a Jewish passenger on deck he cursed him too, and ordered him below until San Francisco with a warning as to what might happen should he again wander on deck.

Victoria and New Westminster (above) competed for the honor of being named capital of the united colony of British Columbia. When the Royal City lost the contest, its residents held mass rallies and burned in effigy the members of the legislative assembly who had voted against them. Among these was the member for Cariboo, Robert Smith, who, upon the Columbian's including his name in a blacklist of the offending MLAs, assaulted its editor with his walking stick.

Suddenly aware that he was being watched, the captain turned and glowered at his audience of two, Higgins and Smith glaring back with open distaste.

"What in the hell are you doing there?" roared the captain. "Get down below, damn you!"

"Are you speaking to me?" Smith asked indifferently.

When the blasphemous mariner again ordered them below and advanced with a menacing expression, Smith calmly stood his ground. Just then a lurching of the ship threw a passing seaman against his superior who, beside himself with rage, began to beat him with his fists — at least, such was his intent, his assault being cut short when the crewman pulled a large knife. Instantly, the captain backed off, the blustering bully of a few moments before becoming a quivering coward.

But the man was not to be denied and lunged forward. The captain turned and ran, the murderous sailor and sheath-knife at his heels. Seconds later, as Smith and Higgins watched, transfixed, the captain and his pursuer circled the deck and were on their second lap about the ship, then a third. Despite the captain's screams for help not a single crewman went to his assistance and he was fast running out of breath, and the gap between hunter and hunted rapidly closing, when Smith, moving swiftly, caught the would-be assassin by the arm. With a flick of his wrist the man was disarmed, his knife over the rail.

The seaman then turned his attention to Smith but the burly passenger soon wrestled him to the deck, where he lay exhausted. At this sudden turn of events the captain regained his courage and, ignoring Smith's and Higgins' violent protests, kicked the man's face into a unrecognizable pulp, when the cowardly crew put him in irons in the forecastle.

"Smith and I," said Higgins, "turned away sick at heart at the cowardice and brutality of the captain and the time-serving crew, who as soon as the sailor had fallen into the clutches of the captain, assisted in carrying him to the forecastle and imprisoning him. While the chase was on, they had wished him success. We remained on deck and came and went as we pleased, and the captain did not again molest us, nor did he thank Smith for his life or speak to us at all until we reached San Francisco. The incident with the sailor had humbled him somewhat, and he treated the passengers with some consideration; but he was as hard as ever on the crew...."

Upon the decrepit *Continental*'s docking in the Bay City, Smith and Higgins went their own way. When next the journalist heard of Smith he was in Utah and, according to reports, doing extremely well. Not only was Smith a financial success at last but he was in love with the territorial lieutenant-governor's daughter.

Alas, it was too good to be true, poor Smith's luck holding true to form. Although he had become rich the object of his affection rejected his proposal of marriage. In fact, the young lady who, until that time, had given him every encouragement, dismissed him from her life rather abruptly. When the bewildered suitor asked why the sudden change of heart she simply referred him to his rival, a Dr. Snedecker. With famous temper to the fore, Smith called upon that gentleman. Just what Snedecker had to say is not known, although it was a matter of public record that, when R.T. Smith left him, he was livid and loudly informed the doctor that "Utah was not big enough to hold them both."

Ironically, not two days later, both rivals chanced to board the same train at the same station at the same moment. According to the record, "They glared at each other, hot words were exchanged, and both drew their pistols."

Although older, Dr. Snedecker seems to have been the more agile as he was first to draw and fire, his pistol ball striking Smith in the chest and puncturing a lung. Crashing backward to the floor, Smith struggled with his remaining breath to raise his gun, when, with a superhuman effort, he aimed and fired. A second later he was dead — unaware that his single shot had caught Snedecker in the heart. "The enemies," it was reported, "breath(ed) their last sighs at the same moment."

With that, Robert T. Smith belonged to the ages, his vast wealth passing to needy relatives in Scotland. One can only hope that the ill-fated Smith's heirs enjoyed happier circumstances than did the bluff but warm-hearted pioneer whose death in a Wild West shoot-out ended a remarkable and tragic career. ●

To his superiors, he was a rebel, a troublemaker and a bore; to his students, he was a stern taskmaster whose word was law and whose temper, uncertain at the best of times, was to be avoided at all costs.

Amor de Cosmos, long a thorn in Governor James Douglas's side, paid honorable mention to the pioneer efforts of Rev. Staines, of whom Douglas had raged: "The Rev. Mr. Staines is a formentor of mischief and I believe a preacher of sedition."

REV. ROBERT STAINES

HISTORIANS view Rev. Robert John Staines as being something between a martyr for democracy and a pompous ass.

Whatever Staines' true claim to fame, there is no denying that, during his brief and stormy tenure as chaplain and schoolmaster for the Hudson's Bay Company, there were few dull moments in the Fort Victoria of a century and more ago.

A "Don Quixote in broadcloth," as one writer has colorfully described him, Staines' background must have suggested anything but a rebel and "fomentor of mischief" to his new employers when he was accepted for duty in outpost Vancouver Island, half a world away. Thirty years of age, married, and a Cambridge graduate, his previous teaching experience had been gained at Derby Grammar School.

Although a classical—and brilliant—scholar, Staines originally lacked the main requirement for

(Opposite page and below) Fort Victoria.
(Right) Rev. Staines' classroom occupied the upper storey of Fort Victoria's "Bachelors' Hall," where company employees such as Dr. J.S. Helmcken, were often victims of childish pranks, such as pouring water through cracks in the flooring.

the colonial posting: that he be a man of the cloth. He easily surmounted this obstacle (thereby demonstrating himself to be a man of adaptability) by applying for, and receiving, holy orders. Thus armed, he obtained the dual posting as HBC post chaplain (for 100 pounds annually) and as schoolteacher to the children of the fort (at 340 pounds per annum); the former stipend to be paid by the company, the latter to be the responsibility of his students' parents.

As Mrs. Staines also was a qualified teacher, this arrangement included her instruction of the post's young ladies.

Little, unfortunately, is known of Staines' background in the Old Country beyond the fact that he had proven himself a gifted scholar. Likely his parents ("nothing of consequence," according to one historian) were of limited means and status, the young Staines having had to justify his university entrance through hard work and high marks; perhaps his obvious abilities attracted the attention of a wealthy sponsor.

Whatever the case, he graduated from Cambridge with honors and secured a teaching position at Derby Grammar School; the post he held when he learned of the opening in far-off Fort Victoria.

But if full particulars as to Robert Staines' family and early career are lacking, it is possible to form a vivid mental image of the 30-year-old preacher-teacher who eventually found his way to isolated Vancouver Island. For his actions and manner soon revealed him to be vain, arrogant and ambitious—in short, a man of limited means, unlimited energy and great pretensions.

This is not to say, however, that he was not a sympathetic figure. Rather, he has left the impression of a rather pathetic character unable to obtain the material and social rewards his education and abilities warranted. Continually thwarted in his attempts to achieve all that he was sure himself capable of—and entitled to—Staines' adult life seems to have been one of frustration and, ultimately, tragedy.

Perhaps the most revealing glimpse at the real Rev. R.J. Staines was that provided during the voyage from England to Victoria: a humiliating episode which, we can imagine, never failed to amuse his critics in Victoria.

Despite the fact that they left several outstanding debts in England, the Staines' were not alone during the outbound voyage, being accompanied by two servants. Upon reaching the Hawaiian (or Sandwich) Islands, Staines decided, like all good tourists, that he would like to meet the "king of the cannibal isles" and, for the occasion, outfitted his manservant in a splendid new livery.

Dressed in conservative broadcloth, as befitted his new calling, Rev. Staines and his brightly costumed servant announced themselves to the King's court. Moments later, that good-natured monarch appeared and, spotting his visitors, rushed forward in welcome. Well over a century after, one can imagine Staines' disappointment and discomfort when the king, overawed by the servant's costume, hurried right by Staines to embrace the other!

To say the least, Staines was unhappy. Hurt by what he felt to have been a deliberate snub, he must have sulked for much of the voyage to Victoria. His feelings, and those of his wife, were not revived by their first glimpse of their new home.

In fact, their arrival in Fort Victoria could only have been traumatic. Assured—in England—by company officials that comfortable quarters would be awaiting them at the trading post, they were distressed to find that Victoria boasted few of the amenities of the Old Country. In fact, their initial impression, as recorded by Chief Trader Roderick Finlayson years afterward, was one of "mud and mire." As there were no streets, narrow tracks of mud which served as thoroughfares made seaboots the order of the day.

As it was his duty to receive the couple, Finlayson had the unenviable job of introducing them to their quarters. Although he felt little enough sympathy for Staines, he did admit to feeling "ashamed to see the lady come ashore," and saw to the laying of planks through the mud "in order to get them safely to the Fort."

Once inside the stockade, the couple looked about in surprise and dismay at the "bare walls of the buildings...stating that the company in England had told them this and that and had promised them such and such." But Finlayson could do no more than apologize for the spartan facilities and assure both that "their rooms were fitted as best could be done."

Their quarters and the schoolroom, recalled Dr. J.S. Helmcken, who shared the same building, occupied a "large portion" of the two-storey log structure known as Bachelors' Hall. This double occupancy led to some hectic moments for Helmcken, his roommate and their guests, as the students slept overhead, and "the little mischiefs used to play pranks, occasionally pouring water on us through cracks in the flooring. By the same token, our proceedings may have amazed them, too, for Bachelors' Hall was pretty noisy."

Regardless of distractions caused by the boisterous bachelors, Rev. and Mrs. Staines maintained a firm grip upon their young charges from the very beginning. For, if nothing else, Staines was a strict disciplinarian, wielding his cane with energy for the slightest infraction. He was, according to one of his students, James R. Anderson, "of rather uncertain temper, and disposed to be unduly severe in administering corporal punishment;" a tendency towards violence that Anderson suffered first-hand more than once. Particularly on those long, tedious summer afternoons when "learning the collects," when, despite the hardness of his seat, Anderson found it impossible to remain awake—"and woe betide me" if Staines caught him dozing.

Three-quarters of a century after, Anderson described Vancouver Island's first classroom as spartan. Heated only by an old, and ineffective, box stove in winter (the older students hogging the warmer seats from their smaller fellows), and stifling in summer, the school had little to offer in the way of comfort.

Upstairs, the dormitory was little better equipped, the tedium and homesickness being relieved only by the antics of bachelors Helmcken, McKay and company, whose "mild orgies," as viewed through a piece of loose flooring, proved, as can be imagined, to be highly entertaining. Between orgies, the students had to content themselves with catching rats, Staines having posted a bounty of a shilling for each dozen killed. Unfortunately, despite the fact that the fort was overrun by vermin, Anderson ruefully recounted that the animals were cunning and hard to catch with the students' home-made traps. Consequently, few earned the shilling and many a night's sleep was disturbed by the pitter-patter of tiny feet—sometimes across one's face.

As for Staines, he had sought his own diversion in the form of a 16-acre farm at Mount Tolmie, then a 400-acre estate at Metchosin. Casually ignoring the fact that the Hudson's Bay Company owned all of Vancouver Island (and employed him), Staines was a squatter. Sure that the land must eventually be released for settlement, he refused to pay the company's exorbitant price and proceeded to raise pigs and cattle between classes. Then, as the farm demanded more of his time, the duties of schoolteacher descended more and more upon Mrs. Staines.

On Sundays, he could not escape, serving in the dual capacity of parson for the morning and afternoon services, and as schoolteacher in between. For his students, Sunday was the longest day of the week—"A day of terror." After a breakfast of bread, treacle and tea without milk, they attended the a.m. service. That over, they turned to lunch—potatoes, meat "and sometimes fish"—when they suffered through the "collects." Following an afternoon service, the students again had tea, bread and treacle before retiring to their hard beds consisting of a single blanket atop a board as mattress, and another for cover against the winter chill.

Amazingly, all survived, Anderson boasting: "We were hardy young beggars and did not mind it."

Despite Staines' ready temper and ready switch, Anderson conceded long afterward that he was "nevertheless a good teacher." Staines even proved himself to be more than a classroom czar when he organized occasional outings by Indian canoe up the Gorge. Once out of the classroom, and into the forests which surrounded the fort, he became another man. A dedicated student of biology, he imparted his own enthusiasm for natural history to his charges. At night, gathered about the fire, he led his students in song.

It was during such outings that Staines was able to relax, it seems, and be himself. At such times, said Anderson, he became quite likable. But, once back in the classroom, he reverted to the tyrant of before.

Obviously, Staines found this same method of escape on his farm, taking more and more time away from his classroom duties, and causing criticism to the effect that he preferred his pigs to his pupils. (Undoubtedly, if the truth were known, this was correct. As far as Chief Factor James Douglas was concerned, he was unquestionably violating his contract and neglecting his duties as teacher).

Actually, Douglas was thoroughly disgusted with his chaplain and schoolteacher, although not strictly on grounds of dereliction of duty. For Staines, between officiating at Sunday service, tutoring the post children, and attending to the care and attention of his beloved pigs, had found time to involve himself in politics. Despite the fact that the HBC reigned supreme over all of Vancouver Island, discouraged all attempts at colonization by "independent settlers" (this, in direct violation of its royal charter), and was his employer, Staines blissfully and vociferously championed the cause of open colonization; a pastime which could hardly be expected to win Douglas' approval.

Their differences had begun with Staines' performing the marriage ceremony for James Cathie and Maria Field, the staid Douglas reprimanding the minister for proceeding with the service when evidence indicated that Miss Field had been married before. Usually—and with increasing frequency—the two—both headstrong and equally sure as to the justice of his cause—differed on company policy. With a growing number of independent settlers, Staines continually voiced criticism of the HBC's efforts to discourage colonization. When, in 1852, he informed the British Consul at San Francisco of gold having been discovered on the mainland, he again raised the ire of Douglas.

As head of the HBC on Vancouver Island, Douglas resented any such publicity which could lead to an influx of settlers. Vancouver Island, the company reasoned (charter notwithstanding), was for fur trading, not farming.

Staines, Douglas penned with disdain, was not performing to expectation. "Had I a selection to make (for teacher) he is not the man I would choose. But it must be admitted we might find a man worse qualified."

Their differences came to a head when, with the resignation of Richard Blanshard as first governor of the crown colony of Vancouver Island, Blanshard agreed to carry with him to England a petition, urging representation, which had been signed by the colony's handful of residents who were unassociated with the company. Among the "independent settlers" whose names were on the petition was that of Rev. Robert Staines—preacher and teacher in the company's employ. Douglas accused the parson of being "a fomentor of mischief and I believe a preacher of sedition."

Moreover, raged Douglas, "His time appears to be devoted to litigation and agitation. He is occasioning dissension between the colonists and the company."

In other words, Staines did not seem to know on which side his bread was buttered. He was a traitor to the company's cause and, with such annoying dissidents as Captain James Cooper, a damned nuisance. Their petition, Douglas said, "slandered" the HBC.

When Staines bravely attacked the fur company's trade monopoly, and continued to defy Douglas' wrath, he was given notice that his services as schoolmaster would not be required as of June 1, 1854.

Finally, with the appointment of a legislative council, the rebels decided that their only recourse lay in taking their case directly to the colonial office. Perhaps because he was now a free spirit, Staines was appointed as "delegate."

The noble assignment got off to an inauspicious start when he missed his boat and had to race to Sooke in hopes of overtaking it. Unfortunately, wind and tide beat him, and he had to arrange passage on another vessel. Weeks passed, Mrs. Staines and his fellow petitioners confident that he was well on his way to the Old Country. But when the master of the barque *George Emery* brought word of having boarded a waterlogged and dismasted wreck off Cape Flattery, they knew it was not to be. For among the lost company was the Rev. Robert Staines.

But there were others to take up the torch. With the arrival of Amor de Cosmos, and the publishing of the British *Colonist*, Douglas, as governor, knew no peace. In the summer of 1859, de Cosmos recounted the struggle for representation and paid honorable mention to the pioneer efforts of Rev. Staines and company.

Today, Staines presents something of an anomaly to historians. On the one hand, it can be argued that he was arrogant, irascible and disloyal to the company he had agreed to serve; certainly he was guilty of not having had the honor to resign his position before campaigning for a cause directly opposed to the aims of his employer and benefactor.

Perhaps the career and character of Rev. Robert John Staines have best been summed up by historian James K. Nesbitt, who wrote: ". . .Mr. Staines, whatever his faults of character, could see plainly the need for reform if Vancouver Island and British Columbia ever were to prosper. Land reforms, but particularly an end of monopoly, were his aims.

"People said he was disloyal to the company, his benefactor and employer. But he was loyal to his principles."

Many men have had worse epitaphs. ●

The satellite communities of Chilliwack, Hope (above) and Princeton were not slow to discover the potential of their proximity to the new diggings.

STEAMBOAT MOUNTAIN
TALE OF THREE CITIES

Overnight, progress and prosperity came to Steamboat Mountain and environs, with not one but three townships springing up where, but weeks before, had been virgin wilderness.

FEW British Columbians must have heard of Steamboat Mountain. Yet, less than three-quarters of a century ago, it was the site of the richest gold strike in provincial history.

At least, such was the claim made for it by its promoters. For, when the bubble burst, thousands were heartbroken to find that this latest El Dorado was but a myth—a gold rush which never existed except in the minds of two American confidence men!

The story behind the rush to Steamboat Mountain (now Mount Shawatum) is as intriguing as the way in which this hummock of stone in south-central British Columbia won its first name. According to legend, it was christened back in the days when Fort Hope was operated as a Hudson's Bay Company fur trading post. As late as 1858, the isolated fort, some 80 miles up the Fraser from what was to become New Westminster, remained far off the beaten track; its only visitors the annual fur brigades, company officials, and neighboring Indians, all of whom travelled overland by canoe.

Thus it came with some surprise to officers of the fort, early in June of that year, when natives informed them that they had observed great puffs of white smoke rising from the river, like smoke signals. Although he found it hard to believe, the post factor, a man named Walker, concluded that the strange smoke must have been that of a steamboat attempting to beat its way upriver. Due to the fact that the river below the fort arched in a horseshoe and formed a strong current, Walker knew that any visiting steamer would be some time in arriving.

The following day the little steamer *Surprise* puffed into view, whistle blowing, crew cheering. But, much to the crew's amazement, those at the fort greeted them with polite restraint. The *Surprise* had not lived up to her name, and the steamboat's captain was mystified by their reception until Walker grinned that all of the fort's inhabitants had known of the vessel's impending arrival 24 hours in advance. The cool reception had been planned as a joke.

Some British Columbia gold mines, such as the famous Sheepshead of William Creek, shown here, were spectacular producers. But the "golden fleece" of Steamboat Mountain was just that — a fleece!

With that, all present marked the historic event with cheers and whoops. Hours later, the Ss. *Sea Bird* moored off the fort, and Hope's link to the outside world by riverboat was forged. With this development, Steamboat Mountain appeared on the maps; a name which was, half a century after, to make headlines across the continent.

Actually, there is another legend concerning the christening of Steamboat Mountain. According to this source, what is now known as Mount Shawatum was originally named after two prospectors named W.L. Wood and James Corrigan. Apparently the two built a raft on which to navigate the Skagit River as far as their claim on Ruby Creek, a tributary. For reasons lost to history, Wood and Corrigan christened their raft "Steamboat," and its place of launching became known locally as Steamboat Landing. In due course the adjacent mountain also was named in honor of this occasion.

Whatever the case, the Steamboat Mountain area slept peacefully until the 1880s, when British Columbia's golden treasury drew more and more prospectors to the area in search of fame and fortune. Gold was not to be found in paying quantities, however, with the result that, after the initial interest, Steamboat Mountain was allowed to rest undisturbed; at least until 1910, when two American miners, Dan Greenwald and W.A. Stevens, reported a fabulously rich discovery on the mountain's slopes. They had, they said, been tipped off to a previously unreported rich strike by a dying prospector in Nevada, and had travelled to British Columbia to see for themselves.

The result of their survey was a wild stampede to Steamboat Mountain, as hundreds, upon hearing of the new El Dorado, poured into the area by riverboat, on horseback, and on foot.

The rush gained in momentum when respected Vancouver mining promoter C.D. Rand announced that he had "acquired substantial interest in the discovered claim. . .that development work on the mine would proceed during the winter months and a stamp-mill was planned for the following year."

Jumping onto the bandwagon, Hope newspapers heralded the strike as a genuine El Dorado, reached by following the "trail of the gods" (this heavenly goat track more or less following what is now the busy Hope-Princeton highway to Mile 120, before turning south along the Skagit River to a point within a few miles of the American border).

Overnight, progress and prosperity came to Steamboat Mountain and environs, with not one, but three, townships springing up where, but weeks before, had been virgin wilderness. Although small enough by today's standards, each of the "towns" boasted a hotel, store, and the inevitable saloons, as well as sundry other buildings and residences (many of these tents). As mining and real estate promoters worked around the clock to push the area as the province's latest mecca for the enterprising and adventurous, more and more people—and more and more money—flowed into the region; all convinced that this was indeed El Dorado, the biggest strike since the Klondike.

Typical of that halcyon era, the new communities —Steamboat, Steamboat Mountain, and Steamboat City—vied for supremacy, each proclaiming itself to be the capital of the new gold fields. Messrs. Stevens and Greenwald, not unnaturally, enjoyed immense popularity throughout the Fraser Valley. Whenever they arrived in Hope, it was to enjoy a reception such as usually reserved for royalty. Crowds turned out to cheer, and the beaming prospectors turned promoters basked in the glory of their discovery.

By the spring of 1911, the rush to Steamboat Mountain had swelled into a wave of humanity, and the competing communities of Steamboat, Steamboat Mountain and Steamboat City became household words throughout the Pacific Northwest. Unfortunately, due to their similarity of names, confusion began to grow among those farther afield; a problem which the Hope *News* tried to eliminate by designating the townsites by their hotels. Thus the three settlements became, in turn: McIntyre and Raymond's Hotel; Still and Raymond's Hotel; and the Jarvis Hotel.

The former hostelry proudly announced itself as the "Steamboat with buildings," although the promotional releases prepared by hotelier Jarvis were not far behind with their glowing descriptions of the aerial tramways and double-track railways leading from the mines.

Of the three communities, Steamboat was the first to form a board of trade, under the guiding hand of David Sloan, to act as city council and to oversee the "care of sanitation, fire protection, street paving and lighting;" in short, all of the modern conveniences. Not to be outdone, the leading citizens of Steamboat Mountain advertised their mines as being richer than those of Ontario's famous producers at Porcupine.

The satellite communities of Chilliwack, Hope and Princeton were not slow to discover the potential of their proximity to the new diggings, and soon began to herald themselves as the gateway to Steamboat Mountain. But only Hope enjoyed the talents of Harvey P. Leonard, who poetically penned that it would soon become famous for its skyscrapers and be linked to the Canadian Northern Railway.

Business continued to boom, with something like seven companies being incorporated, with as many millions in capital, to search for the golden fleece of Steamboat Mountain. When winter snows brought a halt to further development, most of those involved settled back to await spring thaw, confident that, with the snows gone, they would strike it rich. Those who had already staked their claims on likely looking creeks throughout the vicinity undoubtedly felt the most confident as it was rumored that, come spring, at least 5,000 more gold seekers would be on the scene. The more broad-minded of those taking part in the stampede were open to possibilities of silver, platinum, copper, lead and zinc, which also were thought to exist in the locality. For that matter, a geologist named Camsell went so far as to report the discovery of diamonds on nearby Olivine Mountain.

Finally it was spring, and the diggings roared to life with renewed energy. Steamboat City now boasted its very own newspaper, the Hope-Steamboat *Nugget*, edited by R.J. Clark. Among the newcomers to camp was the well-known "Alaska Jack" Ginnin, who opined that, after mining throughout the continent, he had never seen more likely looking prospects than those of Steamboat Mountain.

But—ever so vaguely at first—an undercurrent of confusion began to manifest itself throughout the various camps. More and more, questions were being asked by old hands and newcomers alike. Questions such as: where was the gold?

For, amazingly, all of the excitement, all of the commotion and all of the optimism had not turned up so much as one single rich strike!

Slowly, then with greater urgency, word began to spread that there was something seriously wrong on Steamboat Mountain. For all of the glowing reports made to date, no one other than Messrs. Greenwald and Stevens seemed to have found anything beyond "color." Finally mining entrepreneur Rand, head of Steamboat Gold Mining Company Limited, became worried enough to call upon the partners at their mine—to be turned away by an armed guard. Now alarmed, Rand waited until nightfall and attempted to sneak inside for a look, only to be discovered and again ordered off the property.

By then it was July, and the questions—then accusations—were flying thick and fast. When someone at last admitted aloud that he had not seen any real gold since he arrived, someone else remarked that he had not seen either Greenwald or Stevens for some time, either.

With this observation, panic swept the camps of Steamboat Mountain and Steamboat City. It did not take long to discover that the partners had secretly disposed of their holdings for good sums and had vanished; Greenwald later turning up in South America, then New York, Stevens popping back into the public view in California. Only then was it realized that all had been a hoax, that the Americans had salted their claims by hack-sawing gold coins into fragments, loading them into shotguns, and peppering the rocks with high-grade "ore," courtesy of the United States mint. To the uninitiated (and to many who should have known better), this was a sure-fire method of turning worthless rock into a gold mine.

Sadly, it was all over. The golden dreams of Steamboat Mountain were nothing more than empty air and, disheartened, the thousands of fortune hunters turned sadly homeward, or moved on to newer, more promising fields. Within months, the three little townsites were virtually deserted. By this time the evil Mr. Greenwald thought all had been forgiven, or at least forgotten, and returned to New York where, playing to the hilt the role of the successful mining promoter, he was interviewed by a newspaper reporter. Piously, he told his interviewer how much he hated those "wicked men who lure poor miners to worthless ground by sending out false reports(!)"

Upon the interview being picked up by Canadian newspapers, the West Yale *Review* grimly noted: "Dan's nerve food is a success."

Greenwald then seems to have dropped out of sight. As for ex-partner Stevens, things had not gone as well. Upon losing his ill-gotten gains in another mining venture in California, the destitute and despondent swindler committed suicide.

As the years passed, Steamboat Mountain and its short-lived gold rush became a memory. Then even its name was changed.

Yet, some must remember the ill-starred gold camps of Steamboat Mountain. As poet Laureate Leonard penned 80 long years ago:

Take me down, down
Where the Steamboat trail goes
There we'll bury our sorrows
Our cares and our woes.
Get a claim while you can
And the diggings are new
If you linger long, all you'll get is a view,
Instead of the rain we've the real 'Mountain Dew'
Down where the Steamboat Trail goes.

DUEL IN VICTORIA

Clutching Liverpool Jack about the throat with his left hand, young Sloane pummelled him about the face with his right, a dozen pile-driving blows soon reducing the gambler to a bloodied, semi-conscious pulp.

Pioneer journalist David W. Higgins, whose offbeat news beat enabled him to record the thousand and one events, large and small, which occurred during British Columbia's tumultous birth — including the historic day that two men fought the only duel on provincial soil.

FROM Fraser River tent-town, to condemned murderer's cell, to legislative "birdcage:" such was the fascinating—offbeat—news beat of pioneer journalist David Williams Higgins. For almost half a century, this stocky, genial newsman covered much of the province; first in the role of frustrated prospector, then as a reporter, editor and publisher; finally, as legislative member and Speaker of the House.

Throughout those tumultous years of British Columbia's infancy, Higgins had been on the scene, pen in hand, to record all the news fit to print: the topical, the trivial, the political and pathetic—the thousand and one events, large and small, which occurred during the exotic era of a century and more ago when a flash of yellow on a Fraser River sandbar changed the course of Canadian—and, to a considerable degree, American—history.

Halifax-born, Higgins landed in the outpost of Fort Victoria after a round-about journey which had taken all of 20 years; the reason for the delay, even considering the difficulties of transportation, being the fact that his exodus had begun as a child, his family having moved to Brooklyn where he first enrolled in school. At the age of 18 he was on his own, a young publisher answering the call of adventure which drew him irresistably, like tens of thousands of others, to San Francisco.

But even his own fledgling newspaper, the *Morning Call*, could not keep him there when the magic cry of "Gold!" resounded from distant Cariboo, the New Eldorado. Thus it was, after a memorable stay in California, that the 22-year-old scribe headed northward to Victoria and to the Cariboo.

During his stay in the Bay City, Higgins had enjoyed a front-row seat in the brawling arena that was San Francisco during this period. As one historian has noted, Higgins, "from the moment he landed in the west...seemed to have the knack of meeting extraordinary people in extraordinary situations." As an example of those lusty days, Higgins could recall such minor occurrences as the murders, muggings and armed robberies which finally moved the vigilantes to end the reign of terror by commencing a bloody cleanup campaign. This they accomplished through such harsh measures as summarily hanging the likes of editor James King's murderer—from the window-sill of their upper storey headquarters.

Ironically, Higgins' arrival in Victoria proved to be almost as violent. For, among the 1,200 passengers who rowed ashore from the steamer *Sierra Nevada* one July morning in 1858, was a desperado named Liverpool Jack. At least three illustrious souls have shouldered this title in Victoria's history, by far the worst being the first. This worthy, a San Francisco "bad man," immediately endeared himself to residents of the booming colony by challenging a fellow passenger, and friend of Higgins', to a duel—the one and only such contest in provincial lore.

Forty years after, Higgins had recalled that hazardous passage up the Pacific coast in a decrepit steamer so packed with human cargo that every last square foot of deck space, the saloon and passageways had been pressed into use as sleeping accomodation. Men, women and children sprawled on bedrolls, or on no more mattress than the clothes they wore "in the abandon of despair and hopelessness," as seasickness plagued all but a fortunate handful.

Higgins' finances had allowed him the comparative luxury of sharing a stateroom with but two others: George Wright, who was to become a successful businessman, and a young Englishman named George Sloane. Fresh from college, the latter amused himself by displaying his knowledge of

Victoria's Inner Harbor at the time of the duel between George Sloane and the notorious Liverpool Jack. Armed with a borrowed revolver, Sloane squinted into the setting sun, Liverpool having enjoyed the choice of positions. When both acknowledged their readiness, a second gave the order to fire and two shots exploded in the stillness.

Greek, Latin and poetry.

The adjoining stateroom had been occupied by two Americans and a second young Englishman, known to his fellow passengers as John Liverpool, or Liverpool Jack. Unlike his countryman, Sloane, Liverpool's pastime consisted of smoking and tipping back a demijohn of brandy, which was his constant companion. Once primed, he would entertain the few not suffering from seasickness with anecdotes of his rollicking career, Higgins heartily joining in the laughter. Aboard a ship which was overcrowded to the point of suffocation, without adequate sanitation facilities, with little food—and that of wretched quality—Liverpool's wealth of stories proved to be a Godsend, allowing Higgins and company to forget—at least temporarily—the stench and discomfort of their surroundings.

Another passenger of interest was a young woman. Pale and thin, her expression one of "wret-

chedness and misery," she first attracted Higgins' attention one afternoon while slumped dejectedly in a chair on deck. Despite her obvious sorrow and harried appearance, she was attractive and he had been about to approach her when pushed aside by a burly figure who, without so much as a blush, introduced himself as Liverpool Jack.

From that moment on Miss Bradford, as she was named, and the garrulous gambler were inseparable —at least, such was the relationship Jack tried to establish by seldom leaving her side. He did take a moment out from his attentions, however, to mention to Higgins that her mother had died but days before. The woman had planned to open a boardinghouse in Victoria but now she would have to return to San Francisco, alone and penniless as she had been robbed of her savings while aboard.

And so it went, day after day, as the puffing *Sierra Nevada* labored northward. Upon another

bright morning, the observant Higgins noticed that Miss Bradford had found a new friend, his roomate George Sloane. When the exuberant youth told him of their meeting, George Wright cautioned him against antagonizing Liverpool Jack. But Sloane was unimpressed, replying with the suggestion that they take up a collection to relieve the girl's financial embarrassment, beginning with his own donation of 20 dollars. Within 10 minutes, he had collected 100 dollars.

Then, subscription in hand, Higgins at his side, Sloane approached the girl as she sat in her usual chair and a glowering Liverpool stood behind and watched their arrival with undisguised hostility. When a stammering, blushing Sloane extended the proceeds of his campaign with a halting explanation, Liverpool responded angrily. Grabbing the money from Sloane's hand, he threw it over the side and shouted, "Look here! This girl is not a beggar, and if she stands in need of money I have enough for both."

Outraged, Sloane replied, "You damned cad!"

As Miss Bradford threatened to faint, Liverpool lashed out with a right hook, catching Sloane squarely between—and blackening—both eyes. Staggered by the blow, Sloane stumbled backward when, shaking his head and recovering his balance, he lunged forward. Clutching Liverpool about the throat with his left hand, he pummelled him about the face with his right. A dozen pile-driving blows instantly reduced the gambler to a bloodied, semi-conscious pulp which his antagonist unceremoniously dumped into the chair hastily evacuated by the object of their struggle; at which point Higgins helped his friend to their stateroom, where a steward attended to his blackened eyes with a piece of raw meat.

Early the next morning, the *Sierra Nevada* disgorged her motley cargo at Esquimalt. Throughout the disorganized evacuation, Higgins kept his eyes open for either Liverpool or Miss Bradford, noting in his memoirs that he fervently hoped to sight neither. The reason for his aversion to the fair young lady was not because she repelled him—quite the contrary—but because of his concern for Sloane. Higgins was convinced that if the men met again, the result would be tragic.

But afternoon arrived without the dreaded meeting coming to pass and the relieved journalist headed for Victoria with his companions. Hours later, the tiring hike completed, they gazed upon the boom town for the first time. Even 40 years after, Higgins had marvelled at the incredible scene of 10,000 persons, from each quarter of the globe, of every nationality and hue, teeming restlessly as they prepared to move on to the gold fields of Fraser River.

The dirty streets of town, he recalled, were "alive" with people; even the swamplands of upper Fort and Johnson Streets crowded with tents and lean-tos, as was the forest of oak, cedar and fir where the Parliament Buildings now stand.

With Sloane's two companions, Crickmer and Johns, Higgins pitched camp at the present site of the Dominion Hotel; then just a clearing in the trees. Later, at their suggestion, Sloane rejoined the adventurers and, after a comfortable night on beds of fir boughs, they built a fire. To Crickmer went the honor of cooking breakfast and the American industriously set to work.

Minutes later, he joined his comrades in the tent. Carefully dropping the flap over the doorway, he whispered: "Boys, who do you think are our next door neighbors? Guess?"

When the others shrugged, he exclaimed that the adjoining tent was shared by none other than John Liverpool and Miss Bradford.

With an oath Sloane jumped up, vowing that if Liverpool had wronged her he would kill him. Instantly, his three older, wiser companions were on their feet and restrained him from storming into the other tent. Higgins and the others pleaded with him to forget Miss Bradford, advising him that, when he had been around more, he would come to accept such things without wonder. Slowly the youth calmed down and finally promised them that he would scrupulously avoid both the girl and Liverpool Jack.

At this precise moment, their tent flap was lifted to reveal a grinning visitor who identified himself as a neighbor and said he had been in Victoria for all of a month. Then he was gone, after warning them to watch for a desperado from San Francisco whom he had just spotted in the vicinity: Liverpool Jack.

His friendly tip was forgotten, however, as the four finished breakfast, each deep in thought. Then they looked about town, bought lunch, and returned to their tent about 5 p.m. to begin a supper of bacon, beans and flapjacks. During dinner, their neighbors appeared briefly, Miss Bradford hurrying into the tent without looking over or speaking.

At 7 o'clock, Higgins and Johns left Sloane and Crickmer to attend a minstrel show at the Star and Garter Hotel. When they emerged two hours later, they noticed an excited crowd streaming toward camp and followed, to be met by a fearful Crickmer and grim tidings. He and Sloane had been smoking their pipes beside the fire, he recounted between sobs, when Liverpool appeared with several companions. The object of their visit, Liverpool made deadly clear by challenging Sloane to a duel. As a final insult, he informed the youth that he and Miss Bradford had been married that morning.

At first Sloane refused, denying that he owed Liverpool satisfaction. The latter replied that he would brand him as a coward and, advancing to within inches of the other, spat in his face.

"No!" cried Crickmer, who vainly implored his comrade, now shaking with fury, to ignore Liverpool. Minutes later, as the gambler's companions force-

fully restrained Crickmer, the two combatants squared off. Armed with a borrowed revolver, Sloane squinted into the setting sun, Liverpool having enjoyed the choice of positions. When both acknowledged readiness, a second gave the order to fire.

Two shots exploded in the stillness and Sloane pitched to the ground with a cry of agony. His shot had spun harmlessly into space. Liverpool's had found its mark in his heart.

By the time Higgins and Wright viewed the forlorn body, George Sloane was cold, his handsome features glazed with a fine dew. All that remained to be done was for them to arrange his burial. The coroner's inquest ruled murder but Liverpool Jack, his bride and henchmen had vanished and no trial was held.

Although Jack escaped Canadian justice, his time was running out. Upon his return to San Francisco, he made the mistake of killing a seaman, for which he was swiftly executed. Crickmer, who also returned to California immediately upon Sloane's death, later wrote Higgins that he often saw the hapless girl who had inadvertently caused the tragedy—haunting the streets at night, eyes aglow, as if possessed by an evil spirit.

So ended the case of poor George Sloane, ill-starred hero of D.W. Higgins' first adventure in outpost Victoria. As events were to prove, time and again, as has been noted, Higgins "seemed to have the knack of meeting extraordinary people in extraordinary situations." He demonstrated this from Victoria to Fort Yale: as disappointed prospector, freight clerk, reporter, publisher and member of the legislature.

It was during retirement, almost half a century after his arrival in Victoria, that Higgins recounted many of his exciting tales in a series of articles in the Victoria *Colonist*, then in book form. Never had he missed a chance to record some curious twist of speech, an acquaintance's description, the ofttimes hilarious little incidents which had made frontier life anything but dull for a newsman. As a result of his labors, modern-day historians enjoy a unique opportunity of knowing life as it really was in pioneer British Columbia: the forgotten men and women who helped to carve a province from rugged wilderness. Statistics, Higgins left to others. His concern lay in the people about him, their triumphs and tragedies.

In short, the pioneers Higgins has sketched are full-blooded people in living color. Like a master playwright, he brings them to life once again so that, today, a century afterward, his readers can know them personally. His magic pen has immortalized such fascinating characters as Terrible Jim McLaughlin, Yale's "Terror of the Tenderloins," Caledonia Collins, Happy Tom, Captain John, Victoria's "haunted man,"—not to mention murderous Liverpool Jack—and so many, many others. ●

Victoria's castellated police barracks. Here, John Butts, the capital's hilarious town crier, was reported to be dying, having been found in his cell, paralyzed from the knees down. But, typically, John was far from finished!

He was a "blot, a disgrace, a moral leper and a curse. . .a greater scourge than cholera or smallpox." Such is the glowing epithet pioneer Victoria paid her most illustrious, and ignoble, resident, the one and only—thank the stars for that!—John Butts.

VICTORIA'S
TOWN CRIER

JOHN Charles Butts, "Town Cryer to Her Brittanic Majesty," this delightful rogue preferred to call himself. Victoria has known more than a few characters over the years, but to this day John is its undisputed king of knaves, a lovable blackguard whose antics still bring laughter more than a century later.

He was fat, incurably lazy, a drunkard, thief, beggar and bootlegger...and Victoria loved him. His usual haunt was the corner of Yates and Government Streets where, in uniform of baggy, dirty clothes and belt that was two notches too loose about his protruding belly, and ringing a large bell, he held court before the town's idle.

As town crier it was his duty to announce details of coming events and sales in his "magnificent" tenor voice, in English and in Chinook. Unfortunately, John suffered from a chronic case of ad-libbing; he just couldn't deliver a sales pitch without adding a ribald witticism—at the expense of some prominent citizen. Should any of his audience have the slightest doubt as to the target's identity, John would end the mystery by bawling the gentleman's name at the top of his lungs: a popular pastime

which ended in disaster for him more than once!

He was an Englishman from Australia, most agreed, having come to Victoria in 1858 after fleeing San Francisco vigilantes. Some even went so far as to hint at respectable, if not noble, birth. And the fact John could turn a mean phrase when occasion demanded would indicate something of a literate upbringing. Whatever John's heritage, his brief but boisterous career in Victoria is unparalleled.

The first printed report of John's activities appeared in the *Colonist* of June 6, 1859, with the news he had offered himself as candidate in the forthcoming election of assemblymen. His campaign got off to a rather rocky start with his being summonsed a week later for having struck a little boy. He settled this affair out of court; one of the few times he escaped an appearance before the bench.

Three months later, election time was drawing near and the *Colonist* announced John ready to address the public. "Having an intimate knowledge of government, being no putty-head, and withal, having accumulated considerable money, he is no 'man of straw;' and hence fully believing that this constituency has common sense enough to canvass the merits of all the candidates, he hopes to successfully oppose both the learned gentlemen now in the field."

In typical Don Quixote fashion, John had challenged no less than solicitor George Wight and Attorney-General George Cary. The result of his venture into the realm of politics is not given, although it is easy to imagine.

Within five months he was in court again, charged with "one of the most abominable crimes in the calendar" involving a 16-year-old boy. Exact nature of the charge was unprintable, indicating it was one of indecent assault. We're happy to report, however, that John defended himself eloquently, the three prosecution witnesses contradicted each other admirably, and the case was dismissed. Only John Butts, despite acquittal, would inform the newspaper of "his intention of receiving visitors at the city prison a few days longer!"

A month later, he was in trouble again, charged with having foully threatened and assaulted one Frederick F. Davis—with a kick in the rear. On this occasion, John's eloquence failed him, the magistrate fining him three pounds or a month, disbelieving his defence that he was victim of a conspiracy.

By now, John was well on the downhill path to iniquity. Said the newspaper in May, 1860: "Alas, poor Butts...has again fallen into the hands of the Philistines. Yesterday afternoon Sgt. Taylor nabbed him in the very act of selling liquor to Indians across the bridge, and marched him off to jail. John will hardly escape the chain gang this time."

He was a victim of misfortune, said John to the magistrate, using for the first time an excuse he would belabor to death. He had, by "patient industry," saved the grand sum of $4.87 toward the $5 needed to buy passage for Australia. Unable to raise the balance of a quarter, he had, in desperation, stooped to bootlegging. The judge unsympathetically sentenced him to six pounds of iron around his right ankle.

No sooner was he released than John was again in durance vile, charged with selling tangle-leg to a squaw on Johnson Street. In a rare moment of humor, an austere Magistrate Augustus Pemberton gave him "three moons."

Word of his latest tragedy did not reach San Francisco as, only two weeks later, a Bay City newspaper warned its citizens: "John Butts announces his intention of paying us a visit from Victoria. Secure your mutton!"

With December, a blushing Butts again graced the dock in the police barracks, accused, as usual, of selling whisky to Indians. Looking the "picture of injured innocence," John heard his arresting officer inform Magistrate Pemberton the principal witnesses were not present.

This was all he needed. Surely such a fair man as

Magistrate Augustus Pemberton. He fell for John Butts' blarney time and again.

His Honor would not convict him on the word of a mere constable? After all, he sobbed: "Haven't I always pleaded guilty when I was convicted? Did I ever grumble at Your Honor's decision? Never! Never! Allow me to remind your worship of a good old saying—one that I learned at school—that says: 'While the lamp holds out to burn, the vilest sinner may return,' and do not convict me of a charge of which I am totally innocent."

Replied Pemberton: "Well, Butts, I don't wish to injure your good character; you may go." With which a beaming Butts danced from the dock, to the laughter of the galleries.

This time liberty lasted all of two weeks when Sergeant Taylor accused him of vagrancy and bootlegging. For once, John had no defence, pleaded guilty, and begged Magistrate Pemberton to let him leave for Australia. Delighted at a chance of being rid of him once and for all, Pemberton agreed instantly.

A slight error in judgement, as John bounded from the court and disappeared—without the slightest intention of forsaking Victoria. Nothing was heard of him for three weeks, when a suspicious soul, signing himself "Fort Street," wrote the

Colonist of John's newest dodge—as a missionary!

It seems Butts had turned his modest cottage into the "Congregational Church." Collecting a group of devout natives, he would "lead off with a prayer, followed by singing a hymn. John then makes a short and feeling address; follows it with another hymn, a collection is taken up, and the congregation dismissed with a benediction.

"After the services, dancing, smoking and drinking whiskey are the order of the evening—Butts acting as barkeeper with as much grace as he a few moments before officiated as clergyman. It is quite an ingenious plan and the inventor is, no doubt, making a 'good thing' by administering spiritual comfort to his flock in two totally different ways."

The editor recommended "Fort Street" inform police.

Despite this advertisement, however, officers did not act until three weeks after, when they arrested John for bootlegging and "a general inclination towards loaferism."

As ever, John had an answer. His eloquent speech was liberally spiced with biblical quotations and poetry, ending with the promise that if freed he would catch the first boat to Port Townsend, there to board a ship for Australia. But this was not all. Pointing to fellow prisoner "Scotty," charged with being "too drunk to navigate," John magnanimously offered to "take this poor, lost wretch with me to the American side and thereby relieve the town of a nuisance.

"I'll buy him a new suit of clothes before he leaves here, and I'll give him one pound before he gets there, in order that he may not land a pauper. As for myself, I have only one ambition left: It is to reach my native land and die in peace at the old homestead."

An emotional Magistrate Pemberton bound John over in the sum of $50 to appear a week later. Stirred by Butts' description of his unfortunate friend, he ordered Scotty freed.

Pemberton apparently changed his mind about the week-long remand for, three days later, John was sentenced to three months.

Then...horrifying news shocked Victoria: John Butts was dying!

The poor soul had been found in his cell, paralyzed from the knees down. Doctors pronounced no hope of recovery and sadly gave him but a short time to live. Taken to hospital in a handcart, John received that institution's every attention. Upon arrival, he had been subjected to various painful tests to determine the authenticity of his ailment. Finally satisfied he was indeed paralyzed, the staff showered him with every care and luxury at their disposal. Most of the time John lay in his soft bed, reading "religious works." On fine days he would painfully drag himself by his hands to the front steps to bask in the spring sunshine.

In short, John played the part to the hilt until the eagle eye of Dr. James Trimble detected a suspicious movement on the part of his lower limbs. Instantly assuming the worst, the evil practitioner ordered John seized, stripped, and placed in a chair in the yard. Then, from a second-storey balcony, attendants laughingly poured the contents of 18 buckets of frigid sea water—over John's head!

"Butts shivered and shook, but declared that he could not budge an inch, although he begged the doctor to discontinue the treatment. It was no use. The doctor was inexorable."

Eight more buckets followed, the trembling patient moaning all the while that he could not move. It was not until the 36th pail that John threw in the sponge, leaped from the chair and hid, to the laughter of the staff and inmates. Any lesser man would have then dressed and shuffled away in shame. But not John Butts!

Leisurely pulling on his trousers, the impudent scamp "deliberately, in full sight of a dozen or more persons, laid down on the grass and slowly dragged himself again into the hospital!" The *Colonist* informed readers "much fun" was expected the next day when eviction of the humbugging patient was to be effected.

This time Butts, still dragging himself about the hospital on hands and knees and occasionally uttering a piteous moan, lowered his colors without a struggle when alerted by another patient, who had been carefully prompted by Dr. Trimble, that he was to be subjected to the water cure again. When John sneered defiance, his informant whispered: "If that does not answer, you are to bound to a red hot stove and kept there till you're roasted!"

That was enough for John! Forgetting his paralysis, he bolted for the door. Once outside, he proceeded to roundly curse the institution and all within until an attendant appeared with a club. By this time he had drawn a large crowd, so commenced to entertain by hobbling away, leaning heavily on his cane, and stopping every few steps as if very weak. Back on Johnson Street, his old comrades greeted him with cheers and laughter, at which John held forth on how he had hoodwinked one and all with his malingering, and that he fully intended to bootleg as much as ever.

"Whisky," said he, "is an old enemy of mine; it killed my big brother, and caused me to serve nine months on the chain gang. Consequently, whenever I see a bottle of it I feel as if I'd like to catch it round the neck and take satisfaction out of it!"

Moaned the *Colonist*, "We don't believe a greater villain ever drew breath. He was a nuisance in California, and he is a nuisance here. We cannot get rid of him because he is so great a scamp no captain can be found to take him to a far distant country aboard of his vessel for fear of a mutiny or something as bad; at San Francisco detectives want him as a state prison recruit; and our American neighbors on the Sound say that if he comes there they will box him up and send him back. If he is put in prison he is continually raising a row and causing trouble among the convicts.

"In short, he is a blot, a disgrace, a moral leper and a curse. The authorities feel, when thinking of him, like the man who bought the elephant and didn't know what to do with it. What *shall* we do with him?"

A week after, John again faced the magistrate. Not, as in the past, for vagrancy or bootlegging, but on the curious complaint of being a "rogue and a vagabond." It would almost appear the weary court was inventing charges to be used exclusively against John! He faced the magistrate calmly, made his usual speech in which he denounced the *Colonist* for exposing his malingering and promised to leave the colony. This time, Pemberton was not falling for the old line and gave him three months.

Released in time for July 4, when most Victorians attended horse races in Beacon Hill Park, he celebrated by stealing three turkeys from the house of John Yerman. Hence another three months with the chain gang.

Upon liberation, the "reformed" John Butts found himself in court again, to answer a charge of having assaulted an Indian and his squaw. Despite testimony that he had been provoked beyond endurance by the couple's having called him names and thrown rocks at him, the magistrate fined him 50 shillings.

Miraculously, however, John was a new man. Re-elected to his former position of town crier, he fulfilled the duty with zeal and nary a misdemeanor. But, typically, it was too good to last. Six months later he was ending his "cries" with unflattering remarks concerning one Captain Simpson before a delighted audience. He was enjoying himself immensely until none other than Captain Simpson chanced along, heard his name linked to a "celebrated banjo-player" (the significance of which has been lost, sadly) and promptly proceeded to beat John lustily with his cane!

The bruised Butts answered the "foul and cowardly" attack by having that gentleman arrested for assault. Much to his chagrin, Magistrate Pemberton made short work of his complaint, delivering "a most scathing rebuke." Then, to his regret, Pemberton had to fine Simpson 40 shillings, the captain paying "with the air of a man who had got his money's worth."

John's subsequent arrests are many, the *Colonist* ruefully noting "his habits require a kind of moral tinkering from the magisterial hands of Mr. Pemberton at least once a month." For biting an Indian assistant, he was fined one pound; he had only pushed the native away for fear of catching smallpox, he said.

For slandering another leading citizen John was charged court costs and released after a tearful

apology. He left the court "with smiles of joy illumining (sic) his jocund face and the teardrops glistening like a puddle of dirty water in a Yates Street gutter when visited by a gleam of sunshine."

The excitement of election day in August, 1862, caused John to erupt again, spewing forth insults in the direction of a Mr. Carswell. By the time of his court appearance, John was repentant, blaming his outburst on overwork and drink. Mr. Carswell, a forgiving soul, asked that he be released. Noting he was "not so great a nuisance as formerly," and that the jailors could tolerate him no longer, Mr. Pemberton agreed.

The charges seem endless: Theft of two bottles of brandy, of which he was acquitted; appropriating a photographer's equipment; looting a building at the corner of Douglas and View; possession of a stolen bed. For theft of a goose, he received a month at hard labor. John's "hard labor" lasted precisely a day when he rebelled, indignantly informing guards such toil was beneath his station as a gentleman. Placed on a diet of bread and water, he whiled away the time in his cell by singing hymns and the national anthem in "the most penitent tones."

Out exactly a week, he was arrested for stealing 200 newspapers. The result: a severe lecture and a month. However, informed a ship had been found to take Butts to Australia, the magistrate spoke softly to the sobbing prisoner and "besought him to mend his ways before he became too hardened in vice." John should have been an actor, for by now there was not a dry eye in town.

Then...the notorious John Butts was "gone from our gaze!" With two other worthies he had signed aboard the ship *Rodoma* for China. There had been a tearful farewell ceremony at the jail, a sobbing John bidding farewell to convicts and guards. All the way to the dock, where a large crowd had gathered to see him off, he wept freely. But upon seeing his reception, he regained his spirits, shouting jokes from the ship's rail. Then he retired from view, never again to be seen by Victorians.

Even the *Colonist* was moved to regret at the loss of the city's gayest rogue, saying: "Adieu! poor houseless, homeless vagrant.

"Your offences against society have been many, and your punishment often severe; but God created you for some purpose, and you may yet become a shining light in the national councils of the land of Confucius."

We can be assured that it was a long, long time before pioneer Victorians forgot their incorrigible town crier who was fired for ending his spiels with "God Save John Butts!" instead of "God Save the Queen;" the inebriate who ended a temperance meeting of churchwomen by spiking the teapots with two bottles of brandy; the rascal who lost a contract for cleaning mud from Government Street when caught dumping it in Yates!

Pity the poor Chinese! ●

Looking something like a mosque, the Bank of Montreal at the corner of Church and Columbia in New Westminster. Through these windows, the two lookouts had watched for any sign of an alarm after McNamara and Dean blew the safe during the "most collosal robbery in the history of Canada." Less than a hundred feet away, Police Constable Burrows slept through the entire drama.

B.C.'S BIGGEST BANK ROBBERY

"Big John" McNamara looked to be anything but a criminal mastermind. But when he and his gang were finished, their night's work had netted them more than a quarter of a million dollars and made Canadian criminal history.

SEPTEMBER 14, 1911, dawned like many another September morning for the citizens of New Westminster: with rain. A grey drizzle continued throughout the day until evening, when it became a downpour.

Soon the streets were deserted — but for a Columbia Street doorway, where four men huddled together, sheltering from the rain. Across the street, at the corner of Columbia and Church, lights in the Bank of Montreal showed that an employee was working late and, with a show of impatience, the leader of the quartet glanced at his watch.

It was almost midnight and John McNamara was becoming anxious. Six feet tall, 250 pounds with greying brown hair and moustache, "Australian Mac," or "Big John," as he was known to the underworld and police of two continents, looked to be anything but a criminal mastermind. Rather, he gave every impression of being just what he claimed:

a prosperous businessman in town on a business-pleasure trip....

From the time of his arrival in Vancouver six months before, when he had registered at the Strand Hotel, McNamara had enjoyed the good life and earned the respect of hotel and restaurant staff by his genial manner and generous tips. After three months he had been joined by Charles Dean, his attractive wife, children and dogs, who moved into a cottage McNamara had rented at 1047 W. Broadway. Then all three adults made the rounds of Vancouver social life, enjoying the sights and attending such sporting events as the horse races.

At least, such was their schedule by day. By night, McNamara, who had moved in with them, the Deans, and two younger accomplices named Powell and Martin, finalized the plans that were their real reason for being in town: the biggest bank robbery in Canadian history.

Many other details had already been completed by "McNamara's Band," all of whom were experts in their fields. Throughout their daily sightseeing excursions, McNamara and the Deans had been alert to any and all information that would be helpful to their scheme. One of their first steps called for Mrs. Dean to open an account in New Westminster's Columbia and Church branch of the Bank of Montreal. That done, the eagle-eyed Mrs. Dean paid regular visits to the bank so as to study its layout. Husband Charles studied the routine of staff members, to learn that the bank employed 17 persons under Manager G.D. Brymner.

Of these, the routines of Joe Turner and Hong, the Chinese janitor, were the more interesting: Turner because he slept on the premises when not serving as relief for the Cloverdale branch, and Hong because he arrived at the bank to clean up at 4 a.m. and left two hours later. The latter employee was also one of the crucial links in the entire scheme, as he possessed a key to the front door— a key which McNamara, by unknown means, had duplicated.

The meticulous McNamara had also had his gang monitor the movements of the Royal City police. Due to the bank's proximity to the police station, some 90 feet to the rear, no alarm system had been installed. At the station house, one policeman was on duty all night. Columbia Street was patrolled from midnight to 8 a.m. by a constable who faithfully checked the front door of the bank each time he passed.

Access to the safe had to be gained by the use of an electric drill and explosives after they had penetrated a brick wall and an iron grill. This was Dean's specialty. The robbery also demanded that they overpower the janitor when he reported for duty at 4 o'clock in the morning.

Finally all was ready and, on the evening of September 14, McNamara, Dean, Martin and Powell waited anxiously in a doorway opposite the bank. For what seemed an eternity they waited as, across the street, a bank employee unwittingly frustrated their plan. McNamara was about to call it off for the night when, about 12 o'clock, the lights were extinguished. Moments later, the employee locked the front door behind him and, drawing his hat down upon his head, hunched off into the rain.

Making sure that he was gone, and that the officer on the beat was not coming, they hurried across the street, where McNamara thrust the duplicate key into the lock, gave a twist and all stepped inside.

No instructions were necessary as all had memorized their roles. Martin and Powell, detailed to sentry duty, made for a back room where two ladders, used to wash windows, were kept. These were placed beside the mosque-like structure's high windows, where each took his station to observe traffic on Columbia and Church streets.

McNamara and Dean had immediately proceeded to the room where Joe Turner slept when not working as relief at the Cloverdale branch. To their delight they found it empty and surmised that Turner was in Cloverdale. Returning to the vault, they punched their way through a 16-inch-thick brick wall and picked the lock to the iron grill, Dean, with few wasted motions, then drilling several holes in the vault door. That done, he set the charges, covered them with Turner's mattress, and ran the detonator wires to the bedroom. When all this was in readiness, the sentries signalled the all clear and Dean made the connection between wires and battery.

With a muffled boom and choking cloud of smoke, fumes and debris, the vault door buckled. For several agonizing minutes not a man moved; all poised rigidly as they listened for the sounds of an alarm. But the lookouts, perched atop their ladders and peering through the windows, reported that nothing was to be seen. They had not been heard.

As the Vancouver *Daily Province* was to report with undisguised sarcasm, the thieves had blown the safe under the very noses of the Royal City police: "Not 10 yards away from where the safe was blown to pieces, Police Constable Burrows, who had a room in the Lavery Block next door, lay sleeping. He did not hear a sound. Twenty men lay sleeping in the same building. They heard nothing.

"All night long the jailer in the police station with his window open where 30 yards away the yegg men were busy at work, lay fast asleep and heard nothing."

Cruelly, the Bank of Montreal's confidence in its 20-year-old "burglar-proof" vault had not been justified. After the great New Westminster fire of 1898 the safe and its contents had been found, "practically uninjured," in the ruins of the bank. But the thick steel plates which had defied the "attacks of nature" had been no match for the expertise and explosives of safecracker Dean. In a moment it had been reduced to a twisted, broken pile of rubble: "When the explosion occurred, the half of the door containing the time lock was blown to pieces and there was nothing left of the door but the spring. The safe door was blown from its hinges."

By the time the *Province* went to press the next day, "It had not been determined whether or not the burglars had to blow the doors leading to the cash compartments which are also equipped with combination locks, but it is presumed that the force of the first explosion was sufficient to loosen the doors to such an extent that there was no trouble in removing them...."

Due to the blinding, choking fumes, McNamara and Dean experienced considerable difficulty in emptying the vault. Gagging fitfully, they worked as quickly as possible to dump the contents of the cash boxes into a blanket which they then dragged into the bedroom. There, McNamara and one of the lookouts calmly sifted through the treasure, discarding almost $150,000 in bills of unusually high

Ironically, the Bank of Montreal's confidence in its 20-year-old "burglar proof" vault had not been justified. After the great New Westminster fire of 1898 (shown here) the safe and its contents had been found, "practically uninjured," in the ruins of the bank. But the thick steel plates which had defied the great fire had been no match for the expertise and explosives of safecracker Charles Dean.

denomination and those bills and coins which, damaged in the explosion, could be traced.

As they methodically sorted the money, the city slept undisturbed. At 2 o'clock Constable Capps made his rounds, walking along Columbia and checking the bank's front door before turning the corner onto Church. Totally unaware of what was happening inside, he rounded the rear of the building, turned onto Clarkson Street, and continued to the police station, less than a hundred feet away.

Two hours later, Constable Bourke, one of the oldest members of the New Westminster force, met Hong in front of the Fraser Valley Meat Market, directly opposite the bank. After exchanging greetings, Bourke proceeded down the street as far as the next corner, when he glanced back. The janitor was not to be seen.

He had already entered the bank—to find himself "gazing with terrified eyes into the muzzle of a loaded revolver. A moment later, instead of sweeping out the office, (he) sat in helpless misery bound to a heavy chair in the dark cellar, his own handkerchief half choking him, and strong cords cutting into his flesh."

Throughout this brief drama, McNamara and his assistant had continued to sort and count their take— more than a quarter of a million dollars, and weighing over 200 pounds, which had been intended to meet cannery payrolls. This completed at last, they quietly made their way to the garage of Tom Trapp, near the corner of Royal and 4th. There, they knew, the pioneer McLaughlin-Buick dealer kept his speedy new McLaughlin motor car.

Arriving at the garage, which resembled a small barn, shortly after daybreak, they checked to see that the coast was clear, entered the garage, threw their booty, which was stuffed into two pillow slips, into the back seat, released the car's hand-brake and pushed it into the street. After rolling some 50 yards down the roadway, McNamara braked to a stop, leaped out and gave a heave of the crank handle. When the engine failed to catch, he cranked again. And again. But the grey McLaughlin refused to start, McNamara being unaware that one of Trapp's sons had cleaned the sparkplugs earlier that day and had not replaced all of them.

Time and again, as the others watched in growing desperation, McNamara cranked the engine. By this time they were no longer alone. Donald Ferguson, a teamster on his way to work, stopped to watch the drama for several minutes before continuing on his way. Ferguson, who worked with horses, saw nothing suspicious or unusual in McNamara's actions and, after a silent thought as to the horseless carriage's efficiency, he left them to their task. He did, however, note the time: 5:40 a.m.

In the meantime, the hapless Hong had been struggling to free himself from his bonds. Shortly before 6 o'clock he was able to untie himself and run to the neighboring police station. There, he frantically informed Constable Bourke, with whom he had exchanged greetings earlier that morning, of the robbery. Bourke was the first to reach the scene. But when he entered the bank he found it to be so thick with smoke that he was unable to see the damage or even to find a telephone and had to run back to the station house to give the alarm.

Chief of Police Bradshaw, Manager Brymner and accountant Phipps reached the bank simultaneously, when the chief reported the robbery to Vancouver police, who relayed the alarm to all Pacific Northwest police detachments on both sides of the border.

As this was being done, the bank staff reported for work and, after airing out the building and cleaning up much of the rubble, opened the bank on schedule at 10 o'clock.

On September 16 the *Province* reported that "No 'definite' clue, is the sorrowful admission this morning of the police officials here after a day and a night of fruitless search for the men implicated in the most colossal robbery in the history of Canada. One quarter of a million dollars and eight or ten thousand more were taken by the safecrackers of the Bank of Montreal and there is no clue...."

As no arrests had been made, the manhunt had been extended throughout the northwest and two private detective firms, including the famous Pinkertons, had joined in the search for McNamara and company. In the hours immediately following discovery of the robbery, a harried Brymner and staff had ascertained that $258,000 was missing—

Columbia Street in New Westminster around the time of the robbery. Notice the T.J. Trapp store on the left-hand side of the street. It was car dealer Tom Trapp's new McLaughlin motor car which proved to be "Big John" McNamara's nemesis.

making it the largest bank theft in Canadian history. Further investigation revealed that the money was in the form of $150,000 in new Bank of Montreal bills; $86,000 in American gold coins; and $2,000 in new Dominion of Canada one- and two-dollar notes.

The bank had immediately posted a reward of $5,000 and five per cent of the money recovered for the arrest and conviction of those responsible. It was this generous offer which had attracted the interest of private detectives and Pinkerton agents who, upon learning of Ferguson's chance encounter with the robbers as they were attempting to steal Trapp's McLaughlin, found the first solid clue. Shown mugshots of leading criminals, Ferguson quickly identified John McNamara as the man he had seen cranking the engine. He also picked out Charles Dean, although he was unable to identify the others as they had been standing behind the car.

As the police searched far and wide, McNamara and Dean waited out the storm in their rented house on Broadway. By the time police were alerted by a

suspicious landlord, the trail was cold and a continental manhunt failed to locate either man. Months passed, then a year, without a clue as to the whereabouts of Canada's most wanted bank robbers. When at last police did pick up McNamara's trail, it was in Buffalo, New York, where a gambling house included among its daily deposit $10,000 in crisp new Bank of Montreal bills. They were quickly tied to the New Westminster job, but too late to catch the elusive Australian.

The stolen money also led to the arrest of Charles Dean in a plush Los Angles apartment when police recovered some $20 gold pieces. But McNamara and the bulk of the loot remained at large. Finally he was located in New York. Detectives, hoping to recover the rest of the money, kept him under surveillance for two months before arresting him. But, when taken into custody, McNamara had only $1,000

Returned to British Columbia to stand trial, McNamara found himself facing a charge of having broken into Tom Trapp's garage and stolen his $3,000 McLaughlin— this, because the Crown lacked sufficient evidence with which to tie him to the robbery of the bank of Montreal!

Despite a determined defence (he produced witnesses who swore that he was attending a prize fight in New York's Madison Square Gardens on the night of September 14, 1911), McNamara was found guilty of breaking and entering and car theft. If he considered himself fortunate to have escaped the more serious charge his relief was short-lived. Mr. Justice Morrison, in deference to the Crown's valiant attempts to link McNamara to the bank robbery by innuendo, explained that, "This is not an ordinary case of theft, if there is such a thing as an ordinary case of theft, because my mind is charged with the feeling that this was part of a very grave crime; and under the circumstances I feel justified in imposing the fullest extent of the penalty which the law permits in cases of this sort. I therefore sentence you to nine years in the penitentiary."

Should McNamara successfully appeal his sentence, Morrison continued, he hoped that it would not be amiss for him, "talking as one intelligent man to another, to express the hope that, should you regain your liberty, you will remember this particular occasion."

When McNamara interjected to assure him that he would indeed remember this particular occasion, Morrison concluded: "And endeavor to turn your talents to better use. I am extremely sorry, but I have a certain duty to perform and I must perform it. But no hard feeling of any kind prompts me in the passing of this sentence."

Charles Dean's joust with Canadian justice ended on a much happier note for the American safecracker. When his first trial ended in deadlock, he faced a jury of his peers for a second time— and was acquitted. ●

Bugling in fury, the enraged Tillie galloped to the attack, the earth trembling before her advance. For a split second Charlie Sunrise stood fast, unable to move. Then, as his bellowing attacker closed with every thundering step, he began to run.

The colossal extravaganza that the Sells-Floto Circus inadvertently staged completely overshadowed the greatest act it had ever headlined beneath its big-top!

THE GREAT ELEPHANT HUNT

FROM far and wide they came, that summer of 1926. Expectant children, reminiscing adults, and intrigued Indians, by car, train and wagon, they poured into Cranbrook for that greatest of occasions, Circus Day. The colossal extravaganza Sells-Floto Circus inadvertently staged was to make history and completely overshadow the greatest act it had ever headlined beneath its big-top.

To this day, many British Columbians remember with affection and a smile that riotous time when seven grey monsters terrorized a countryside—the Great Elephant Hunt.

For most of its western tour, Sells-Floto had been troubled by its 14 pachyderms. The nervous giants had created disturbances at Edmonton and Calgary, but it was the high altitude and smoke from forest fires—some maintain a barking dog was to blame—that triggered the stampede at Cranbrook when they were being unloaded from their boxcars.

Instantly, the quiet community was plunged into bedlam, as 14 trumpeting elephants charged through the streets in every direction, ears wide, trunks erect.

Within seconds, doorways, culverts—anything that afforded cover—were crowded with scrambling circus hands and spectators. Several roustabouts who had not jumped aside quickly enough were slightly injured and rushed to hospital.

The great chase was on.

Hours later, reports of enormous footprints were flooding in from as far away as Yahk, 40 miles to the southwest, the lumbering fugitives having made good time by following the Canadian Pacific right-of-way, and prompting what is considered the most unusual telegraph message in North American railway history:

"All trains East: Keep lookout for elephants on track; advise if sighted from first telegraph office giving location."

Seven of the mammals were soon safely under wraps, some having been captured in the Cranbrook cemetery. But the remaining seven had scattered even farther, as harried circus officials issued contradictory orders, charged madly off in all directions and swallowed aspirin by the bottle.

Delighted newspapers gave the breathless details in glaring headlines: "Hundreds of men now hunting elephants in B.C. Five hunters hospitalized, many others hurt. Another Indian has miraculous escape from being gored by rampaging female elephant."

Hampering the search most, according to the

Cranbrook *Courier*, were "dense woods, deep ravines and steep hillsides...Luckily no one joining in the chase of the huge beasts has been seriously hurt so far, though several men have been more or less bruised in attempting their capture.

"In the first rush of the breakaway, Dooley, one of the trainers, received minor injury, and Abel, Kootenay Indian, had an exciting experience when suddenly swept from his horse by one of the runaways which charged him from a thicket."

As elephant trainer "Cheerful" Gardner flew north from Wichita, Kansas, to direct the hunt, circus employees and volunteers scoured the rugged countryside with ropes, nets and chains. Gardner finally arrived by train, his plane having been grounded by poor weather.

In the meantime—much to her regret—60-year-old Kootenay squaw Mary Janet had located three of the missing mammals, the cows Bessie and Virginia, and the bull Cicero.

With neither newspaper nor radio, poor Mary had not heard of the notorious escape. When she looked up from her labors in her little orchard to see three towering, grey monsters watching her curiously, the old woman had almost fainted.

Looking about wildly for a means of escape, the terrified woman glanced upward, decided it was her only course, and scrambled up an apple tree to await further developments. Cicero, Bessie and Virginia watched her antics placidly, then, scenting the apples Mary had shaken loose in her flight, shuffled forward. Plucking the fruit from the grass with their trunks, the towering trio munched contentedly as Mary watched in awed silence from her perch.

As the monsters continued their repast peacefully, Mary's terror subsided somewhat to a sense of wonder. And with wonder came a plan. Noticing how they devoured her apples, the old woman began throwing the fruit to the ground, each time farther from her tree. The elephants followed her succulent missiles eagerly, each step taking them that much farther from Mary.

When they had ambled off to what she thought a safe distance Mary clambered down and ran as fast as she could to the cabin of her nearest neighbor, Charlie Sunrise, to find he was not home.

Poor Charlie was, in fact, at that very moment running for his life. This unhappy turn of events had resulted from an overwhelming curiosity.

Earlier, Charlie had encountered enormous tracks, of a shape and size he had never seen before, although he had hunted bear and cougar for years. But these prints—and a wide swathe bulldozed through brush and undergrowth—were unbelievable.

Hair tingling, the frightened man had followed the mangled trail for some distance, until he came to a thick grove of cedar and hemlock. Suddenly, he looked back—to see the cow Tillie, maddened by cold and hunger, charging!

Bugling in fury, the enraged mammal galloped to the attack, earth trembling before her advance. For a split second, Charlie stood fast, unable to move. then, the distance between them narrowing with every moment, he began running.

In his panic, Charlie left the comparative shelter of the cedar grove, fleeing instead through the tangled undergrowth as his bellowing attacker closed with every thundering step.

On and on he ran, lungs heaving violently, but he could not stop for breath. On and on came Tillie, now at his heels, trampling young trees and brush.

Breaking into a clearing, Charlie came to a deep

Few remember the historic day of half a century ago when seven grey monsters terrified the Cranbrook countryside — the Great Elephant Hunt.

gorge, spanned by a rickety foot bridge. On the far side, exhausted, he slumped to his knees in despair. He could run no more.

Long seconds passed. A minute. Still he had not been grabbed skyward and crushed by the snaking trunk. Looking back, he saw the elephant place a tentative foot on the slender frame, then withdraw. Balefully the cow looked across the ravine, at the bridge, and at Charlie again. Then, decision made, she slid carefully down the side of the draw and charged eagerly up the other bank, trumpeting victory.

Her earsplitting boast instantly gave way to a scream of outrage when she topped the rise to find Charley had moved—onto the narrow bridge. Once again, Tillie tested her weight on the span. And once again she realized it could not support her.

Then began an almost comical dance of death as Charley inched back and forth across the bridge, the frustrated cow vainly charging up one bank and down the other. Time and again they repeated the eerie performance until, at last, Tillie tired and, with a last bellow of anger, rumbled off into the trees, Charlie was alone.

But he waited some time, to make sure she had really departed, before venturing off the bridge. Fleeing to town, the exhausted brave told of his narrow escape and heard of Mary's adventure with Cicero, Virginia and Bessie. When trainers surrounded Mary's orchard, they found the threesome still there, happily gorging on her fruit. For her loss and ordeal, Mary received an award of $300.

"Vicious monsters roam the Rocky Mountains," continued newspaper headlines as the hunt intensified. Anxious circus officials, now worried someone would be seriously hurt, offered generous

cash bonuses to local Indians to act as guides. But the scheme became disaster when, paid in advance, the natives, forgetting all about the recalcitrant pachyderms, embarked on a wild spree, allowing the fugitives to wander ever farther afield.

The celebrating Indians created a greater headache when Frieda was captured. As trainers cautiously coaxed the nervous cow up a ramp to her freight car, watching natives gave a rousing cheer, spooking Frieda and sending her galloping down the ramp, up the street, and out of sight.

Cursing roustabouts finally recaptured her and urged her up the ramp a second time—in complete silence.

In the meantime, murderous Tillie had attacked a second victim, Charlie Buckbone. He managed to escape when Tillie turned on his horse—after she had ripped the shirt from his back with her lashing trunk.

Circus employees finally tricked her into surrender by using two tamer sisters as decoys. Said the *Courier*: "Spotted by Indians and finally coaxed into civilization by her keepers, Tillie...was brought into the stockyards here on sunday.

"Contrary to general expectations, Tillie, though restless, exhibited no inclination to attack Dooley and Cheerful Gardner, sent by the circus management to assist effecting her capture. Last reports are to the effect that Charlie Ed and Myrtle are ranging in the vicinity of Finlayson's ranch on the Gold Creek road."

When keepers bandaged her cut feet in gunny sacks and children treated her with apples, belligerent Tillie's temper cooled and she accepted captivity without protest.

Another Indian, Salmon Jack, had spotted one of the runaways while picking raspberries with his wife and grandchildren. Hugging their baskets of berries without thinking, they had fled to their cabin as the starving elephant, aroused by the berries' scent, lumbered along behind.

Reaching his cabin, Jack bolted the door, then huddled in a corner with his panic stricken family as the beast fought frantically to enter the house for the fruit. Timbers groaned and cracked as the giant shouldered the cabin, rocking it to and fro like a ship at sea.

Then it tried a different tack, thrusting its snout through a broken window to probe the interior. A grave strategical error as Jack, emboldened by the sight of the trunk, grabbed up an iron poker from his fireplace and brought it down with all his might across the writhing grey form.

With a banshee wail of pain, the elephant thundered off into the trees, leaving the terrified Indians to enjoy their miraculous escape from what had seemed impending doom.

When trainers at last found Myrtle, they were too late. "Located by Indians at a spot close to the base of Moyie Mountain...she is reported to be a physical wreck; all her toenails are worn off, her knees terribly bruised, and two or three bullet wounds in her hip. It is thought that Indians, panicked by being charged several days ago, fired several shots into her. She was in extremely exhausted condition and in great pain."

Calmed with morphine injected by an heroic trainer, Myrtle was securely chained. Then circus men faced the herculean problem of how to extricate her bulk from the jungle of slash and rock. Alas, unfortunate Myrtle solved the problem for them by dying on the spot of pneumonia, the result of her wounds.

With Myrtle's demise, Sells-Floto officials had but one fugitive to track down, young Charlie Ed. Most prized of the herd, as he was a talented clown, the bull had been suffering from an infected tusk when he escaped. Officials worried he would perish like Myrtle if not found soon.

Happily, Charlie was traced to Smith Lake. The Cranbrook *Herald* gave details of his capture: He "recognized (his) own trainer Charlie Morgan, and on hearing his voice whimpered a little, and showing signs of friendliness, was coaxed along with bread.

"The mountain air, however, did apparently make Charlie somewhat more frisky than was anticipated, with the result that, before Morgan and (Spot) Griffith succeeded in getting him properly chained, the former had his shoulder hurt, while Griffith was injured in the ribs. (In the Edmonton melee, Morgan had been 'laid out' by the 'obstreperous Mary' and had not yet fully recuperated).

"Charlie was being brought to Cranbrook on Wednesday, and by the courtesy of the Sells-Floto Circus, through their representative here, Mr. A.J. Ironsides, and their assistant manager, Mr. Orville Stewart, the animal will be shown at the Cranbrook Fall Fair the last three days of this week. On this occasion it is the intention to have Charlie Ed rechristened 'Cranbrook Ed.'

"The managers of the circus feel that they would like to do this in recognition of the many courtesies received by them in this city during their stay and subsequent to the loss of their...elephants."

Later that week, a beaming Mayor T.M. Roberts renamed Cranbrook Ed in a colorful ceremony. The Great Elephant Hunt was history.

When Sells-Floto management totalled the costs of the six-week adventure, they found themselves out the staggering sum of $50,000. This through the loss of Myrtle, cancelled bookings, and compensation for damages and rewards.

More than half a century has passed since that exciting summer, but the memory of East Kootenay's rampaging elephants lives on. Each summer Pacific Northwest skeet shooters and marksmen travel to Kimberley to compete and commemorate those outrageous weeks of 1926— British Columbia's wildest "big game" hunt ever. ●

FIRST AIR FATALITY

Canadian aviation history was made in October of 1894 when the daring young man in pink tights met with tragedy while performing over the New Westminster fairgrounds.

BRITISH Columbia made aviation history, August 6, 1913, when barnstormer Milton Bryant crashed his converted Curtiss seaplane onto a Victoria rooftop while attempting to land in the Inner Harbor. Killed instantly, Bryant was officially listed as Canada's first aviation fatality.

In point of fact, he undoubtedly is Canada's first aircraft victim. But he certainly is not our first *aviation* fatality, as a little-known drama in New Westminster, 20 years earlier, would indicate. For this dubious distinction must go to a young balloonist named Charles Marble who, according to an account of the time, "sold his life for a trifle."

Thousands of spectators, young and old, crowded onto the Royal City fairgrounds, that warm October day in 1894, to view the hundreds of exhibits and competitions. Unquestionably the most eye-catching display was that of Professor Soper's balloon. Almost as intriguing was the young man who strutted about the fairgrounds in shocking pink tights. Head held high, and with a barely concealed smile of satisfaction, he marched through the crowd and basked in the glow of the amazed stares of those about him.

Perhaps he would not have been quite so smug had he known the gist of the many comments which followed him:

"There's the fool that's going to risk his neck in a balloon."

"Such things shouldn't be allowed."

"He gets $300 for three ascensions."

"He'll drop in the river, sure."

Then it was time for his first "ascension," and Marble forgot about his admiring audience as he readied the balloon for the first flight of the exhibition. After carefully examining the "immense canvas monster" for leaks, he patched a few small holes with thread and needle and hauled the collapsed balloon into position over a fire of wood and coal oil. The resulting gas and smoke, with Marble's help, entered the hole at the base of the balloon and, ever so slowly, the great bulk of canvas began to swell.

As Marble continued to "inspect... minutely every detail," the balloon gradually became buoyant and assumed the shape of a giant, inverted light-bulb. Finally, about 4 o'clock in the afternoon, the "monster was full, swollen, bulging and anxious to be off." By this time, no fewer than 8,000 persons had gathered to witness the great launching.

When all was in readiness, Marble entered the basket slung underneath the balloon and freed the guy wires which anchored his ungainly craft to the ground. Immediately the lines were released, the balloon "ascended swift as a rocket. First the large bulk, then yards of rope, then the folded parachute, then more yards of rope, than a trapeze, and dangling in the air at the end of all was the figure of Marble."

All, according to our breathless eyewitness account, had happened so swiftly that, in less than 10 seconds, the soaring balloon had reached such an altitude that Marble "assumed the proportions of a large doll, performing like a marionette at a giddy height above the surging crowd, who, silent as death, kept their fascinated yet unwilling eyes on the daring aeronaut."

For an undetermined length of time, the magnificent Marble thrilled his audience with death-defying stunts as the balloon, apparently having reached its maximum altitude, drifted out, over the Fraser and, becalmed, hovered in mid-air.

William Wallace Gibson, British Columbia's flying birdman, who, on September 8, 1910, flew the first Canadian-built airplane in all of Canada. During his second flight his "Twin-plane" crashed in a Victoria cow pasture. But Gibson lived, leaving the dubious distinction of becoming Canada's first aircraft victim to Milton Bryant, three years later.

Then the aeronaut could be seen busying himself with the ropes as, hundreds of feet below, thousands of upturned faces watched in breathless silence and anxiously awaited the highlight of his performance, when Marble would leap from the balloon and descend by parachute.

Suddenly a murmuring rippled through the crowd, as it became apparent to those watching from below that the balloon was again moving— not away, but downward. Slowly, steadily, the craft lost altitude as Marble continued to cling to the trapeze. Moments later, the "canvas giant of the air" had crossed the river and dropped from sight below the tree-line.

But, no sooner had the balloon vanished from view, than it reappeared above the trees and soared skyward, with smoke pouring from its emptying valve.

Again, an excited murmur swept the crowd: "He fell in the river!" exclaimed one. "He fell safely on the other side; he knows how to control that balloon," countered another, as a third spectator disgustedly argued, "That's no parachute drop— he shouldn't get paid a cent."

And with that, the spectators turned away, forgetting all about the marvellous Marble and his balloon as they watched the Vancouver and New Westminster seniors take the field.

In Town, many of those whose duties had prevented their attending the fair had had a better view of the balloon's erratic performance. Upon losing altitude directly above the river, the bulging craft seemed to be headed right for the water— "straight down, with terrible certainty, without a breath of air to sweep it to the land."

Immediately upon realizing that Marble was in serious difficulty, eager hands launched a small fleet of boats and rowed frantically for the balloon, which was yet sufficiently inflated that it bobbed safely on the current. Of Marble, however, there was not a sign and, as the first rescuers came alongside, they noticed his parachute floating on the surface. Upon pulling it in, one of the boatmen found it to be entangled. Moments later, he learned why. For there, at the end of "the long ropes the inanimate form of the aeronaut was found tied fast."

Amazingly, Marble was alive, and he was rushed to the nearby Guichon Hotel where, minutes after, he expired. Curiously, a news account of the incident attributes his death to faulty treatment: "Still alive, he was taken to the Guichon Hotel, to a warm room, a mistake so often made in the case of threatened death by drowning, for the patient should always be attended in the open air." Whatever the case, poor Marble never regained consciousness.

A newcomer to British Columbia, the young aeronaut had been hired by Professor Soper in Seattle. Formerly of Saginaw, Michigan, the Puget Sound balloonist, as the professor was billed, toured the continent with his balloon, astounding country fairgoers with his aeronautical exploits. Marble was believed to be 21-years-old, and was said to have left a mother and stepfather in Auburn, Washington.

"What makes his death particularly sad," observed one newspaper correspondent, was the fact that he had been "hired, it is said, for a paltry sum to make the ascensions, his employer, Professor Soper, pocketing the $300 received from the fair authorities."

Within an hour of Marble's ill-fated flight, the balloon was returned to its launch pad on the fairgrounds— where the professor waited with a second "reckless daredevil" to complete Marble's parachute jump. This time, when the deflated balloon, described as a "limp mass of dirty canvas," was stretched over the oven to be inflated, an even larger crowd, prompted by morbid curiousity, waited expectantly for the launch. But all were doomed to disappointment as, at this precise moment, customs officials seized the balloon and refused to surrender it until Soper paid $24 in duty. The professor and officials were debating the matter when darkness "happily came over the scene."

The tragedy of Charles Marble, it would seem, was even greater than the loss of a life in a fairground stunt, as the young American was said to have been so desperate that he had asked Soper to let him make the ascent for only $10. "There is little doubt," it was reported, "that Marble had never made a balloon ascension before. Soper admits that he did everything wrong, got rattled, and waited too long before he dropped…" An autopsy added to the magnitude of the tragedy by showing that Marble had not drowned, his heart having stopped— or almost so— before he hit the water. Death, the doctors said, had resulted from shock, Marble "probably being frightened to death."

The next day, Professor Soper, customs difficulties apparently resolved, proceeded with plans for further ascensions, as Marble's mother wired New Westminster authorities for her son's remains. That afternoon, the balloon was launched on schedule with its regular aeronaut, named Markeberg, contributing a "decidedly pretty feature" to the fair by completing a perfect ascent.

So relieved were spectators upon his safe descent that a willing mob carried the beaming German about on their shoulders, all present seeming to experience "an almost irrepressible desire to demonstratively welcome back the aeronaut from his perilous trip."

Minutes later, Markeberg, who was described as a mild-mannered veteran of 138 trips "into the ether," chatted with a reporter. Modestly, the seasoned balloonist remarked that he was callous to danger, that, aside from a pleasant sense of exhilaration, he felt the same when 4,000 feet above the earth as on it.

His own flight had been to an altitude of 2,000 feet. Once over the river, the balloon had encountered an opposing air current and been carried to 4,500 feet before it was swept back towards the fairgrounds. There, almost a mile above the ground, it had remained motionless for some moments until a warmer air current had caused the craft to make a gradual descent.

Marble, the aeronaut revealed, had not been quite the novice as indicated in initial reports, having been his ground assistant for some time. The younger man's experience, however, had been limited to preparing the balloon for flight, and he had lost his life during his first actual ascent, said Markeberg, by failing to begin his descent before reaching the river.

For his own part, Markeberg had thrilled his audience by leaving the basket to hang by his teeth from a strap as he waved two flags and performed other "hair-raising feats." Then, performance concluded, he had landed in a private garden, after a 72-second-long descent, "as if alighting from a coach." His return to the fairgrounds, as noted, was accompanied by an immense ovation.

In town an inquest into Marble's death ruled that he died accidentally and attached no blame to any of those involved. Professor Soper, in discussing the accident, emphasized that he had warned Marble "over and over again to drop before he got to the river."

But the fledgling aeronaut apparently had panicked when he was carried out over the river and lost control of the balloon when he attempted to reach the other side. ●

PHOENIX: A

FORGOTTEN CITY

(Opposite page) A view of Phoenix, looking towards the Stemwinder Mine, in its infancy. Before long, the ladies of Phoenix were "delicately holding up their skirts as they crossed from boardwalk to boardwalk on dusty Old Ironsides Avenue."
(Above) The same general view in the 1970s.

With the coming of the railroad, the great mining boom was on. As production soared, so did the town of Phoenix. From an area of just two square miles, in a single generation, the Phoenix mines yielded an amazing $100 million in copper, gold and silver ore.

"IT was a camp that for several years at least shipped more ore than all other mining camps of Canada combined; a camp whose principal mine was opened by a man (virtually) broke, but in a few years paid $10 million in dividends; a camp that. . . started professional hockey in the province, where $1,000 bets on games were not uncommon; (and the camp) which originated skiing in British Columbia...."

The pioneer "camp" of these impressive distinctions was Phoenix, in its day the "highest incorporated city in Canada." Like its legendary namesake, it flourished, then died—not in flames, to be born anew, but a victim of cold business logic. For a time it appeared that Phoenix would live up to its name and boom again. But, alas, this dreamed-of resurrection has not occurred and the former mining camp seems fated to remain but a memory to its former residents and their descendants.

Situated in the Boundary District of British Columbia, about 20 miles north of the international border, Phoenix, at an elevation of 4,500 feet, overshadowed, in fact and in production, its nearest neighbors, Midway, Greenwood and Grand Forks.

Although built on a mountain of copper, it was the eternal search for gold which led to the founding of Phoenix late in the 1880s. After the placer strikes on the Fraser and in the Barkerville region, prospectors had looked farther to the east, pouring into the Boundary District from the western part of the province and from Washington by way of the Dewdney Trail. The first placer strikes were made on Boundary and Rock creeks; when these played out, lode deposits were discovered at Midway and Greenwood. During this period the miners had noticed that the gold, while present, was greatly surpassed in quantity by deposits of copper. (Copper, however, unlike its yellow and more precious cousin, required large scale production. This in turn required an efficient and economical transportation system and, at that time, there was no railway).

In July of 1891 Matthew Hotter and Henry White staked the Old Ironsides and Knob Hill gold claims, James Schofield and James Atwood located the Stemwinder, and Joe Taylor and S. Mangott staked the Brooklyn property. Three years later, John Stevens located the Victoria claim. In the meantime the Silver King property, which adjoined the Old Ironsides, had been allowed to lapse. Relocated by Robert Denzler, who named it the Phoenix, it and the other three claims were the first of hundreds of properties to be staked in the immediate vicinity. But the Old Ironsides, Knob Hill, Victoria and Phoenix properties—when mined for their copper—proved to be the richest of them all and be the foundation—literally—on which the bustling town of Phoenix was built.

The shift in emphasis from gold to copper came about with the construction of the Spokane Falls and Northern Railroad. Although this new line ended at Marcus, Washington, a full 60 miles to the southeast, it made the mining of copper far more appealing to speculators and attracted development. In the meantime, work on the original four claims had required considerable capital and control of all four had been assumed by Jay P. Graves and A.L. White of Spokane who in turn sought further financing. This they received from the aptly-named S.H.C. Miner, president of the Granby Rubber Company of Granby, Quebec. With the money advanced by Miner's business associates in Eastern Canada, the Miner-Graves Syndicate reorganized in 1899 to become the Granby Consolidated Mining, Smelting and Power Company Limited.

Such massive financing had been required by the fact that mining in this region was by the "square-set" method, meaning that all excavation had to be done by tunnel. These required massive amounts of timbering—as demonstrated by the fact that, in 1902, one Phoenix worker in 10 was a "timberman." Fortunately, the area was well provided with pine and tamarac, and the logs for the thousands of 10 x 12-inch timbers were readily available.

This left the expensive matter of a railway. As crews of miners blasted their way underground and built up extensive stockpiles of copper ore, the Canadian Pacific Railway linked Phoenix and Greenwood with a 25-mile-long right-of-way. On May 21, 1900, the last spike was driven in the spur to the Old Ironsides bunkers. Reported the Greenwood *Times*: "Amid the shrieking of steam whistles and the cheers of assembled miners and other citizens of Phoenix, and with the ore bunkers gaily decorated with flags, the last piece of steel was laid to the Old Ironsides ore bins at noon today. Immediately after the last spike was driven the deep basso profundo whistle of the Ironsides shaft house heralded the welcome news, quickly followed by the Knob Hill, and in turn taken up by the War Eagle, Gold Drop, Golden Crown and other mines. The terrible ear-splitting din was not lessened by numerous explosions of dynamite and CPR locomotive whistles. The citizens of Phoenix sent 10 barrels of Phoenix beer to the workmen immediately after completion. This marks a new era here and its effect has already been felt, about 14 lots having been sold in the three townsites in the last two weeks."

Almost immediately, smelters were completed at Grand Forks, Greenwood and Boundary Falls, and the great boom was on. As the mines boomed, so did the town of Phoenix, which sprang up immediately adjacent to the Knob Hill and Old Ironsides mines, as the owners of the Cimeron, Phoenix and New York claims also surveyed and sold their surplus land for residential and commercial development.

By this time, notes Midway writer Susan Hilliard, "the ladies of Phoenix were delicately holding up their skirts as they crossed from boardwalk to boardwalk on dusty Old Ironsides Avenue. Phoenix Stage Lines—MacIntyre and Macdonald, proprietors—made two daily round trips from Greenwood to Phoenix, and visitors to Phoenix might choose from a variety of hotel accommodation.

" 'Finest Wines, Liquor and Cigars' were offered at the Brooklyn (the town's leading hotel), at the Bellevue, the Mint, the Union, the Imperial (table board seven dollars a week), at the Morden, the Maple Leaf, the Butte, the Cottage, Black's, the Golden, King's, Queen's, and Victoria House. By September 1900 the city's newspaper, *The Phoenix Pioneer*, was appearing weekly, and in its mining articles, social notes, and advertisements it struck a note of exuberant optimism...."

Besides hotels and saloons, Phoenix had its more respectable side as well, with four churches—Congregational, Presbyterian, Anglican and Roman

Grand Forks. With the copper boom at Phoenix, and the coming of the railway, smelters were constructed here, at Greenwood and Boundary Falls.

Catholic—a hospital and school. The three-storey Miner's Union Hall boasted a theatre, banquet hall and "the finest ballroom in the interior of the province." There also were the usual business establishments, and services, a brewery, shops and a covered skating and curling rink.

In short, Phoenix was no fly-by-night mining camp, but a substantial community with fine buildings of brick and wood. By the fall of 1900, George Rumberger, the town's first mayor, and the man who had given it its name, in honor of Denzler's claim, enthusiastically described the production of the leading mines and expressed his faith in the future of Phoenix in the *Pioneer*. At that time, he said, the various mines were shipping a total of 3,500 tons of gold and copper ore per week, of which the Knob Hill and Old Ironsides mines contributed 300 tons daily, and the B.C. Mine 150 tons per day: "The shipments from Phoenix alone

far exceed the combined output of all other mining camps in B.C., outside of Rossland," gushed Rumberger. "*Yet Phoenix is only in its earliest infancy.*"

While the Granby Company was the undisputed leader, with its Old Ironsides, Knob Hill, Curlew, Snowshoe and Gold Drop mines, there was also the Dominion Copper Company, owners of the Brooklyn, Stemwinder and Idaho mines; the Rawhide and Athelstan mines were operated by the British Columbia Copper Company. As all ore had to be loaded into cars capable of holding a ton each, hauled to the shaft house, then caged, hoisted and taken to the bins for dumping, there was keen rivalry between mining crews to see who could load the most ore in an eight-hour shift. Average tonnage hauled to the surface in a 24-hour period seems to have been 500 tons, although one shaft produced an amazing 18,000 tons in a single month, at the rate of 600 tons per day.

Phoenix in its glory. At its peak it boasted a population of about 4,000 persons and was the backbone to the economics of Greenwood, Grand Forks and Boundary Falls. But with the decrease in ore values and a world-wide drop in the price of copper, its mines closed and Phoenix was no more.

As production soared, the tunnels of the original Granby properties were linked underground and the horses, used to haul the ore cars to the base of each shaft, were superseded by the more efficient electric motor. Progress had also meant the layoffs of many of the timbermen, it having been discovered that some of the later workings did not require the excessive amounts of timbering. This development, according to Mrs. L.M. Haggen, MLA, in an address to the British Columbia Historical Association in 1957, had been welcomed by the company timekeeper, who, until that time, had had to devote hours of record keeping to keep the timbering accounts straight.

In July of 1900, noted Mrs. Haggen, the CPR reached Phoenix and the first ore train made the 25-mile-long, downhill haul to the smelter at Grand Forks. Because of the steep grade, the CPR used a Shay locomotive. Although slow, it could pull twice the number of cars of a regular locomotive as every wheel on the engine and tender were drive wheels. Nevertheless, the CPR experienced its share of difficulty on this stretch of track. On one occasion, Mrs. Haggen recounted, "a shay engine and 24 cars ran away, jumped the track, and everything was smashed to pieces. The track was so littered that instead of clearing away the debris to keep the ore moving, the company built a temproary detour track. Another train which ran away sailed merrily

down the mountain till it came to a level spot and just simply stopped, with no damage done. A few years later the Great Northern built into Phoenix and for nearly 20 years *two* railways ran night and day getting ore from Phoenix to the smelter."

By 1905 no fewer than 26 mining companies were in operation, as well as the smelters at Grand Forks, Greenwood and Boundary Falls, making the Boundary District one of the busiest in the country. Beneath the city of Phoenix, 50 miles of tunnels were interconnected in a giant maze and employed 1,500 miners.

When not on shift, many of the men spent their time in one of the city's 17 saloons, all of which were open around the clock, where they indulged themselves in drinking and gambling; joined one of the 16 secret lodges; skated; skied; or curled. Hockey games, particularly those between the Phoenix team and that of their arch-rivals from Grand Forks, drew such capacity crowds that special excursion trains had to be run between the communities. For spectators, hockey meant an opportunity for placing bets—some as high as $1,000—on the outcome of the game, and many a goal meant the winning or losing of a small fortune.

By 1911 the population of Phoenix had grown to 4,000 souls, the town enjoyed electricity, a modern water system, its number of churches had grown by one, and the future looked rosy. Between 1909 and

1911 the town shipped half of all the crude copper ore mined in Canada, about 7,000 tons daily, making it the largest producer in the country.

But, as early as 1909, dark clouds had formed on the horizon. Although the town continued to prosper, the Granby Company's engineers had warned that the ore deposits were decreasing in metal values, and the company had devoted increasing attention to its Anyox properties on Observatory Inlet, as well as some coal reserves on Vancouver Island. Also, the Grand Forks smelter was becoming obsolete and the Dominion government was considering additional taxes on ores. Consequently the Granby Company decided to push development of its Anyox and Cassidy properties.

At this time copper was bringing 11 cents per pound; at the outbreak of the First World War this had risen to 13 cents. But war also brought a complete shutdown for a period of four months before the mines resumed full production and the price of copper, now a vital commodity, steadily increased until it peaked at 28 cents a pound in 1918. By this time also the mines and smelter had broken all production records. But, with Armistice, the price of copper on the world market plunged to 14 cents and the Granby Company, saddled with the high costs of financing its Anyox operation, considered the possibility of shutting its Phoenix mines until the Anyox plant was self-supporting.

The decision was made for them in the summer of 1919, when a strike at Fernie closed the coke ovens and forced the smelters at Grand Forks, Greenwood and Boundary Falls to cease production. With the smelters out of operation the mines at Phoenix were also idled. When the Fernie strike dragged into autumn, many of the workers at Phoenix, becoming desperate for work, packed up their families and moved away. Most thought their moving would be temporary and left their homes virtually intact. But, when the strike did end, the world price of copper had fallen so low that the Granby Company decided against reopening.

The closing of the Granby mines meant ruin for Phoenix, as the other operations soon followed suit. From an area of just two square miles, in a single generation, the Phoenix mines had yielded an amazing $100 million in ore.

The end of Phoenix was rapid and ruthless. In a race against winter, salvage crews began to tear up railway tracks, as residents packed up what belongings they could take with them and the city council of the community which had boasted of being the highest incorporated city in Canada concluded the work of wrapping up the town's affairs by selling the skating rink to a Vancouver company for $1,200. The rink had been paid for by public subscription and the money recovered was invested in building a cenotaph which, despite the fact that Phoenix was no more, would continue to honor those of the town who had died for their country during the war.

Of the $1,200, $400 was turned over to the Royal Canadian Legion in Grand Forks to insure that the cenotaph would be looked after, and a further portion was used to create a fund to pay someone to serve as town watchman for a year, by which time all Phoenix residents would have moved away. This post went to an old resident, Adolph Cirque, better known to Phoenix citizens as "Forepaw" because of the crude iron hook and braces he wore after losing most of an arm.

Issued a billy club and a home-made star cut from a tomato tin, Forepaw moved into the steepled city hall and proudly announced himself as mayor and constable of Phoenix. Two others remained also: carpenter W.H. Bambury and Robert Denzler, the miner who had coined the name Phoenix for his claim. Then Banbury took up permanent residence on the Greenwood-Grand Forks road, Denzler and Forepaw died, and Phoenix was alone with its memories.

Even before this, salvagers from neighboring communities had stripped many of the buildings of their contents, and tore down homes and business establishments for their lumber and bricks. Those that were left began to fall away and once busy streets became overgrown until only rusting fire hydrants and rubble remained to show where they had been. Before long, only the cenotaph, cemetery and the old shaft houses were left to tell their tale of boom and bust.

In the autumn of 1927 an Oroville, Washington newspaper reporter visited the ghost town "situated in the clouds." On an October Saturday, the newsman made the long, steep drive to Phoenix: "As the car purred up the steep grade the fog fell behind and in a few minutes the outskirts of Phoenix were in view. Soon one gazed on a spectacle that can be duplicated in but few places in the world.

"Phoenix's two streets were once lined solid with buildings, but since the boom died some 200 buildings have been torn down and carted away. Many buildings, however, remain, and are an impressive sight, boarded, ghostly and silent in the canyon. The Brooklyn Hotel, a three-story structure, still stands in good condition, but across the street the old Morrin-Thompson hardware store has crumbled to pieces. The city had two important streets divided by a deep canyon, bridged at several places.

"The main street, on the west side of the canyon, is still lined with huge frame buildings, many of which have fallen to pieces. A splendid brick building still bears the sign "Morrin-Thompson." Higher up on the hill, looking spick and span, is the hospital, although the inside is in ruins.

"In the main part of the city and flanking the hills are scores of beautiful residences, boarded and ghostly, while in the lower end of town is the remains of an old brewery. As one stands on a knoll at the upper end of the canyon, across and high up

(Top) When the mining operations at Phoenix were shut down by the falling price of copper, it meant ruin for neighboring communities as well. The Dominion Copper Company's smelter at Boundary Falls, shown here, was also closed. When the miners moved on the townsite gradually disappeared. Today, only the slag heaps and some foundations mark this historic townsite.
(Bottom) The mines lie deserted in this photograph, taken in 1919.

on the hillside rears the mammoth building of the Granby Company, which alone at one time employed a thousand men...."

At the time of the *Gazette* reporter's visit, only Forepaw and Bob Denzler where living there, although Denzler had simply moved in from his claims, four miles away, for the winter.

Both men remained loyal to the Phoenix that was and assured their interviewer that "there is untold wealth still left underground." But for a single tunnel which had reached the 500-foot level, they said none of the mining companies had gone very deep. Forepaw estimated that as much as 2.5 million tons of ore remained in the Granby mine, and about a million tons in the Brooklyn, not to mention the numerous other workings. Yet, despite his confidence in the ore reserves remaining beneath the streets of Phoenix, Forepaw did not think that the city would ever regain its former glory, as it was extremely unlikely that a railway would ever be rebuilt. He did believe, however, that "some day concentrators will be put up and the ore hauled out by trucks, or shot down a tramway to Greenwood."

According to the *Gazette*, a "well-known mining company of British Columbia" was expected to do some diamond drilling in the area. But, in the meantime, Phoenix slept on: "Nothing breaks the stillness except the low of a cow, the rustle of the wind, and perhaps, now and then, the crash of some building, becoming weary of life, crumbles away."

Actually, one other Phoenix resident had remained. This was Bob Forshaw, who had settled on a farm several miles down the valley. Although driven to farming with the closure of the mines, he never lost his interest, or faith, in the area's mining potential. Over the years he continued to search the hills for promising signs of mineralization and bought up mineral claims as they lapsed. In this way he obtained rights to the old Brooklyn and Stemwinder properties. In 1924 he succeeded in interesting a Vancouver group in resuming work on the properties. This time they were after gold, not copper. For Bob Forshaw's extensive research had uncovered two amazing facts: that the most promising ground had not been tapped for its gold content and—even more remarkable—that the Brooklyn mine was "in high pay ore when it was closed." Test shots by the Depression-era firm had confirmed highly promising veins of gold, silver and copper.

Two years later, W.E. McArthur, for many years mayor of Greenwood and "a well-known figure in British Columbia's mining circles," bought the Phoenix properties. He operated on a small scale until the Second World War when a shortage of manpower brought quiet to Phoenix once more.

This silence reigned until 1955 when history came full cycle. With an upswing in copper prices, interest in the old Phoenix workings was reawakened and McArthur's properties were sold yet again—to the Granby Consolidated Company.

In August of 1956 it was announced that the Granby Company was preparing to build a concentrating plant capable of processing 50 tons per day. The new operation would be an open pit mine, rather than underground. The plant was to be constructed of surplus equipment from the company's Copper Mountain operation and was intended to be in production early in 1957. Once in full swing the operation, which would utilize the old Snowshoe and Ironside mines, would employ 40 men, the ore, after concentration, being shipped to Tacoma for smelting. Surveys indicated that the operation would produce 500 tons per day for about 10 years.

By 1969 Phoenix's third lease on life had produced 5.6 million tons of ore, worth about $30 million, and employed 120 workers. Daily production had been stepped up to 2,400 milled tons per day, the price of copper having soared to 60 cents a pound. Although the grade of ore recovered was just half that mined half a century before, quarrying methods and modern equipment made it a profitable venture until the fall of 1976, when the firm announced that its ore reserves at Phoenix were nearing exhaustion. Since resuming operations at Phoenix, Granby Consolidated had milled more than 140 million pounds of copper, 1.4 million ounces of gold, and 200,000 ounces of silver, with an aggregate value of more than $80 million.

Throughout this period miners had not lived on the site but commuted from neighboring townships and only those buildings necessary to the mining operation had been constructed. Rather than having been rebuilt, the Phoenix of old had vanished in the maw of the great open pit gouged from the mountainside.

Thus Phoenix passed into history. Never again would it know the hustle and bustle of a boom town. But some of its memories live on, in the hearts of those who lived and worked there and their descendants. Some of its citizens, such as six-foot, 10-inch W.R. Williams, onetime police magistrate, have left memories of their own. Williams, who was widely known for his unorthodox judicial decisions, when chided by an army officer for not having recognized his rank, had indignantly retorted: "Judge Williams, if you please; I want you to understand that I am the *highest* judge of the *highest* court in the *highest* city in Canada." ●

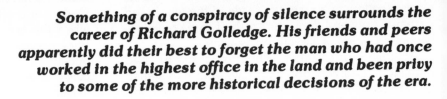

(Below) Lieutenant Peter Leech, whose discovery of gold on the Leech River created a stampede in Victoria's backyard — and a second chance for Richard Golledge, formerly private secretary to Governor Douglas. (Right) Chinese washing gold in the Leech River — 1909.

Something of a conspiracy of silence surrounds the career of Richard Golledge. His friends and peers apparently did their best to forget the man who had once worked in the highest office in the land and been privy to some of the more historical decisions of the era.

(Opposite Page) With the stampede of miners to Leech River, Richard Golledge was appointed Acting Gold Commissioner for Sooke mining district. Despite later difficulties, Golledge seems to have filled this post reasonably well, although many of the independent-minded miners resented having to buy mining licences and register their claims. Alas, the riches of Leech River were fleeting—as were the fortunes of Richard Golledge. (Right Top) W. Ward & Co. camp scene—mining at Leech River, B.C. (Right Bottom) First log house on Leech River—Mountain Rose claim.

The Fall Of

RICHARD GOLLEDGE

TWENTY years. To most people 20 years represent a generation—one chapter in a long and full life.

But for Richard Golledge 20 years meant a lifetime: a period that marked the height of his career and the depth of his fall from grace.

One of the most infuriating aspects of history is the matter of missing links, when the existing record reveals little of the who, what and when. One of these unhappy ommissions is Richard Golledge, at one time Governor James Douglas' private secretary.

The record does show that he landed in Victoria from the bark *Tory* in 1851 as an employee of the Hudson's Bay Company. Then about 20 years of age, young Golledge came from a respectable family, had had a full education, and was immediately made Douglas' right hand. For seven years he served in this demanding capacity, seeing to the dozens of major and minor details with which Douglas had to contend daily. As far as can be determined, he served the governor well until 1858. It is not known whether his return to private life was by his own decision or that of Douglas.

For something of a conspiracy of silence surrounds the career of Richard Golledge. It seems apparent that, embarrassed by his antics in later years, his former peers and acquaintances did their best to forget the former secretary who had worked in the highest office in the land and had been privy to some of the more historic decisions of this era. Only the briefest mention (and then only in reference to his official capacity) is made of him in records and personal memoirs.

Not until July of 1864 is he again referred to officially when, with the discovery of gold on Leech River, it was announced that "His Excellency

(Governor Arthur Edward Kennedy) has been pleased to appoint Mr. Richard Golledge to be Acting Gold Commissioner for Sooke mining district."

A week after the Colonist reported that C.J. Hughes, Esq., "a gentleman whose initials are well known by all readers of the Victoria papers," had been appointed as justice of the peace and acting magistrate for Sooke mining district and Acting Gold Commissioner Golledge had also been "placed on the commission of the police."

Within days of accepting his new post, Golledge submitted his first report to Governor Kennedy from Leech River. From various parties along the river, many of whom he knew and trusted, he had learned that "Coarse gold…is to be found everywhere on the Leech River from the hilltops to the bed of the stream, and the right hand side of the river (upstream) is said to contain the most gold. The nugget found by Booth and about $200 worth of very coarse gold (button gold), which have been found above were mostly taken from the crevices of the bedrock on the river. It is the general opinion however that the largest quantities of gold will be taken from the hills and bed near the mouth of the river, on account of the scarcity of dirt above; the hills and bed of the stream a few miles up being almost bare…"

To date, he reported, only 20 licences and claims had been applied for and registered, although he was confident that the fiercely independent miners would soon resign themselves to both requirements. Those of the miners who had rockers and who were satisfied with the ground they were working would, he was sure, take out their licences the next day.

He concluded his report with the expressed hope that Kennedy would approve of his actions and assured him that his efforts would benefit the miners and "be the means of preventing much speculation."

But a day later, he wrote a second dispatch to Victoria in which he assured the government that "affairs are progressing in a very satisfactory manner, both in regard to the finding of gold paying prospects, the numbers of miners gradually coming upstream, and the working of the present mining regulations.

"With respect to the former I may mention that miners even in prospecting their claims are taking out sufficient to pay their daily expenses; when they commence working the benches and hillsides good wages may be expected, and should the many who are sinking shafts for the bedrock, strike gold in the old bed of the river, it is more than probable that very rich and extensive gold diggings will be the result. A small particle of silver attached to a piece of coarse gold was to-day washed out within half a mile of our encampment."

For all of his assurances that the new mining regulations were working well, he had to admit that he had been so besieged by inquiries that he had found it necessary to draw up a notice outlining the requirements for those wishing to stake claims. New gold strikes invariably experienced disputes over the question of claim jumping and he was determined to see that no such problems presented themselves on the Leech River.

"Miners complain of the hardship of having to possess a License before they select a permanent spot, this however is done for the purpose of obtaining a promise from the Commissioner to secure to them the place wherever their prospects are good, while they either take out enough to pay for their licenses and registration fees, or proceed to Victoria for the same—this is rather a nice point, and if allowed would without doubt be an injustice to those who come forward immediately upon their arrival and pay their fees, and therefore their complaints cannot be attended to."

Up until 6 o'clock in the evening of August 3, he had issued 77 licences and registration receipts. That same day, some 76 newcomers arrived on the river and Golledge anticipated a busy day.

Alas, the riches of Leech River were fleeting…as were the fortunes of Richard Golledge, onetime private secretary to Governor Douglas, acting gold commissioner for Sooke mining district and justice of the peace. Exactly 20 years after his appointment as commissioner, 52-year-old Richard Golledge appeared before an Esquimalt magistrate to answer a charge of having stolen an Indian canoe.

It was a long, long way from having had a position in the highest office in the land and a disgusted newspaper reporter summed up his career in three cruel words: "Fallen so low!"

Convicted of stealing the canoe, Golledge was fined 10 dollars and ordered to appear before Justice Fisher in two weeks' time. "Meanwhile," sneered the newspaper, "it is hoped that Golledge will rid the province of his presence, which has become very distasteful to respectable people. Golledge received the education of a gentleman, was highly educated and connected. He took to drink and prowling about Indian villages nearly 20 years ago, and has become a confirmed vagrant."

However, the fallen Golledge did not rid the province of his presence. When he did take his departure, three years after, it was for keeps. This time the Colonist reported his passing at St. Joseph's Hospital, where he had been under the care of the Sisters of St. Ann for the past year. Death, at the age of 55, was said to have been the result of heart disease. It was a sad end for the man who had begun his career in the province with such promise, a quarter of a century before. Out of respect for his memory, the obituary notice mentioned nothing of his troubles in later years, merely noting that, once, he had enjoyed wealth and prominence, that his "connections are prominent people."

On September 8, 1887, Richard Golledge was quietly laid to rest. ●

A fellow sealer, and kindred spirit of the "Flying Dutchman," was "Sea Wolf" Alex McLean. Between them they took on the American, British and Russian navies. McLean was immortalized by Jack London, but poor Gustav Hansen has all but been forgotten.

Gustav Hansen:
THE
FLYING
DUTCHMAN

The record shows that Captain Gustav Hansen had all the glamor and excitement of a Captain Kidd, with the single exception that he had a heart of pure gold when it came to dealing with — most — fellow men.

B RITISH Columbia's famous sealing industry was a grim business. Not only for the poor seal, slaughtered almost to extinction, but for the seamen who braved distant and dangerous seas to follow the elusive prize. For sealing demanded men—real men.

Then there were sealers of a different cloth. This tiny fraternity thumbed noses at more than storm and killing fog—little obstacles like international law and three navies!

Rogues like Alex "Sea Wolf" McLean. And Captain Gustav Hansen, the "Flying Dutchman."

Unlike the ill-fated mariner of legend, doomed to sail his phantom ship forever, the Flying Dutchman of provincial lore was quite human. And, like all humans, he had his weaknesses: such as a total inability to read Keep Out signs or earn an honest dollar. Still, legitimate sealers admitted to reluctant admiration for the Northwest's last, if not only, real pirate.

Strangely, although he became a legend the length of the Pacific coast in his lifetime, today there is little record of this amazing man's exploits. But the scant details on file show that Hollywood has overlooked an honest-to-goodness latter-day buccaneer with all the glamor and excitement of a Captain Kidd

or Blackbeard. With the single exception that Gustav Hansen had a heart of pure gold when it came to dealing with fellow men. Well...with most fellow men.

When it became known that fortunes were to be made, sealing had passed from an international free-for-all to closed competition. While American warships jealously guarded Alaskan territorial waters, the Tsar's Imperial Navy watchdogged that nation's icebound shores against intrusions by foreign sealers. Confiscation of ships, heavy fines and (or) imprisonment were the price of trespassing. For second offenders the Russians promised a fate worse than death: a journey (usually one-way) to the dreaded salt mines of Siberia. Sometimes without so much as a hearing.

While these arbitrary threats proved to be a poor deterrent to the hardy sealers, they seemed almost to encourage the daring Captain Hansen, who was lured to these shores about 1878. As marine reporter Frank Kelley observed, years ago: "Hansen was the sort of man who would sooner get money by unorthodox methods than by honorable means, no matter how easily it might be earned at the time... There was no risk too great for this astute and courageous rascal."

His five-man crew were of the same reckless cut. Armed only with double-barrelled shotguns, the merry band of freebooters sailed their 35-ton schooner *Adele*, a former Shanghai pilot boat, into stormy northern seas to boldly challenge both nations.

It was about 1890 that the *Adele* slipped from Shanghai under the German flag, bound for the Bering Sea rookery of St. Paul Island in the Pribilofs. As the schooner hove to offshore, Hansen and crew landed in two boats. All went according to plan at first, the poachers coolly battering seals to death left and right. They had collected 80 prime pelts before the shore patrol spotted them.

Rifle bullets shrieking overhead, Hansen and company ran for the boats and rowed desperately for their schooner. It had been a close call—not so close, however, that the raiders had abandoned their furs.

Saner men would have turned to more honest— and safer—pursuits. But not the buccaneering crew of the *Adele*. Two weeks later, under cover of a gale, Hansen again anchored his schooner off St. Paul. This time they landed on the opposite side of the island at night. By dawn they had 400 skins. When the guards finally caught on to the slaughter, a laughing Hansen had the *Adele* running before a brisk wind.

Never one to abandon a profitable business, when next Gustav Hansen returned to work, he was back at St. Paul. As one early story understates: "This was an impertinent affair.

"Armed with. . .shotguns, the sealers landed in the night with fog augmenting the darkness and as daylight neared they surprised the guard, then engaged in preparing breakfast. While some of the raiders stood guard over the Aleuts—to whom Hansen gave a jar of rum he had brought ashore— the raiders broke into the salthouses where skins taken by the natives for the lessees had been baled for shipment and made away with more than 1,000 skins."

Upon docking in Victoria, Captain Hansen duly registered his catch as "from Behring Sea."

Between voyages, Hansen would paint Victoria red. Not one to save or invest his ill-gotten gains, he would embark upon a drinking spree which lasted until he was broke again. Much of it he gave away to

Victoria Harbor. When not on the high seas, raiding seal rookeries, or languishing in a Russian prison, Captain Hansen and his freebooting crew painted the city red. Never one to hoard his ill-gotten gains, Hansen was an easy touch to seamen down on their luck.

seamen down on their luck. No matter what else people thought of him, they had to admit that he "never refused a 'touch'—if he happened to possess the where-withal."

Then it was back to his schooner, to play his banjo and to delight audiences with tales of his daring deeds on the high seas, until once again it was time to sail for some mysterious destination.

Once the American cutters *Richard Rush* and *Bear* found him in forbidden waters. It must have been towards evening, for Hansen waited until dark, then made his escape. But, unlike the Arabs, he was not a man to fold his tent and silently steal away. Almost within earshot of the unsuspecting cutters, he proceeded to take 491 seals! By dawn, he was well on his way toward the Japanese coast.

Hence the title, "Flying Dutchman."

But even Captain Gustav Hansen's phenomenal luck had to end; poor *Adele* pounded to pieces on the rocky Queen Charlotte coast when her anchors dragged in a gale. Two years later, he recounted, "with the schooner *Emma*, I was seized by the Russians off Saghallen Island and with my crew of 10 men taken to Vladivostock. Here we were kept prisoners for six months without being given a hearing. At the end of that time we were all suffering from scurvy.

"When at last we were tried, it was to be sentenced to four months' additional imprisonment. I knew I could not stand any more of the Russian grub without becoming an invalid for the rest of my days, and as luck would have it the day we were sentenced an English and a Japanese steamer in harbor were ready to sail that night. Money will do almost anything with a Russian sub-officer, and I succeeded in bringing the guards (around to) allowing us to reach the steamers.

"Five of the men stowed away on the English steamer while myself and five others were secreted on board the Japanese ship, all hands being safely landed in Yokohama."

Undaunted by this enforced vacation, Hansen was soon back in business. If he had learned anything from his stay in a rat-infested jail, it was to leave the Russians alone—for a while. This voyage, he would pay his respects to the Americans.

This also was his most ambitious scheme to date. But, again, his luck had soured. It was Hansen's intention to raid the Alaska Commercial Company's salthouses. He shrewdly timed his arrival for the end of the season, just before the skins were to be shipped to St. Louis. This meant that the salthouses would be crammed with prime skins.

Unfortunately for Hansen, they also proved to be

well-stocked with guards. There was no buying their freedom this time, and Hansen and crew found themselves in the Sitka lock-up.

There are three versions of what followed: The first says that Hansen was convicted and sentenced to a lengthy stay in the stockade, his schooner confiscated. Then, the story goes, a chastened Flying Dutchman swallowed the anchor, preferring a quieter life ashore to further adventures on the high seas.

The second telling is more to our liking and in keeping with Hansen's record. According to this story, it was the United States revenue cutter *Corwin* which made the capture: "A prize crew was put on board the schooner, instructed to take the vessel to Sitka for seizure, and there the raiders were to be tried. However, Hansen and his crew managed to surprise the prize crew a few days later and its members accepted the alternative of being given a boat to enable their landing on the Alaskan coast as against a voyage to Victoria."

This sounds more like Captain Hansen!

A third account is along the same line. Taken to Sitka, the poachers managed to break jail, reach their impounded schooner, cut her free, and slip out of harbor to freedom.

Whatever the case, Gustav Hansen was back in circulation, albeit with a price on his head. When next he made news, it was in the noble role of injured innocence. "Captain Gustav Hansen, commonly known as 'The Flying Dutchman,' 'piratical sealer,' 'poacher of seal rookeries,' etc., is on his way to Victoria," it was reported in 1896. "He arrived in Portland some days ago on the steamer *Mount Lebanon*, having left his schooner, the *Josephine*, at Yokohama, that he might proceed to Victoria and collect $12,369 which he claims to be due him under the *modus vivendi* for constructive damages for having been driven out of Behring Sea and thus prevented from sealing."

What became of this claim—outrageous when considering its author—is not recorded.

When ill luck continued to plague the buccaneer, he decided at last to turn his talents to a new—and alien—field of endeavor: honest toil. Terrible blow though it must have been to Hansen's pride, still it was in keeping with his adventurous soul. At sea or ashore, Hansen was forever chasing rainbows, the quick money. This time he was after a lost mine.

With veteran prospector Jack Donahue for partner, and the occasional grubstake from Village Island storekeeper Amos Ellis, Hansen poked about the rugged fjords of Vancouver Island's northwest coast. None of his claims came to much and the lost mine remained lost.

As evidence of the extent to which the Flying Dutchman had mellowed, he embarked on the sea of matrimony by marrying a Kyuquot maiden.

When not at home or prospecting, Hansen enjoyed visiting his old mates aboard visiting ships.

"In those days, a majority of Canadian Pacific Navigation Company's skippers and deck officers were ex-sealers, particularly on the west coast run. Whenever the old *Tees* dropped anchor at Village Island in the winter months, Hansen would be a regular visitor, renewing acquaintance with Captain Jack Townsend or Captain Ed Gillam and, as it sometimes happened, when discretion was the better part of chance-taking on stormy nights and the *Tees* rested, passengers were regaled with round, unvarnished tales Hansen had apparently lived in his time. In the telling of them there were no hints of bragadacio, even when the memory was loosened some with a brand labelled 'White Horse'."

Gustav Hansen was now a walking example of respectability. No more was his name linked with midnight sailings and mysterious doings in northern seas. In fact, the only apparent link with his colorful past was a charge of breaking and entering an Indian house at Kyuquot. Held aboard the steamship *Willapa*, the informal hearing (very informal, as all participants were "well primed") came to the conclusion that it was a misunderstanding and the charge was dropped. Firstly, because the lack of a door cancelled the breaking half of the charge, secondly, because the fact that he was a "frequent and welcome visitor" disqualified the entering clause.

Then it was back to mining. One adventure of this period, involved an incredible tale of shipwreck and suffering at forboding Cape Cook, on the northwestern end of Vancouver Island. Prospecting with two companions, Hansen was amazed to see 10 emaciated men stagger into his lonely camp. Survivors of the sunken Peruvian bark *Libertad*, the seamen would have perished but for their chance finding of the miners' camp.

The prospectors risked starvation and drowning to save the Peruvians. As has been mentioned, Captain Hansen may have been a rascal but he never refused a helping hand.

Ironically, Gustav Hansen was to die at sea within a month of his heroic rescue of the *Libertad*'s crew. While returning from some claims at Kashutl Inlet with Jack Donahue, his dog, and James Moir, one stormy January night, their tiny canoe capsized, plunging all three into the wild surf.

Donahue luckily reached a rock, where he clutched the dog to his chest to keep warm. Somehow he clung to the frigid perch until morning, when storekeeper Ellis' sister-in-law, the beautiful daughter of a Kyuquot chief, spotted him. Courageously, the young woman launched her canoe in the foaming breakers and rescued the weakening prospector. Donahue subsequently married his lovely savior and they enjoyed a long, happy partnership.

But poor Hansen and Moir were gone. When last Donahue had seen him, Hansen was swimming strongly for the beach. When the storm passed, he

With the end of the historic sealing industry, many of the little schooners lay at anchor for years until they were hauled onto the beach, stripped of their metal and burned. Their destruction marked the passing of a colorful chapter in British Columbia's marine lore.

was not to be seen.

"It was not until that spring that Hansen's body was found floating near Village Island," wrote Frank Kelley, "and I'm sure if he had his choice he would ask for no finer resting place than the grassy knoll of the little island, near the mouth of (Clanninick) Harbor, looking out over the Pacific on which he had been a bit of a freebooter when seal rookeries

might be raided and salthouses broken into—more for devilment than riches."

The Kyuquots thought highly of the once-notorious Flying Dutchman, burying him with the rites of a chief. A totem pole marked his grave, within sight of the sea he and the carefree *Adele* had conquered with a few reckless comrades and sheer daring.

●

Some of his critics claimed that Captain Stamp (below) "built sawmills in outrageous places. . .in out-of-the-way places that would never, never possibly amount to anything—faraway, isolated places like Alberni (Vancouver Island) and a wilderness arm of the sea called Burrard's Inlet...."

WAS CAPTAIN EDWARD STAMP A NICE GUY?

Whatever one's point of view, few can deny that Captain Edward Stamp was a character or that he made a substantial contribution to the birth of Canada's third largest metropolis.

HISTORIANS hold conflicting opinions of Captain Edward Stamp, pioneer businessman and prominent citizen. Vancouver Island historian James K. Nesbitt has termed him "British Columbia's No. 1 industrialist." On the mainland, authors Alan Morley and Eric Nichol have not taken as kindly to the doughty mariner's earlyday efforts to develop what is now the metropolis of Vancouver.

Whatever one's point of view, few can deny that Captain Stamp was a character or that he made a considerable contribution to the birth of Canada's third largest city.

In fact, modern-day visitors and Vancouver residents alike—inadvertently—owe thanks for the pleasures of Stanley Park to the long-ago businessman who originally held the option to log this magnificent rain forest. Fortunately for posterity, Stamp's original plan to strip Brockton Point was foiled by the tricky currents which occur there and which would have caused continuing headaches for the loggers attempting to secure the timber into rafts. Consequently, stamp renegotiated with Governor Frederick Seymour for a new lease (which put the original to shame) and proceeded to begin operations at Hasting's Mill.

Twenty years ago, Mr. Nesbitt wrote of Stamp: "He had an unshakeable faith in the future of this new land. There were those who scoffed at him because he invested heavily in the future; he was told he was throwing his money away. He was laughed at each new venture he went into.

"He built sawmills in outrageous places, many of his fellow citizens said—in out-of-the-way places that would never, never possibly amount to anything—faraway, isolated places like Alberni and a wilderness arm of the sea called Burrard's Inlet...

He built empires, small compared to those of today, but empires nonetheless, and to his initiative and vision must go in some measure much of the credit for the British Columbia we know today."

Captain Edward Stamp was, in fact, a walking contradiction. He could be charming and ruthless; he made fortunes overnight and lost them almost as easily; he gained wide respect for his daring in business, then proceeded to alienate many of those with whom he had dealings. He was, in short, irascible and vindictive, his photograph showing a mutton-chopped scowl which can only be interpreted as indication of the nature which lurked within. For all of Stamp's courage in business and his interest in public life, he leaves us wondering yet as to whether or not he was a "nice guy!"

A British mariner and hero of the Crimean War, Captain Stamp landed in the Pacific Northwest in 1856, when commissioned to purchase ships' spars in Puget Sound. When, two years later, the discovery of gold on a Fraser River sandbar prompted a stampede for the uncharted interior of New Caledonia, Stamp threw all thought of his maritime career to the winds. It was not the hope of finding his fortune on a riverbank, however, that intrigued him. Rather, he had plans for developing the colony's incredibly rich resources, having realized that gold literally came in many forms other than mineral.

He immediately demonstrated his flair for prophecy by attempting to form a company to pipe water into Victoria, as the shacktown's supply at that time was delivered to the door by tank-wagons for 25 cents a gallon. However, the enterprising mariner's proposal to lay pipes through Victoria's muddy streets met only with the approval of the

House of Assembly. Citizens apparently preferred the rustic, horse-drawn "bucket brigade," and Stamp's proposed waterworks was stillborn.

(Actually, he had not been the first to foresee the effect of such an enterprise, colonial surveyor Joseph Pemberton having previously requested that the Hudson's Bay Company permit him to lay a single water main from Spring Ridge to downtown for "not less than 40 persons.)"

Whatever, by 1859, having made Victoria his headquarters, the industrious Captain Stamp was manager of the Puget Sound Mill Company of Port Gamble, Washington Territory, which furnished "spars for the English markets." Among the company's shipments during this period was the delivery of the lower and topsail yards, the topmasts and two of the lower masts of the then-building mammoth steamship, the *Great Eastern*.

By the following year, Stamp was involved in the establishing of a new sawmill on Alberni Canal, Vancouver Island. However, like most of his ventures, it did not hold his interest for long as, within three years, he sold his shares in Messrs. Edward Stamp and Company. In this instance, at least, Stamp's reputed talent for making enemies apparently did not come to the fore. In fact, it would appear that he had been popular with his men, who held a testimonial for him. It was reported that they "unanimously resolved to present him with a gold watch and chain, with a suitable inscription, as a token of their respect and esteem...

"Yesterday (Capt.) T. Pamphlett and E. Beedle, in the name of the workmen, presented the watch to Captain Stamp, who expressed himself highly gratified with the token of their regard. The watch is valued at $250."

(Which, when one considers that the dollar was worth at least 10 times that of today, was a rather handsome "token" of regard indeed).

Stamp next turned his attention to the wilds of Burrard's Inlet. There, on the North Shore, as shown earlier, "Sue" Moody had purchased the foundering J.O. Smith sawmill and transformed the quiet rain forest into a thriving industry. Captain Stamp held the same hope for the inlet's southern shore, having obtained from Governor Seymour, after the disappointment at Brockton Point, a lease for 30,000 acres. This lease, to be good for 21 years and to cost his British Columbia and Vancouver Island Spar, Lumber and Sawmill Company all of a cent an acre, ably justified the faith Stamp's British backers had in him. Shortly before, he had returned from England with 100,000 pounds capital and, with Seymour's blessing, immediately set to work at carving a fortune from the wilderness.

Seymour also had thrown in permission for him to import all equipment duty-free, and granted his mill status as a port of entry. Thanks to this governmental largess, Stamp's Mill blossomed into existence, comprising, at the start, the sawmill, one

store and four acres of fallen trees, brush, shacks and saloons.

Business boomed immediately; so much so that Stamp ordered construction of the tugboat *Isabel*. Constructed of the "finest timber ever put into a vessel on this coast," the good ship *Isabel* was to enjoy one of the more illustrious careers in Pacific Northwest shipping history. For by now it must be apparent that Stamp believed in doing things well.

But when Stamp's hopes of having the *Isabel* enter the profitable California trade fell through, he resigned the steamer, which had been opulently furnished to accommodate 50 passengers, as well as carry freight, to local service. He then began to invest in real estate by building a "fine block of stores...on Government Street, opposite the Bank of British Columbia," in Victoria. The three-storey block of stores and offices was built entirely upon speculation, Stamp being convinced that, despite his critic's denials, he would be able to rent the premises. Once again he proved himself to be ahead of his time as, even before completion, the building was fully leased.

Thus encouraged by his growing prosperity, Stamp found time to cast his eye upon the political arena. This decision led to something of a puzzle for historians as, although elected originally in Esquimalt, with the union of the colonies of Vancouver Island and British Columbia, he changed his mind and his address to Lillooet, where, by acclamation—"the other candidates, finding they had not the ghost of a chance, resigned rather than continue the contest to the close of the poll"—he was elected to the British Columbia Council.

A Victoria journalist congratulated Lillooet upon its fortune in having "secured a gentleman of wealth, respectability, talent and, above all, unflinching loyalty. The district may well be proud of its representative who will do all that lies in his power to advance the interest of the united colonies. We

(Below and opposite page) *Posterity owes a debt of gratitude to Captain Stamp for having spared what is now Stanley Park from the woodsman's axe. Actually, Stamp, who had a timber lease on Brockton Point, moved his operations because of the tricky currents which occur there and would have hindered loggers when forming the timber into rafts.*

congratulate the honorable gentleman upon his elevation to an honor that has really been 'thrust upon him,' and we compliment the electors of Lillooet for their display of good sense in selecting so fine a representative."

And so it went, Captain Stamp seeming to have the golden touch of Midas. But not all begun under auspicious circumstances achieved financial greatness. His ambitious Hastings Mill folded despite an impressive production of 4,000,000 feet of lumber and 100,000 hand-cut shingles in a single year, with sales as far distant as China and Hawaii. Across the inlet, Sue Moody not only topped these figures but prospered.

Perhaps it was this setback that prompted Stamp to embark upon a new and novel venture, the canning of salmon. Sailing for England on another quest for finances, he returned to Victoria 14 months after, contracts in pocket and eager to begin exporting barrelled and tinned salmon to Europe. He leased the former Royal Engineers' barracks at New Westminster and set to work with his usual enthusiasm. The new plant was soon in production, when a gourmet praised Stamp's piscatorial product as being tastier than any other preserved fish he had ever tasted.

The delighted diner even recommended that the salmon be eaten cold, "or, as some prefer it, warmed up in the tin previous to being served... It constitutes a most convenient article of food for the bachelor who does his own housework, as all trouble in preparation is avoided."

Thus, another first for Captain Stamp: "TV" dinners!

The captain's newest enterprise soon proved to be so successful that, at a time in life when "most men seek repose from active business pursuits," he felt impelled to sail for England to promote the first shipment of canned salmon upon its arrival. Late in November of 1871, he embarked for the Old Country.

It was to be his last great adventure for, two months after, word of his sudden death in London reached Victoria. Mourned the *Colonist*: "Captain Stamp was a most enterprising and energetic citizen and will be greatly missed here, where he had a host of friends. He leaves a wife, two sons and a daughter in England, and two sons in this province."

Ironically, within six months, his son Edward, who had inherited charge of the salmon cannery at New Westminster, died at the age of 35. About the same time, half a world away, Mrs. Stamp, "relic of Captain Edward Stamp," succumbed near London at the age of 60. This, at least for the immediate period, closed the "strange and melancholy fatality (which) appears to have pursued this family in the past few months." Besides Captain Stamp, Mrs. Stamp and son Edward, the captain's brother had passed away less than a month before him.

So ended an illustrious career in British Columbia's early development. Perhaps as much as, if not more so than, any of his peers, Captain Stamp had recognized the future province's potential, its almost limitless treasury of natural resources. Where others had feared to tread, he had rushed in to build sawmills, steamboats and buildings, and had gambled upon a new process for the canning of salmon.

What kind of a man was he? As noted, Vancouver authors Morley and Nichol have dealt rather harshly with Stamp in their respective efforts. In *From Milltown to Metropolis*, Morley has referred to him as the "bumbling, fuming Captain Stamp."

"Well connected, hand-in-glove with the Victoria political clique, captain probably by courtesy (since he once bought a ship he was afraid to sail in) he had unfortunate intervals as a merchant in Victoria and a mill-owner on Alberni Canal..."

In all due respect to Mr. Morley, the reference to Stamp's title and the accusation that he was afraid of the sea is quite inaccurate, Stamp having earned distinction for having saved his command, the troopship *Emu*, from destruction in a savage gale during the Crimean campaign. However, in all fairness, it should be mentioned that, once, when personally commanding the tugboat *Isabel*, Stamp ran out of fuel and got lost in the Gulf Islands!

Mr. Morley seems to base his judgement of Stamp upon the fact that that tycoon filed the "inlet's first civil lawsuit" over the faulty shipment of an important piece of machinery for his mill. He also noted that Stamp fought a mining company over its right to sink a test hole near False Creek—this, despite the fact that his lease covered timber only.

Stamp also had protested the right to a timber lease near Brockton Point. This time, even Governor Seymour was exasperated and wrote: "Captain Stamp has given us a great deal of trouble."

In his more recent *Vancouver*, Eric Nichol also inclines to the opinion that Captain Stamp was, to say the least, difficult. Both authors, however, credit his role as one of Vancouver's founding fathers.

Such views tend to make one wonder at Stamp's widely-touted respectability as a businessman, the presentation of the gold watch by his workers at Alberni, the ease with which he won election in Victoria and in Lillooet, and the public expressions of sadness at his death. What was the true measure of Captain Edward Stamp?

Perhaps, a century after, we should content ourselves with the tribute that was paid him upon the building of his three-storey office block in Victoria. Voiced the *Colonist* at that time: "When so many here systematically decry the country and endeavor to shake the faith of capitalists in its future it is gratifying to see men of colonial experience like Captain Stamp thus silencing the voice of the country's calumniators."

So be it!   ●

In a South Wellington cottage such as these, John Dalton found his daughter's body. She had been shot three times.

THE FIDDLING MURDERER

Although he maintained his innocence until the very end, the case against Robert Featherstone was overwhelming. But he faced his fate bravely and, in the little death cell, played ragtime music and danced a jig for his guards.

AS the aging year of 1906 creaked towards its finale, British Columbians looked forward to the approaching holiday season. But for at least one man—Robert Styles Featherstone—that Christmas Day would never arrive.

For, while Victorians prepared for the festivities, Featherstone whiled away his final hours on earth in a cell of the provincial jail on Topaz. On the morning of December 12, he would take the last few steps to the gallows and pay the ultimate penalty for the murder of Mary Jane Dalton.

As his final hours sped by, Featherstone awaited his end calmly, maintaining his innocence as carpenters put the finishing touches to the scaffold. By the evening of December 10, they were almost done, and hangman Radcliffe completed his own last-minute preparations.

Throughout his waiting, Featherstone stoutly denied his guilt. When a visitor was ushered into his little cell, he swore: "They've doomed me; but I tell you, they're hanging an innocent man." When un-

disturbed, he labored with pen and paper, compiling a rambling statement in which he refuted the evidence which had damned him during his trial, two months before. Upon completion he handed the fulscap document, in a sealed envelope, to Rev. J. Grundy, his spiritual advisor. To be opened after sentence was carried out, officials and the public could only wonder as to the envelope's contents. The latter, at least, assured by rumor that Featherstone intended to make a statement on the gallows, waited almost impatiently for the final scene, when, it was hoped, he might shed more light on the crime which had shocked and appalled British Columbians for more than six months.

Then, seemingly relieved of a heavy burden, Featherstone's spirits, despite his approaching date with Radcliffe, improved immensely. Facing his fate with outward calm, he admitted, "There's no use in prolonging the agony," and, to pass the time, amused himself with a violin borrowed from a guard.

(Left) *Moments after sentence was carried out, Dr. J.S. Helmcken, as prison physician, pronounced the convicted murderer to be dead.*
(Above) *When Robert Featherstone was arrested, miners such as these—"men grown white-haired in the district"—repeatedly rushed the prisoner until wiser heads prevailed.*
(Right) *The Vancouver Island community of Wellington, whose residents were shocked by the cold-blooded murder of pretty Mary Jane Dalton.*

There, in his tiny, third-storey death cell, Featherstone played ragtime and dance music, mostly in the form of jigs, the lively tunes striking a discordant note in the grim corridors of Hillside Jail. Cheered by his own music, the condemned man willingly entertained the guard who shared his cell around the clock, sometimes interrupting his solos with a dance step. And as Robert Featherstone danced, ate heartily and played away the hours, his appointment with eternity drew nearer. . . .

The tragedy of Mary Jane Dalton and her fiddling murderer began on the warm Saturday afternoon of July 21 at South Wellington. Upon returning home, John Dalton had discovered his attractive daughter, Mary Jane, dead on the floor of their home, her "fair hair in a pool of her blood, and the mark of a revolver bullet on her forehead."

Upon the horrified watchman's raising the alarm, neighbors rushed in. When police arrived, they soon noted that, while Miss Dalton had been shot in the forehead, other shots had been fired, as evidenced by bullet holes in the woodwork. Signs of a struggle indicated that the girl died defending her honor, her wrists having been badly bruised in the fatal contest.

First reports of the tragedy indicated that little genuine police work was initially involved, Chief Constable Dave Stephenson, after examining the body with the coroner, Dr. L. T. Davis, proceeding straight to the neighboring boarding house occupied by Featherstone, head sawyer at the Wellington mill. Accompanied by a large and excited crowd, Stephenson found the wavy-haired, goateed suspect collapsed on his bed, fully clothed, in a drunken stupor.

Striding to his bedside, Stephenson rudely awakened him with a shake. As the befuddled sawyer rubbed his eyes, the chief constable tersely informed him that he was under arrest. When the

suspect asked why, Stephenson replied: "For the murder of Mary Jane Dalton."

"Murder in the first degree?" queried Featherstone. Stephenson then repeated the charge, at which the suspect protested "vehemently" that he had not committed any crime, then refused to say more. Curiously, a newspaper reported, "He did not seem to realize that it was for the murder of Mary Dalton that he was being arrested, but thought it was on some other charge preferred from the last place he worked, which was at Sumas, Wash."

A search of his room turned up a handkerchief with what appeared to be fresh bloodstains, and a .38 calibre revolver. According to witnesses, Featherstone had been seen at 3 o'clock that afternoon with a loaded revolver. The seized weapon proved to be empty.

Featherstone later told arresting officers that, the previous evening, he had gone to Nanaimo with some South Wellington cronies for a drinking spree, and spent the night in a hotel room with an unidentified woman.

This story police could readily believe as, since his arrival in South Wellington, three weeks before, the new head sawyer had shown himself to be a determined tippler. Upon word of his arrest, a crowd of excited Wellington residents gathered in groups on street corners, it being reported that a crowd of "sturdy oldtimers—men grown white-haired in (the) district—made a demonstration against the prisoner. Repeatedly, old friends of heartbroken John Dalton rushed at the prisoner and it would have feared ill for the handcuffed man if wiser heads had not stepped in and interfered. . . ."

Two days later, Featherstone appeared in police court, where the authorities presented a case built entirely upon circumstantial—but overwhelming—evidence. Undoubtedly the most damaging circumstance, although superficial, was Featherstone's face. Scratched and bruised, it seemed to substantiate the theory that Mary Jane had fought valiantly for her life. Other marks on his hands indicated that, according to cautious medical testimony, the girl had used both nails and teeth.

According to a Mrs. Dick, Featherstone—drunk, and brandishing a revolver "fiercely"—had entered her bedroom early on Saturday morning. He had mentioned Mary Jane, having been introduced to the pretty girl by her father, at the mill. John Dalton, upon recalling their meeting, then remembered that, upon Mary Jane's departure, Featherstone had watched her walk away, seemingly unable to take his eyes from her.

Featherstone, meanwhile, was reported to be "nervous" and silent, although firm as to his innocence. Detailed medical testimony indicated that the dead girl had been shot not once but three times, the last shot, in the forehead, being fired point-blank as she lay on the floor. The first had struck her in the body, the second in the back of the head. All wounds would have inflicted almost instant death.

The following day, a startling statement attributed to the prisoner seemed to seal his fate. According to the manager of the South Wellington Lumber Company, Featherstone had informed him that, on the afternoon of Mary Dalton's murder, as he had passed the Dalton home, there had been "a hell of a row going on." Mary and her father, he said, had been quarrelling and there would be "something doing" before long. Investigation of Featherstone's story showed it to be totally ficticious, John Dalton having been in Nanaimo on Saturday.

That afternoon, Mary Jane Dalton was laid to rest before a large crowd of relatives, friends and curious onlookers. Earlier, the mourners had been excited by reports that a number of spent .38 cartridges— the same calibre as the gun taken from Featherstone —had been recovered from in front of the Dalton home. Other reports placed the accused man, on the fatal afternoon, in South Wellington where, according to witnesses, he had displayed a revolver and had boasted of having killed a man. His landlord and landlady reported that he had not been too drunk Saturday, having dined with them as usual.

As for Featherstone, it was reported that he had "nothing to say and does not seem unduly nervous, other than a man naturally would who was charged with such a crime."

The preliminary hearing began a week after with Superintendent of British Columbia Provincial Police Fred Hussey watching the case for the crown, Russel Simpson acting for the defence. Little new evidence was revealed, other than the testimony of mill superintendent Karl Berg, who stated that, about 10 days before the murder, Featherstone had told him about having just met Miss Dalton, and had expressed "some evil designs on the girl." Twice

afterward, the sawyer had made remarks of a similar nature. On another occasion, shortly before Mary Jane was shot, Featherstone had seen her walk by and remarked, "There goes my girl."

The accused also had "jollied" John Dalton about becoming his son-in-law, although there had been no apparent relationship between him and the girl.

Earlier, authorities had confirmed the rumor that Featherstone had been, of all things, a Mountie. Described by his employers as being one of the best sawyers in the business, the suspect, according to Superintendent Hussey, would, due to his police background, prove to be a tough nut to crack. Featherstone would, thought the policeman, "be very canny and act with caution." Remarkably, the hard-drinking sawyer's background had held another surprise for investigators, who learned that he had been a gold medalist graduate from a leading Michigan optical college. Such was the man charged with the brutal murder of lovely young Mary Jane Dalton.

The preliminary hearing continued to play before a full house in Nanaimo, the courtroom being crowded "almost to suffocation by an immense number of people, the majority of whom were curious to get a glimpse of the man accused of a horrible murder." Questioned by Superintendent Hussey, Dr. O'Brien described the cuts and scratches on the back of Featherstone's hands, which he had examined shortly after the man's arrest. Although he would not comment definitely as to their origin, he thought it probable that they had been made five or six hours before. Pressed further by the defence he admitted that he thought the scratches to have been wider than would have been caused by a girl fending off an attacker.

Chief Constable Stephenson, the arresting officer, then described the revolver which he had taken from Featherstone's room, and the cartridges found near the murder scene. The Ivor Johnson double-action .38, he said, had been recently fired. Victoria gunsmith W.N. Lenfesty stated that he had examined the weapon in question, that the shells found in Featherstone's room and in front of the Dalton home were of the same manufacture and calibre, although of a standard make.

At the final sitting of the hearing, held in the packed Miner's Hall in South Wellington, Featherstone remained silent at his counsel's instruction. Finally, on the evening of August 3, Magistrate Yarwood committed him to the October assizes for the murder of Mary Jane Dalton.

On October 19, Featherstone's trial opened in Nanaimo, a reporter describing the prisoner as "looking well and dressed in a new tweed suit and spotless linen, and with clear eye and brisk step." Although Russell Simpson continued as defence counsel, Colonel F.B. Gregory of Victoria had assumed charge of his case, Deputy Attorney-General MacLean acting for the crown.

The single new development in the case came in the form of a ban by Mr. Justice A. Morrison of evidence "relating to the moral character of Featherstone." Given by a Miss Meredith, the nature of her testimony was deemed to be "too offensive" for publication.

Finally it was Featherstone's turn in the witness box, where he read a lengthy statement which outlined his movements on the day of the slaying, and in which he claimed to have seen Miss Dalton arguing with another man, a stranger, shortly before she was murdered. Then the jury retired, to return 25 minutes later with their verdict. As the ex-Mountie, ex-sawyer, ex-optician carefully studied the faces of his peers, Foreman Jones pronounced him guilty of first degree murder.

Without so much as a quiver of the lip, or the flicker of an eyelid, Featherstone squared his shoulders and, jaw thrust forward, faced the jury in mute defiance, a reporter terming his ramrod posture and stoic silence as demonstrating "more of his Mounted Police training than he has shown since his arrest."

In a clear, unwavering voice which "penetrated to the farthest corner of the room," Featherstone declared: "I am in the same position as Captain Dreyfus, and am apparently unable to prove that I am innocent. I am unable to prove it, but as God is my witness, I am not guilty of this charge."

Asked if he had anything further to say, he merely refuted the evidence of mill superintendent Karl Berg, who had testified that he had passed an unsavory remark upon seeing Mary Dalton. Berg, he said, had perjured himself. He then listened impassively as sentence was passed and marched out of the courtroom, between his guards, "with a determined air."

Thus Robert Featherstone's December 12 date with the hangman in the "common jail" on Topaz.

As the hours ticked by and the carpenters completed their grim assignment, Featherstone amused himself, and his constant companions, with his borrowed violin and dancing. But, for all of his apparent cheerfulness, he could not deny some anxiety. At one point he informed his guard that, during the night, he had been visited by his dead mother, who instructed him to refuse all food; that by so doing he would, by some unexplained miracle, be reprieved. Consequently, for several days, he neither ate nor drank, until, famished, he received another nocturnal visitor; this time a dead brother, who told him that toast would be permissible. Before long he was eating normally and heartily.

Under the spiritual care of Rev. Grundy, Featherstone developed an abiding interest in the Bible, although his spiritual beliefs were described as being "strange notions." As for the future, he expressed full confidence in a "spiritland" where he would join the ranks of angels in eternity—after he had settled earthly accounts in Nanaimo, South Wellington and

The old provincial jail in Victoria where, on the third floor of the main block, Robert Featherstone, ex-Mountie, ex-honors student, ex-sawyer, and murderer, whiled away his remaining hours by playing his borrowed violin and dancing.

Vancouver.

On the appointed morning, Featherstone was led into the jailyard where hangman Radcliffe and officials awaited him. Mounting the gallows steps with "marked coolness," the convicted murderer faced the end with what one witness described as greater composure than that of those in charge. Asked if he had anything to say, he vowed: "I now declare with my dying breath that I am innocent of the murder of Mary Jane Dalton. I further state that I die in the communion of the Church of England."

From a window overlooking the scene, John Dalton and a son watched the brief ceremony, having been admitted at their own request. Earlier, Dalton had asked to speak with Featherstone, but had been refused.

Standing with Rev. Grundy, Dr. J.S. Helmcken watched silently in his capacity as prison physician. Moments later, Radcliffe released the trap and sentence was carried out.

Upon doctors Helmcken and Hanington pronouncing him dead, his last declaration was opened and read:

"I write the following statement, and it is my dying request that you will have it published for the information of the public. It is this: That I am innocent of the charge of murdering Mary Jane Dalton. I make this statement fully believing in a peaceful hereafter, and I ask my Heavenly Father to judge me when I stand before Him according to the truthfulness or falsity of the above statement.

Robert S. Featherstone." ●

*Father Pat, they called him. Rev Henry Irwin
was neither Patrick nor Catholic, merely Irish.
But to the hundreds of miners, railway construction
workers and settlers throughout British Columbia,
the name Father Pat was one that would unlock any door.*

INTO THE VALLEY

"THE strangest funeral procession that ever passed on earth"—of all the wild and wonderful incidents of a remarkable career, this, according to Rev. Henry Irwin—"Father Pat"—was indeed the "most weird."

Of the many extraordinary men who pioneered the British Columbia wilderness as missionaries, surely Father Pat was the most extraordinary of them all. To this day, he is fondly remembered and so many stories have grown around him that it is difficult to separate fact from fiction.

But there is no disputing that Henry Irwin was every bit as colorful and as exciting as the legends. In

fact, of him it could be said that he was bigger than life.

Although his Christian name was Henry, and he was an Anglican, rather than a Catholic, the miners christened him Father Pat because he was Irish. For that matter, Irwin treated one and all equally, regardless of religious belief. And when, as occasionally happened, he met a skeptic who chose to argue his case with fist, Father Pat was ready, willing and able to oblige.

Born August 2, 1859, the son of a vicar, Irwin was schooled in Dublin to be a missionary, during which time he excelled in sports. This background

When snowploughs failed to clear the track, it was time to rely on the oldest machine in the world, muscle power. This locomotive is merely bogged down by the snow. Others were not as fortunate, being swept from tracks, their crews and passengers crushed or buried alive.

OF DEATH

was to prove invaluable when, years after, and half a world away, he carried the word of God through the wild, woolly and isolated camps of British Columbia.

This career began in 1885, after his service as curate at Rugby, when he was assigned to serve as an assistant to the Bishop of New Westminster. Once in the Royal City, he was sent on to Kamloops, where he embarked upon what was to become a lifelong crusade of administering to the spiritual, and oftimes material, comforts of the miners, railway workers and settlers scattered throughout the British Columbia Interior. . . .

With the coming of the Canadian Pacific Railway,

the boom camp of Donald had appeared on the map and it was in this brawling, bustling settlement that Irwin built a church. And it was near here, so many years ago, that he recorded details of the "strangest funeral procession that ever passed on earth."

"I must write you a line to tell you of one of the most weird things you ever heard of and what I have just gone through today," Irwin wrote to a friend one evening. "A few days ago up here in the Selkirk an avalanche came thundering down Mount Carrol, and came right across the valley and struck the track, turned right up grade and smashed into two

Snow country. Here, high in the Selkirks, Father Pat led an expedition to recover the body of a railwayman killed when his train was buried in an avalanche. "Fancy avalanches rumbling and thundering around," he wrote a friend, "and 12 men trailing across the hills with a coffin swinging on a pole as fast as he could across the 200 yards between the (snow) sheds. . . ."

engines and the snowplough, burying them completely, and 16 men with them. Nothing was to be seen of them but the end of the plow and the smokestack of one engine, which was buried up altogether.

"Well, the slide came down upon the men who were watching it come down the other side before any of them could escape. Of course, when the few men who were around saw this, they set in digging and got out ten, but six of the poor fellows were killed. The men dared not go on digging for long, as avalanches were coming down all around them, and they were in peril of their lives. It was a strange scene, and a heartrending one, too. They now have got all the bodies out. One of them was the husband of a poor woman in Donald whom I knew. I had to break the news to her and as there was no one to hurry up things, I started for Donald yesterday, and after a ride of 12 miles on an engine, I got to Bear Creek last evening late."

Early the next morning he and his companions had pushed on to the camp where the bodies of the avalanche victims were being kept. With 10 men to pack the coffin containing the remains of his friend's husband, he began the return trip to town, as further snowslides continued to roar down about them. ". . .I think of all queer frisks," he marvelled, "this day's was the greatest I ever had."

Encumbered by their heavy clothing, snowshoes and the weighty coffin, the burial party was forced to run from one snow shelter to another, while keeping close watch on the mountainside so as to time their sprints between the avalanches, whose thundering roar resembled an artillery barrage and almost deafened them.

Describing their awesome "frisk" of nature to his friend, Irwin explained that the avalanches were preceded by this roaring and flurries of snow which "always told us when they came. . .exactly like artillery booming away, (with) the smoke curling from the guns, and true to the simile, the great snow or ice balls came thundering down with all the rightful force of cannonballs."

In short, it was a frightened funeral procession that memorable day in the Selkirks.

"Well," he continued, "we had to climb over slides between the snowslides, and that by a bad trail, over perhaps 30 feet of snow and trees, and you fancy that those 200 or 300 yards did not take us long to make. The scene of the accident was too awful and too weird to describe: all snow around, piled up 100 feet, and there down in the hole, the engines, and the graves of the poor six, one of whom we had put in a coffin, and start back along that fearful hillside, and run all the risks again.

"That was the strangest funeral procession that ever passed on earth. Fancy avalanches rumbling and thundering around, and 12 men trailing across the hills with a coffin swinging on a pole, every man listening for the avalanche above him and going as

(Above) *After service as curate at Rugby, Irwin was assigned to serve as an assistant to the Bishop of New Westminster, then was sent to Kamloops where he began a lifelong crusade of administering to the spiritual and material needs of pioneer British Columbians.*
(Left) *Father Pat.*

fast as he could across the 200 yards between the sheds. I can tell you, it made one think of the 600 ride into the valley of death. However, thank God, we got through all safe, but we don't have to do it again. I am going to Donald tomorrow with the coffin."

Days later, in a second letter, Father Pat continued his amazing, and hair-raising, account of escorting the railroadman's body to Donald. But, before describing the final lap of his journey, the missionary again impressed upon his friend the horrors of that funeral procession across the snow, and called it the "weirdest funeral that the wildest imagination could paint." Even at the time of his writing the second letter, when safe in Donald, Irwin continued to relive every terrifying moment of that mad race down the mountain slopes, between snow shed and snowslide.

"You can only think of great, gigantic heights up to 4,000 feet above you, and some 20 feet of snow on the hillsides; then to hear the rumbling like a roll of thunder; you see the smoke rolling from guns and the slide rushes into the gulch below you at 100 miles a minute. No place can give you a better idea of the power of nature and the powerlessness of man. There is no railroad to be seen; the only things to mark the line (are) the tops of telegraph poles or the butt ends here and there where they have been

turned endwise. . . ."

Suffice to say, each and every man of the heroic party had been relieved and thankful to have escaped from "the valley of death" without injury. Those waiting for them also were relieved, as they had witnessed three of the larger slides, and had feared for their safety. For, as all were aware, there was no rescue for a man caught in an avalanche as "they are as solid as granite and just as heavy."

On Sunday morning Irwin decided that it was safe to begin the 28-mile trek along the railway line to Donald with his grim cargo. Dividing his volunteers into three six-man teams, he stationed them at various locations along the route, each taking turns to pull the toboggan with its coffin to the next relay point as Father Pat took his turn on the towline, or broke trail through three feet of packed snow.

Throughout the morning and early afternoon, they struggled on towards Donald at the rate of two miles per hour. At 4 o'clock they met three locomotives plowing their way up the hill. On their return trip, the funeral party was able to hitch a ride for eight miles to a way station, where Irwin wired to Donald for another train. Hours later, the relief train picked them up for the run into Donald, arriving about midnight.

Sighed Irwin: "That was the hardest Sunday's work I've ever done, and (I) hope it will be the last I'll have to (do) of that kind. Of course, I should not have done it unless the poor wife was here fretting her heart away that her husband's body was lying miles away in the snow."

Such, then, was the story of the "strangest" funeral procession—and the measure of a wonderful man, Rev. Henry Irwin—Father Pat. ●

Your Friend,
Edward Gowan

1

2

3

4

(1) Edward "Ned" McGowan, the notorious typesetter, lawyer, politician and badman. Upon life in California becoming "unendurable," he wrote years after, he had headed for the gold fields of British Columbia. His stay in the future province was brief but memorable. After a lifetime of adventure he died in San Francisco in 1893, a garrulous, penniless and pious old man.
(2) Lieutenant Richard Mayne, RN. Originally dispatched to Yale to put down armed insurrection, he and Colonel Moody found that the troubles were virtually over. After McGowan was fined for assault, he generously invited Moody, Mayne and Judge Begbie to a champagne supper, Mayne recalling: ". . .All things considered, I have rarely lunched with better spoken, pleasanter company."
(3) As Colonel Moody headed upriver to Yale aboard the Ss Enterprise, Governor James Douglas met the emergency with a hundred marines, seamen and a field-piece.
(4) Stage preparing to leave for the Cariboo from Barnard's Express office in Yale. Yale's importance as a mining town soon died, although the town enjoyed a second boom during the construction of the CPR. Once again the town became a rip-roaring recreation centre for transients, and recaptured something of the excitement of the day when California desperado Ned McGowan almost sparked a war.

NED McGOWAN'S WAR

Informed that the notorious Ned McGowan was leading a rebellion, Governor James Douglas responded with a hundred marines, bluejackets and a field-piece as Colonel Moody ordered Captain Grant to march on Yale.

NOT all of those attracted to British Columbia by the lure of gold were of sterling character and welcome immigrants to this untamed land. For, hard on the heels of the miner and merchant came the camp followers. Gamblers, thieves, fallen women—and considerably worse—they, too, headed for the riches of the Fraser River.

Unlike the prospectors, these fortune hunters had no intention of stooping to honest toil with pick and shovel. Rather, they hoped to mine the miners with all the temptations of human vice, from loaded cards to loaded gun.

One of the worst—certainly one of the most spectacular—of this motley army was the ubiquitous Ned McGowan. Although his stay in British Columbia was brief, his influence on the provincial course was memorable. For few of the thousands who flocked to Fraser River created so much excitement as the California badman who sparked a "war."

Philadelphia-born of Irish parents, Ned began his tempestuous career promisingly enough by serving an apprenticeship as a typesetter with a printing firm. Young Edward soon proved himself to be fast, hard-working and reliable—the very antithesis of the Ned McGowan of later years—and to all appearances was an honest and up-and-coming young man.

His future as such seemed even more assured when, in 1835, he began to study law. But it was during this period that he also became involved in politics. Here, he quickly demonstrated a natural ability as a speaker and behind-the-scenes manipulator of the Democratic Party. Naturally flamboyant, charming and ambitious, he found the rough and tumble arena of politics far more satisfying and rewarding than either printing or law. Senior Democrats were quick to see his potential and, in 1847, after serving three terms as District Clerk, Ned McGowan was nominated as the party's candidate for a seat in the Pennsylvania legislature. Elected, he again demonstrated his flair for politics by acting as opposition spokesman.

To McGowan, politicking was a war and, even when giving a speech, he went for the Republican jugular. Time and again he viciously attacked the governor, until the editor of the *State Gazette* denounced his muck-raking in a strongly-worded editorial. Ned, who had proven himself to be a master at dishing it out, then proved that he lacked the most essential attribute of a true politician—a thick skin.

He showed this dramatically and violently the day after the editorial, which had called him a bully, by stabbing the *Gazette's* editor. Luckily for all concerned, the editor lived and McGowan, rather than going to jail for attempted murder, enjoyed the full support of the Democrats, who were able to pull the necessary strings. Ned, after resigning his seat, simply left town until the excitement subsided— later returning to Philadelphia as big as life to be made a captain of police.

It may seem an odd role for a would-be murderer, but such was politics in the good old days. Ned, no longer hindered by having to keep up appearances as a legislator, now devoted himself to having a good time. But wine, women and song are a costly pursuit, even for a corrupt police officer and, before long, Ned was in need of money. His solution to this problem became a matter of public record when the erstwhile captain of police vanished immediately after the robbery of a bank. When found, McGowan was disguised as a sheep-herder and loaded down with the bank loot. Arrested, he was quickly arraigned for trial. This time there was no back-room finagling to save him and, upon being convicted, Ned had to escape and head West.

By, this time the great rush was on to California and Ned joined the human exodus to the gold fields. He found his own brand of El Dorado in San Francisco, which was then in the iron grip of a corrupt regime. Upon excercising the political skills he had learned in Philadelphia, Ned quickly rose to the top, being elected an Associate Justice of the

Court of Sessions. He then received a gubernatorial appointment ot the post of Commissioner of Immigrants. Lest anyone from back east question the commissioner's integrity, Judge McGowan even had the territorial legislature pass a special bill declaring his bank robbery conviction to be null and void.

For all of their power, McGowan's powerful associates were not unopposed. Spearheading a reform movement was a newspaper editor named James King, who published the *Evening Bulletin* and daily assaulted the administration. Formerly a banker, King had lost his fortune but not his reputation for integrity, and, through his newspaper, he daily called for a clean-up campaign, among those taking the brunt of his editorials being Judge McGowan. McGowan's team had its own organ, the *Sunday Times*. The city's largest newspaper, it was edited by one of his compatriots, James Casey.

Like McGowan, Casey also came under attack of the *Bulletin*, which, in the spring of 1856, went so far as to publish details of Casey's criminal background. Casey, infuriated by the editorial, stormed into King's office. The two argued violently until Casey left, when King returned to work. At the end of the day, King left his office and began to walk home, as usual, along Montgomery Street. He was approaching the Banker's Exchange, a popular saloon, when he was accosted by Casey.

As King stopped in surprise, Casey drew a revolver from under the coat which was draped over his shoulder and told him to defend himself. Before King could so much as open his mouth to argue, Casey fired. As the dying editor fell to the sidewalk, Casey calmly surrendered to two police officers who had magically appeared at his side and was led away.

From across the street, Judge McGowan and a crony named John Bagley, who also had been vilified in the *Bulletin*, had witnessed the tragedy. Moments later, they went their way.

But the cold-blooded murder of James King was the long-awaited spark for reform. For months, respectable and prominent citizens had become increasingly enraged by the corruption all about them. Within hours of King's shooting, the Vigilantes were on the march and the famous purge of San Francisco's lawless elements underway.

One of their prime targets was the honorable Judge Ned McGowan, who immediately went into hiding when informed that the vigilantes had learned of his role in King's murder. For investigation showed that he and Bagley had virtually staged the shooting by providing King with Casey's criminal record, and the outraged Casey with a loaded revolver. Quite aware of what would happen to him if he fell into the hands of the vigilantes, Ned went underground. Unable to leave the city, he hid in the room of a friend. For 10 days and nights he cowered in the little apartment, and peeked through the curtains at the vigilantes' headquarters, which were in full view of his hiding place. Daily, he saw friends and associates, including James Casey, escorted into the building for quick trial and dispatch. Those found guilty of more serious crimes were promptly dealt with at the end of a rope—a fate which did nothing to ease McGowan's state of mind.

Then, disguised as a priest, he made his way through the vigilantes who were scouring the city for him, and continued to Santa Barbara where, despite being betrayed by a friend, he slipped across the border into Mexico and waited for the vigilantes to lose interest in him. Months later, he turned up in Sacramento. There, safe from justice in the Bay City, he made his headquarters at the Magnolia Saloon and entertained a large following of hangers-ons with stories of his daring escape from the vigilantes. For that matter, Sacramento seemed like a second home to the judge, as many of his fellow refugees from justice had sought refuge there. When asked by a Sacramento newspaper about his disappearance, McGowan cheekily replied that he was afraid that he would be seized by "the Vigilance Committee's sheriffs, and that these well-meaning but mistaken gentlemen would hang me as a felon before an honest man could be found who knew me and could prove my innocence."

This was the "ubiquitous" Ned McGowan who was shortly to make his presence felt in British Columbia. But before seeking his fortune in a foreign land, Ned exhausted every effort to whitewash his past. Through influential contacts in the California Legislature, he won a change of venue from San Francisco to the wide-open settlement of Napa City, where, assured of acquittal by judge and jury bought and paid for, he willingly presented himself for trial in the murder of James King. At this time, Napa was notorious as a haven for the criminal elements of the whole territory and resembled, as the San Francisco *Bulletin* moaned of Sacramento during McGowan's stay there, "one of the Jewish cities of refuge, where murderers and other criminals could flee for shelter from the avengers of blood."

The *Bulletin,* not unnaturally, was embittered by the murder of its editor, and rightfully denounced Ned's trial as a farce: "Ned McGowan, the cunning but cowardly and unprincipled man who has played so conspicuous a part in the villainy that has heretofore been practised in this city, the tool and accomplice of equally as guilty parties now in our midst, has at last been caged in Napa, and is undergoing a farce of a trial, which is only intended to create sympathy for a hardened wretched, totally unfit to be loosed on society.

"Nearly three months since, this fugitive from justice made his appearance on the public streets of Sacramento. Under the eye of the very governor who claims to have offered a reward for his apprehension, he was suffered, although under the indictment of a grand jury, to roam at large, hold levees, and be lionized by men of the same stripe. He was not only persuaded to ask for special legislation in his behalf, but members seemed eager to obtain his favor by granting his request; and he was permitted to occupy a seat within the bar of the assembly, during the sessions, by the side of a boon companion."

Acquitted of any complicity in King's slaying—the court ruled that King died as the result of the doctor's treatment rather than Casey's bullet—McGowan, who now revelled in the role of a public hero, and was delighted by newspaper accounts of his escape from persecution in which he had been termed "ubiquitous," returned to San Francisco to publish a newspaper under this name. The scandal sheet failed within months. San Francisco had changed since the lawless days before the vigilantes and, although legally acquitted of the one and only criminal charge against him, he no longer fitted in. It was time to seek fresher fields, greater challenges, greater fortunes—a decision made all the sooner when a would-be assassin took a shot at him, the bullet passing through the lapel of his coat.

It was time to head for British Columbia.

The discovery of gold on the Fraser River, as shown in preceding chapters, caught the future province ill-prepared for the onslaught of humanity which followed the latest rainbow. Among the vanguard was the illustrious Judge Ned McGowan (who, until his dying day, continued to use this "honorary" title). Upon making his way to Hill's Bar, then the richest and busiest camp, he soon found himself a popular leader of the local mining community and the owner of one of the best-paying claims. Nightly, Ned held court before the inevitable following of barflies and idlers.

Even without a rich claim, Hill's Bar was the likely headquarters for Ned McGowan. Situated just over a mile downstream from Fort Yale, Hill's Bar had mushroomed into a shantytown in the months following the discovery of gold by James Moore and companions. It would in fact prove to be the richest of all Fraser River sandbars, yielding more than $2 million. As it had attracted the first influx of miners, most of whom were American and little inclined to respect British authority, Hill's Bar had also provided Governor James Douglas with his first major challange upon the discovery of gold. Faced with what amounted to an invasion by Americans, Douglas—who, as Governor of Vancouver Island and Chief Factor for the Hudson's Bay Company, had no legal jurisdiction on the mainland—gambled that the colonial secretary would support him when informed of his actions, and issued a proclaimation of authority over the gold fields. To enforce his ultimatum, he appointed George Perrier as magistrate for Hill's Bar, and Henry Hickson as constable. For bustling Fort Yale he named Captain P.B. Whannell justice of the peace, George Donnellan chief of police.

As envisioned by Douglas, both Perrier and Whannell had their own areas of authority. In cases where their jurisdictions overlapped, he expected them to cooperate with each other for the common good. He did not envision the spirit of rivalry which existed between the two camps, or the lengths to which their respective keepers of the peace would go.

But he soon found out. On Christmas Day, 1858, Isaac Dixon, a negro barber in Yale, was pistol-whipped (over a bottle of hair oil) by a miner named Farrell from Hill's Bar. J.P. Whannell quickly issued a warrant for Farrell's arrest, only to be informed that the miner had returned to Hill's Bar. He then ordered a constable to proceed downstream and to arrest Farrell. Because of the competition between the camps, however, Magistrate Perrier rejected Whannell's warrant and—in answer to Farrell's counter-charge that Dixon had, in fact assaulted him

—ordered Constable Hickson to arrest the barber at Yale!

Then, what had begun as petty rivalry became a comedy of errors. Upon reaching Yale, Hickson found that Whannell, so as to insure that nothing happened to his witness, had placed him in protective custody. When Hickson presented his warrant for Dixon's arrest, Whannell was so infuriated by Perrier's disrespect for his authority, and Hickson's insolence, that he had the constable arrested for contempt of (his) court and "insubordination," and thrown into jail with the hapless Dixon!

This move not only marked the height of folly but a first in British jurisprudence, and prompted Magistrate Perrier to make an even more drastic and foolish move. After issuing a warrant for Whannel's arrest on a charge of contempt of court, he swore in a 20-man posse of special constables and placed it under the command of the esteemed Ned McGowan. McGowan, with all of the enthusiasm he

(Above and below) *Various views of the old mining settlement of Yale. After the short-lived "war," Justice of the Peace Whannell resigned before notice of his dismissal could reach him.*

usually showed for the side of the law and order, proceeded to Yale with his small army of special constables. There, they found Captain Whannell's court in session and, without so much as knocking, marched into the courtroom and placed the astonished justice of the peace in custody. As the protesting Whannell was led away, McGowan had his men release Constable Hickson.

Perrier enjoyed his vengeance the next day when Whannell was brought before him, found guilty, and fined $50. He was then released.

Perrier likely thought he had had the last laugh. He had not counted on Whannell's spite. Humiliated and beside himself with anger, the justice of the peace immediately wrote Governor Douglas of the incident. Forgoing all restraint, he denounced Perrier as being unfit for service in Her Majesty's Government, exaggerated McGowan's role in the affair, and painted a picture of open rebellion: "This town and district are in a state bordering on anarchy; my own and the lives of the citizens are in imminent peril. I beg your Excellency will afford us prompt aid. . . ."

Not content with this plea for assistance, Whannell dispatched a copy of his letter to Captain Grant of the Royal Engineers, who was camped at Derby, explaining that his troops could "easily be billeted in this town."

Likely it was the name Ned McGowan, rather than Whannell's hysteria, which prompted Colonel Richard Moody, commander of the Royal Engineers, to take immediate action. Alarmed that this notorious American was planning a rebellion against British authority, he did not even wait to hear from Douglas but ordered Captain Grant to march to Yale with 25 sappers. For his part, Douglas responded with no less alacrity and determination by ordering HMS *Plumper* to proceed to Colonel Moody's assistance with a hundred marines, seamen and a field-piece.

In the meantime, Moody, accompanied by Judge Begbie, was leading his men upriver aboard the steamer *Enterprise*. Hampered by ice in the river, their progress was slow and Moody became increasingly impatient as he had since been informed that McGowan and his "lawless band of ruffians," after occupying Yale by force, had shot Whannell and the town's police force.

If anyone else had been in command of Perrier's posse, neither Douglas nor Moody likely would have been provoked into over-responding to the emergency. But the judge's reputation was such that they were quite willing to believe the worst. It was not until the laboring *Enterprise* reached the mouth of the Harrison River that Moody encountered Billy Ballou, the legendary expressman. Fresh from Yale, Ballou quickly set Moody straight. Nevertheless he continued to push on to Yale. When the riverboat was turned back by low water at Umatilla Snag, they drifted down-river to the mouth of a creek where they sheltered for three days, as one of the passengers, a Hudson's Bay Company storekeeper, hiked overland to Yale. By the time the *Enterprise* was able to get underway again he had returned with confirmation that all was quiet in town.

The *Enterprise* was then overtaken by Lieutenant Mayne and nine men who had been sent ahead by Captain Richards when the *Plumper* was forced to anchor at Fort Langley. With the arrival of Lieutenant Mayne, Moody determined to proceed to Yale by whale-boat as the main of his force marched overland. Upon arriving at Hope, Moody decided that it would be best if, the next morning, just he, Begbie and Mayne completed the journey to Yale.

As expected, their arrival in the mining camp was without incident, the citizens greeting them civilly and without fanfare. They had not altogether forgotten or forgiven the emergency responsible for the officials' arrival, however, as, that very night, the miners held a meeting and passed several resolutions denouncing Magistrate Perrier's actions in the affair. The next morning, a Sunday, 30 or 40 miners attended a church service conducted in the court house by Colonel Moody. That done, all seemed peaceful and the crisis passed. Moody, Begbie and Mayne were about to leave town the following day when McGowan assaulted Dr. Fifer, a former member of the San Francisco Vigilance Committee.

It was nothing more than a case of bodily assault on the part of McGowan but Moody, determined to make a firm stand in the face of what he interpreted to be an intentional slight, ordered Lieutenant Mayne to hasten downstream and bring up the engineers under Captain Grant. These quickly marched on Yale and, early the next morning, the town awoke to find them lined along the riverbank in full dress uniform. Even the ubiquitous Ned McGowan could not mistake Moody's message and he hastened to the colonel with an apology for having assaulted Dr. Fifer. Turning on his vaunted charm, he convinced the colonel that, in arresting Whannell, he had only acted as a legally appointed special constable under the explicit instructions of the Hill's Bar magistrate. Moody had to agree, but this left the matter of the assault on Dr. Fifer. When McGowan magnanimously surrendered to the charge and pleaded guilty before Judge Begbie, he was fined $25 and released.

That done, all retired to Hill's Bar, where Ned conducted Moody, Mayne and Begbie on a tour of the diggings and even gave them a demonstration of gold panning, before inviting them to a champagne supper! The old McGowan charm had not failed him and, by evening, he had convinced his guests that all the stories they had heard about him were absolutely false. Lieutenant Mayne, in his reminiscences, admitted to having been completely won over by the Californian desperado. Although quite aware of McGowan's notoriety, he found him and his cohorts to be gentlemen and, "all things considered, I have rarely lunched with better spoken, pleasanter company."

And that was that. It was, in the opinion of one respected historian, "merely a squabble between two petty officials." In the view of Hill's Bar Constable Henry Hickson, the entire blame for the affair could be laid on Captain Whannell, whose "overbearing manner. . .together with his want of legal knowledge and gentlemanly deportment, totally unfit him for the office he had been appointed to, being more fit for a constable than a magistrate."

Not a shot had been fired, not a casualty marred the landscape (although it has been estimated that the affair cost the government $40,000). But Colonel Moody's show of strength had convinced McGowan that there was to be no leeway with British authority and he once again decided to move on. At least, this is the usual reason given for his abrupt departure. However, according to Chartres Brew, acting chief gold commissioner and chief inspector of police, Ned's decision to return to the United States resulted from an argument with his old friend and accomplice of San Francisco days, John Bagley. With the peaceful conclusion of the "war," Ned and George Perrier, who had been dismissed from his post, decided to celebrate. After promising Brew that they would keep the peace, they received permission to fire a salute of 100 "guns" from an anvil battery in honor of George Washington, and a further 10 as a compliment to Brew for his courtesy.

That night, a grand ball was held, Brew writing that, "The utmost harmony prevailed until the company went to supper, when some jealously arose about precedence for seats. A Mr. Bagly (sic), of Hill's Bar, abused McGowan and called him an old grey-headed scamp. McGowan immediately broke a plate on Bagly's head and Bagly, in return, broke McGowan's head with another plate.

"At once there was a general row and friends on both sides went off to get their pistols (Brew having stipulated that all guests check their weapons before the ball). But when they returned to the scene the affair had subsided into a demand for 'satisfaction' as soon as arrangements could be made."

As neither man, after their introduction to Moody and Begbie, was willing to fight a duel on British soil, it was agreed that they would cross the line into Washington Territory. The time and place were agreed upon and McGowan, to facilitate matters, wound up his affairs by selling his rich claim to a newcomer for "the paltry sum of $500." Before the duel could take place, McGowan and Bagley came to terms but Ned kept his resolve to quit the country.

In March of 1859, the Puget Sound *Herald*, published at Steilacoom, W.T., reported that he was heading for Mexico: "By the politeness of Mr. Saunders of this place, we are in possession of a private letter dated 7th March, from a friend in Victoria, who left Steilacoom about a fortnight since.

Likely it was the name Ned McGowan, rather than Whannell's hysteria, which prompted Colonel Moody to take immediate action. Alarmed that this notorious American was planning a rebellion, he ordered Captain John Marshall Grant, shown in this handsome portrait, to march to Yale with 25 sappers.

Judge Matthew Bailie Begbie. When McGowan pleaded guilty to a charge of having assaulted Dr. Fifer, he was fined $25. But he escaped all criminal liability for his part in the arrest of Justice of the Peace Whannell, pleading that he had been "regularly commissioned 'on her majesty's service' at the time."

Old Fort Langley where Captain Stamp and his men were stationed when they received Whannell's hysterical plea for rescue from "imminent peril."

We extract from the letter the following: 'Ned McGowan, Sam Banty and others, arrived here last night (6th inst.) from Hill's Bar. Ned is bound for Sonora by the first vessel, where he goes to meet his son George McGowan, who is *en route* for Sonora as a bearer of dispatches. Ned reports favorably of the mines; but hearing a man gas is one thing, and seeing the product of his labor is another. I saw the latter, which amounts to $47,000, all in dust. Pretty good for an old man of 50." (Other reports place his "poke" at $4,700).

Pretty good indeed for an old man of whom Chief Inspector Brew had previously reported that he "kept himself shut up and is seldom seen out," and of whom it was suspected that he spent much of his time drinking and gambling.

Whatever the source of McGowan's money (sadly, details of his obtaining and working his claim on Hill's Bar are virtually non-existent), he was no longer a source of trouble to Governor Douglas or anyone else above the 49th parallel. In fact, he seems to have troubled no one further, apparently having, with his new wealth, turned over a new leaf. When next British Columbians heard of him, five months later, he was serving in the duel capacity of lawyer and compositor in Tuscon, Arizona, where he was elected to Congress. Two years later it was reported that he had been killed by Apaches—not so, as he returned to Pennsylvania where, it would seem, all of his sins had been forgiven. Not only was his stabbing of the *Gazette's* editor forgotten, but he was made Sergeant-at-Arms in the House of Representatives!

A quarter of a century after his stormy stay in British Columbia, Ned gave his own version of that memorable period: "Life in California becoming unendurable, I went to Fraser's River, in British Columbia, at that time the scene of the tremendous mining excitement. While there I met with a singular and amusing adventure. In 'Hill's Bar' as our little mining town, largely settled by Californians, was called, there was an English magistrate who, though it sounds like a 'Paddyism' to say it, was a French-Canadian, a good fellow named Perier (sic). There was another English magistrate, a bona fide Britisher, this one at Fort Yale, a few miles away, who hated Americans, put on lots of dignity, insisted on the miners touching their hats to him, and was pretty generally disliked. He would have our boys arrested, and lock them up without due process of law, and make himself generally disagreeable. I represented to Perier that, taking a man from the jurisdiction of his court was a contempt of court, and that one magistrate could not be in contempt of another. Perier swore me in as a special officer of her majesty, and with a body of picked men I went over to Fort Yale, took the key from the jailer, and liberated all the Americans confined, and brought the objectionable magistrate a prisoner before his confrere Perier.

" 'What did you do with him?' (asked the reporter).

" 'Fined him $50 for contempt.'

" 'And the money?'

" 'Was spent in drinks for the crowd. It was a Christmas Eve and the miners were taking a holiday.'

" 'And so that ended it?'

" 'No, indeed. They sent for troops. Colonel Moody, afterwards Lieutenant-Governor Moody, was in command. I was arrested and tried for a breach of the peace. Judge Begbie, afterwards Sir Matthew Bailey Begbie, was on the bench. I made them put Perier on the stand, who testified that I was regularly commissioned "on her majesty's service" at the time of the alleged outrage. I got off, but Begbie denounced the proceedings as "a clever Yankee trick." ' "

In the early 1880s Ned returned to San Francisco, the scene of his near-escape from the Vigilance Committee and an assassin's bullet, almost 30 years before. It was there he died on June 4, 1893, a "garrulous, penniless (and) pious old man."

The incredible Lillian Alling poses with Bruno, whose stuffed carcass she carried with her throughout the Far North. He was, she said, her first companion.

Her route, 6,000 miles from New York City to Siberia, was as ridiculous as her means of travel. But by attempting the impossible Lillian Alling won immortality.

THE INCREDIBLE LILLIAN ALLING

SOME called her a heroine, a human homing pigeon. Others were less charitable; they said she was crazy.

Whatever the true definition of Lillian Alling, there is no dispute on one point: that she is one of the most, if not the most, incredible women ever to set foot in British Columbia.

For the young Russian woman, driven by some primeval need to return to her homeland, set out to do just that—by walking from New York City to Siberia. Her route, 6,000 miles long, was as ridiculous as her means of travel. But north, north to the top of the world, she went. Whether she ultimately achieved her goal is not known. But by attempting the impossible Lillian Alling, who sought anonymity throughout her odyssey, achieved immortality.

Even her background is a puzzle. It is known that, in 1927, she was about 25-years-old, a Russian national, apparently well educated, and working as a maid in New York. Upon becoming homesick for her native land, and unable to raise the price of a steamer ticker (or so she told an inquiring British Columbia Provincial Police officer) she determined to hike overland from New York to Siberia.

And this, after studying maps in the public library, she proceeded to do, apparently setting out early that year. With two $10 bills, a small packsack on her back, and dressed plainly, simply in skirt, shirt, jacket, headscarf and running shoes, she marched westward, at an average of 30 miles a day, passing through Chicago, Minneapolis St. Paul, then crossing the border and continuing through Winnipeg to Vancouver, where she headed northward to Siberia.

It was in British Columbia that her incredible attempt to hike to the Canadian Arctic first came to official attention when, on the autumn afternoon of September 10, 1927, she appeared at a lineshack of the British Columbia-Yukon Telegraph line. When lineman Bill Blackstock answered a knock on the door of Cabin 2, second in a chain of such cabins spaced about 20 miles apart, he was astonished to be greeted by a tiny young woman. Although she spoke English fluently, she had a strong Russian accent.

But it was not the woman's accent nor her sudden arrival in the middle of the wilderness that staggered the lineman. Rather, it was her appearance. For she was a walking scare-crow, her clothing virtually in shreds, her feet showing through the holes in her shoes. Blackstock quickly invited her into his cabin and without asking if she were hungry, prepared a meal. Only when she had finished, did he venture to ask her her name and destination. When Lillian calmly replied that she was on her way to Siberia, her host was shocked speechless.

Even then winter had begun to assert its hold on the northland. Soon it would begin to snow and the country would become an icy prison to all but the most experienced travellers. Yet here was this woman, less than five feet tall, dressed in rags, ill-equipped, but determined to proceed on her way. Such a venture was suicide and, alarmed for her safety, the lineman telegraphed the provincial police detachment at Hazelton for advice.

His urgent query was answered by Constable J.A. Wyman who, shocked that anyone, let alone a woman, would attempt such a feat, instructed his informant to keep her there. Then Wyman headed for Cabin 2. When he arrived, Lillian was still there, emaciated, exhausted but determined to continue her journey. At first she pleaded for him to let her go her own way. When he insisted that she return with him to Hazelton, she became defiant but had to comply and, once back in Hazelton, he handed her over to Sergeant W.J. Service.

Then it was Service's turn to be amazed, and appalled, by her obsession to hike to Siberia. Lillian was obviously suffering from malnutrition, the only clothes she had were those on her back, and she was down to three loaves of bread and some tea. When he bluntly warned her that she would be risking her life by continuing with winter so near, she tearfully replied that go on she must. Despite his every argument she remained firm in her resolve and insisted that he release her.

For that matter, Service had no legal right to hold her as she had not broken any laws. But, in desperation, and determined to save her from herself, he charged her with vagrancy and placed her in custody. Even this move was on tender legal ground as a search by a police matron showed that Lillian had $20. The search had also uncovered a light-weight 18-inch-long iron bar which she wore, suspended from a cord, under her skirt. When the bemused sergeant asked her about the bar, she tersely replied that it was to protect her from men.

Upon her appearing in court Justice of the Peace William Grant agreed with Sergeant Service's action and accepting the trumped-up vagrancy charge, found her guilty, and fined her $25 and $1.75 costs. Lillian, of course, could not meet the fine and the ingenious JP sentenced her to two months in Okalla Prison Farm in Vancouver.

Thus Grant hoped to at least delay her journey. By the time she was released it would be November and too late in the season for her to travel. By spring, it was hoped, she would have come to her senses and abandoned her quest.

However for all of the lawmen's good intentions, Lillian was not to be dissuaded. Immediately upon her release from prison (she was granted 10 days off for good behavior) she went to work in the kitchen of a restaurant in Vancouver. Had the provincial police oficers or JP Grant known of her

employment, they might have been forgiven for thinking that their counsel had convinced the woman of the madness of attempting to hike to Siberia. In fact, Lillian was only marking time by working for a grubstake while she waited for spring. As soon as she had enough money, and the snows in the hills began to melt, she resumed her journey.

No sooner had she hit the trail than word of her departure was flashed to provincial police detachments along her proposed route. Although she was not a criminal and could not be handled as such, the police could do their best to see that she was safe, and when Sergeant Andy Fairbairn, at Smithers, received word of her coming he resolved to watch for her. He did not have long to wait. By mid-July, Lillian was reported to be nearing Smithers.

Glancing at a map, Fairbairn made a rough calculation of her speed from Vancouver. The strange Russian, by following the Cariboo Road, had achieved an average of 35 miles a day!

When he first set eyes on the woman, the sergeant's incredulity gave way to suspicion and he asked her if she had hitch-hiked. Scornfully, Lillian replied that she had walked every step of the way.

Fairbairn then found himself agonizing over the same dilemma as that which had faced Sergeant Service the previous year. Lillian had broken no laws — and this time there could be no pretence of a vagrancy charge as her winter's work in Vancouver had earned her sufficient travelling money. Neither could Fairbairn use the threat of winter to dissuade her, as it was only the middle of July, and she would have until mid-September, two full months distant, to cross the mountains into the Yukon. When Lillian calmly assured him that she could maintain her rapid pace, Fairbairn had no choice but to let her proceed. He did, however, make her promise that she would check in at every line cabin along the telegraph trail.

Then, as a final gesture of concern, he dispatched word of her approach to each of the linemen stationed along the telegraph route and asked that they do what they could for her as she reached them.

Within days Lillian was in Hazelton, the Omineca *Herald* reporting: "Lillian Alling, an old friend of the police force, blew into Hazelton this week en route to Echo Lake. She is on foot and makes an average 20 miles a day. Last year she was in Hazelton and after a reasonable stay she was charged with vagrancy and drew a six months term in Okalla from the magistrate. Lillie is a small woman, wiry and quite capable of taking care of herself."

Then Lillian hit the Telegraph Trail and, keeping her word to Sergeant Fairbairn, faithfully reported to each cabin in turn. By September 12 she had achieved 140 miles and checked in at Cabin 8.

But Lillian, for all of her determined spirit, was not superhuman. By the time she reached the eighth cabin it was snowing heavily. Linemen Jim Christie

(Left) *Hazelton, where British Columbia Provincial Police Constable Wyman turned Lillian over to Sergeant Service. When she insisted on going on, despite the fact that winter was approaching, Service charged her with vagrancy and placed her in custody. It was a trumped-up charge but forced Lillian to wait until the following spring.*
(Below) *A busy street scene in Telegraph Creek in 1928. According to an RCMP officer, this was Lillian's goal, not Siberia, as her fiance was supposed to be waiting for her there.*

and Charlie Janze, who were expecting her, suffered the same shock as that experienced by the lineman at Cabin 2 the previous year. For Lillian was almost dead on her feet. Exhausted, weak from hunger, burned by wind and sun, and her eyes almost swollen shut by insect bites, her clothes were torn, her little packsack almost empty. But the same fanatical light shone from her eyes and Christie and Janze quickly abandoned all attempts to dissuade her from continuing. Instead, they decided to do all in their power to assist her.

The first step was to persuade her to at least remain with them until she was rested. This time—for the first time—Lillian made but a token

protest and, while she regained her strength, the linemen outfitted her with a change of clothing. For the next few days, while Lillian recuperated in one of their two cabins, they plied her with food and did their best to improvise an outfit from their own clothes, the slightly built Janze volunteering a pair of his work boots which, when stuffed with two thick pairs of woollen socks, fit her comfortably. In addition to a handkerchief, to replace her worn-out scarf, Janze gave her a hat. Christie, unable to contribute much in the way of clothing as he was too big, contributed his small dog, Bruno, and the two improvised saddlebags as a travelling companion, when both filled her knapsack with food.

Touched by the gift of the dog, Lillian showed as much emotion as she ever had: "My first companion," she said. "He will always remain with me," and she warmly thanked the linemen for their concern and generosity. Then it was time for her to leave for her next stop on the trail, Telegraph Creek. Christie insisted upon accompanying her over the fog-bound, 8,000-foot Summit Pass to Cabin 9 which, like the other odd-numbered cabins on the Telegraph Trail, was not occupied. Before they set out, word of her coming was flashed to the occupants of Cabin 10 at Echo Lake, Drysdale "Scotty" Ogilvie and Cyril J. Tooley.

As Christie and Lillian headed over the summit, Ogilvie and his dog headed to meet them at Cabin 9. But Scotty did not show. Days passed without word of his arrival and Tooley, becoming alarmed, set out to trace his route. At the Ningunsaw River cable crossing he found the bridge submerged. A dog's barking attracted his attention and, heading downstream, he found where the raging river had undercut its banks. Farther down river he found his partner's body, Scotty having been plunged into the river when the bank collapsed under him.

Meeting Lillian and Christie at Cabin 9, 24-year-old Tooley informed them of Scotty's death, when Christie accompanied him to the scene. Almost half a century after, Tooley recalled: "It was with a great deal of difficulty that Jim Christie and I managed to get the body across to the north side of the river, on a hand-made stretcher, where we wrapped the body in a Hudson Bay blanket and a canvas and buried same with a little prayer and great sorrow. . . ."

Lillian then accompanied Tooley to the gravesite. There, the strange woman, whose distaste for men generally had been apparent to everyone she met, was heartbroken by the death of a complete stranger who had died while attempting to help her. After tearfully placing some wild flowers on his grave, she knelt and prayed.

Then she pushed on to Telegraph Creek and the former boom town of Atlin, in the northwestern corner of the province and within 20 air miles of the Yukon border. Although she apparently arrived in good shape, her little black and white companion had not been as fortunate, Bruno having died on the trail. In the only photograph of Lillian Alling, taken by Jim Christie, she is shown, stout walking stick in hand, as she poses with Bruno, who looked to be something like a border collie cross. Upon reaching Atlin her pack was on her back as before—with the grass-stuffed carcass of her ill-fated companion strapped to its top. It was there when she left town, bound for Dawson.

Even before she reached the former Klondike capital, Lillian had become something of a celebrity, the Whitehorse *Star* calling her "The Mystery Woman," and monitoring her progress as she approached Dawson. Although Lillian shunned notoriety, Yukoners followed her in the pages of

their newspaper. On September 6, 1928, H. Chambers informed the *Star* that he had encountered her some distance east of Tahkinna several days after she left Whitehorse. He offered her a lift but she declined.

A week after, word reached the *Star* that Lillian had passed through Carmacks "but she maintained her silence." Upon arriving at Yukon Crossing she allowed H.O. Lokken to ferry her across the river. She then had the Pelly and Stewart Rivers to cross.

On October 19, she reached Dawson, whose residents had been looking forward "with an unusual degree of curiosity for her arrival." According to the *Star*, Lillian "made some meagre purchases (at Carmacks) and continued her journey; at Yukon Crossing H.O. Lokken put her over the river in a small boat; at Pelly Crossing A. Shafer performed a similar service for her; at Stewart T.A. Dickson's survey party was camped and the boys cared for her for three days during a

It was at isolated camps such as this along the Yukon Telegraph line that Lillian stopped to rest. The linemen, upon recovering from their shock at meeting such a tiny woman in the wilderness, went out of their way to help her once they realized they could not talk her out of her mad scheme.

bad storm, and from this point she went down the river in a small boat to Dawson, arriving there in the morning of October 5th. She left Whitehorse on the morning of August 28 and as far as was known the only provisions she had was a loaf of bread, which she had cut in three pieces, as she said she was not carrying a rifle. . . ."

In all, it had taken Lillian 39 days to travel between Whitehorse and Dawson, during which time she kept in the open. Upon reaching Dawson she was wearing a different style of men's shoe on each foot.

Winter was well advanced and Lillian, now a veteran traveller, decided to wait until spring thaw. Obtaining a job as a waitress, she spent the winter working on an old rowboat she had bought, and kept to herself.

The mighty Yukon River has witnessed some strange sights, and some unusual craft, since the day the first gold seekers braved its rapids with whip-sawed nightmares in their rush to the diggings. Few could have been more unusual than the skiff in which Lillian, crowded between her supplies—and her stuffed dog—headed downstream to Nome the following spring.

For mile after mile she drifted downriver. Once at Nome, she abandoned her boat, shouldered her pack and stuffed companion and marched into the Arctic—and into oblivion. For, somewhere in the ice-bound wastes of the Alaskan Arctic, Lillian Alling disappeared. She was last seen by an Eskimo who was terrified by the strange apparition of a white woman, in the middle of nowhere, pulling a crude two-wheeled cart. Even more unnerving had been the sight of the stuffed dog, atop her cart.

The supersitious Eskimo did not dare speak to her and, as he reported later, the last he saw of her she was moving steadily along the shoreline near Teller, form bent slightly forward as she pushed ever northward. Shortly afterward he saw her tracks beside a river in flood. When Alaskan authorities were informed of this sighting they concluded that she had drowned.

But there were those who wondered. She was then within reach of Bering Strait, the last major hurdle between her and her homeland. According to one rumor she had managed to obtain a kayak. Those familiar with her incredible 6,000-mile trek across the continent and through the British Columbia-Yukon-Alaska wilds could not help but wonder if any woman capable of such a feat was not quite capable of crossing Bering Strait.

Others have pondered the overwhelming drive which compelled Lillian Alling to brave danger and to endure months of hardship while attempting such a preposterous thing as walking to Siberia. Most accounts mention that she was simply homesick and unable to save enough for steamer fare. Another version is to the effect that her family had been sent to a Siberian labor camp in a Stalinist purge and she was attempting to join them.

But one man had an even more intriguing idea as to her motive. In fact, he declared that the reason he gave came straight from the horse's mouth—from Lillian Alling herself.

Although several of the salient details given by former RCMP officer T.E.E. Greenfield vary from the accepted record, he offered an interesting insight into Lillian's incredible odyssey. In a letter to the Vancouver *Province* in 1973, Greenfield queried both Lillian's nationality and the spelling of her name. She was Polish, not Russian, he said, and her correct name was Ailing (others have spelled it 'Ayling'). Her goal had not been Siberia, but Telegraph Creek, British Columbia, to which she had hiked from North Dakota to "marry a countryman boyfriend…but he had departed before her arrival. She then walked through Alberta and B.C. via Jasper and Prince George and had reached Kispiox on the Yukon Telegraph Line about 30 miles north of Hazelton, when B.C. Prov. Police Constable George Wyman received a phone call and he immediately went to Kispiox by car and picked her up and brought her to Hazelton.

"He locked her up on a vagrancy charge. It was at this point that I came into the picture. Const. Wyman had to go out of town on an urgent matter and he asked me to do the gaol guard duty until his return. I happened to be in Hazelton on patrol duties and it was not infrequent that members of the R.C. Mounted Police were asked and readily gave the necessary assistance to the provincial police.

"When she appeared before Justice of the Peace Grant, she was sentenced to five days to be served in Okalla prison farm. She was then escorted to Okalla by police matron Constance Cox and after the five days had elapsed Lillian was released immediately. I believe she spent the winter of 1927-28 in Vancouver.

"In 1928, Lillian walked through the Bulkley Valley again, this time by night and over the Yukon Telegraph Line to Telegraph Creek, early in the summer. In the latter part of October, 1928, I received a letter addressed to 'Policeman Greenfield, Hazelton,' from Lillian. She wrote in poor English that she had not found her beloved in Telegraph Creek as he had departed before her arrival. She had, however, found and married a kind man there. She thanked me for delaying her a year from meeting her beloved. She said she remembered my name but couldn't recall the name of the other policeman.

"The letter was addressed to Hazelton but was sent on to me at Kitwanga where I had been transferred.

"Lillian's effects consisted of a man's heavy cloth overcoat that hung to ankle length in which she slept. She carried an iron bar about 16 inches long for defence purposes. She had a landing card showing her arrival at New York early in 1927 and showing her to be Polish. Her name on the card was spelled Ailing. She wore a pair of men's 8 inch top boots.

"I know nothing further after her letter to me in 1928."

In conclusion, Greenfield noted that Lillian had been "very much in need of a bath, maybe one would not have sufficed!"

And on that personal note the file on Lillian Alling (Ailing, Ayling) is closed. Did she perish in the Far North? Or did this amazing woman make it across Bering Strait to her homeland? Sadly, we likely will never know. . . .

The incredible saga of Lillian Alling was recalled in December of 1969 when it was reported that Esther Gaschk, a 55-year-old Los Angeles widow, accompanied by her 18-year-old parrot, Elmer Fudd, was hiking from California to Alaska. She left Los Angeles in July and intended to give two and a half years to the 3,000-mile journey after wintering in Tacoma, Washington.

"I'm not a nut," Mrs. Gaschk told a reporter. "I'm doing it for adventure and the challenge. I have friends who thought I'd never make it this far, but I'm awfully determined."

However, unlike Lillian Alling, who had refused all offers of a ride, Mrs. Gaschk had accepted lifts from passing motorists. She said she intended to write a book about her experiences, with a special section on camping tips for women.   ●

Today visitors to the provincial museum can view in amazement the internationally famous legacy that this amazing father and son team bequeathed to posterity.

GENTLEMEN SCIENTISTS

IF a weathered mansion on Dallas Road in Victoria could speak, it would tell tales of the fierce Haida; of the wild British Columbia coast when sail yet challenged steam and shipwreck was common; and of bloodchilling rites which hinted of human sacrifice. It could tell, also, of a remarkable father and son team which contributed more to northwest history, in their chosen fields, than any other. They were Dr. Charles Frederick Newcombe, and his son, William Arnold Newcombe.

Although honored as British Columbia's "first psychiatrist," Dr. Newcombe's immense contribution to provincial heritage was not in the field of medicine, but rather in the fields of anthropology and biology.

Perhaps the personable physician is best remembered for the time he took seven Vancouver Island natives to the St. Louis World Fair, in 1904, and almost caused a riot. This unexpected state of affairs had resulted from the realistic demonstrations of the party's fierce-looking medicine man and magician, Chief Atliu.

"In addition to their ceremonial robes, headdress, face-masks, animal-skin clothing and grass rugs," George Nicholson wrote in *Vancouver Island's West Coast*, "they took with them a forty-foot canoe named Heitl-hei-yachisht, which means Sea Serpent, totem poles and house figures. Also a knocked-down Indian dwelling-house and trunks filled with baskets, beadware, matting and other articles of native art."

Before an awed American audience, the party erected its "prefabricated" house, and totem poles, creating "a village typical of the B.C. coast Indians." Here they lived and conducted their displays, the men carving totems, house figures and dugout canoes as the women wove baskets and matting, and stitched beadware and clothing.

Star of the unique show was Chief Atliu, his "heap strong medicine" baffling laymen and professional magicians alike. In one act, to again quote Major Nicholson, the mystifying chieftain "ran a red-hot poker through the belly of an Indian (an accomplice no doubt) and had it come—still steaming hot—out the middle of the man's back, without his suffering any apparent discomfort!"

Another time, Atliu "sacrificed" a young boy. As no children had accompanied the party, a negro stand-in had been disguised as an Indian. Before the evil rite, volunteers from the audience were invited to satisfy themselves that he was indeed alive. This confirmed, the natives began their dance. Suddenly, to the spectators' screams of horror and disbelief, they seized the "child" and threw him into a roaring oven!

As men gasped and women fainted, demoniac Atliu withdrew the corpse from the fire, cut off its head, and then, blood gushing from the wound, calmly proceeded to eat the flesh.

The audience hadn't noticed that the lad had been switched, that the "body" was made of mutton and vegetables, and that the blood was that of a bullock.

"Some called 'Police', " continued Nicholson. "However, the chief managed to becalm them by declaring that he would bring the 'boy' back to life.

"More dancing and the beating of drums, another mysterious switch and there stood the boy, bewildered, but very much alive. Handed some peanuts and bananas, and a five-dollar gold piece for his mother, the little negro boy went home quite happy. And he required no coaxing for future performances."

Throughout the incredible exhibition, watching over all, was Dr. Charles Newcombe. Although the St. Louis performances drew the most publicity, it is for his research and field work that the gentlemanly scientist is appreciated by modern authorities.

Surprisingly, Newcombe's background would seem to make his career one of contrasts, rather than that of a natural progression of events. Born at Newcastle on Tyne, September 14, 1851, he studied medicine at Aberdeen University. After post graduate studies in Germany, he joined the staff of a Yorkshire hospital and later practised at Rain Hill Mental Hospital, Liverpool.

Marrying Marion Arnold in 1879, the 28-year-old physician and psychiatrist moved to Windermere, then Twickenham, during which period he crossed the Atlantic to study American advances in medicine. Impressed with the New World, he returned for his family, now comprising two daughters and a son, and moved to Hood River, Oregon, via steamship, train and stagecoach.

Hanging up his shingle, the good doctor soon had an extensive—and scattered—practise. On horseback and by buggy, he made his rounds, crossing the Columbia River when necessary in a 14-foot boat he had built himself.

Despite the exhaustive demands of a frontier practice, Dr. Newcombe found time to indulge a growing interest in natural history. Between calls, or, perhaps, while travelling to and from patients, he began to study the flora and fauna of the region, completing several expeditions to Mount Hood in quest of wild flowers, and carefully preserving fragile blue and white lupins, blue bells and yellow erithroniums in air-tight bottles.

Putting his observations to practice, he turned his home into a small fruit farm, complete with clover field for his bees, and the Newcombe residence became known for its succulent strawberries and bright, attractive flower gardens.

It was in Oregon that Dr. Newcombe began the collection of Indian artifacts that was to become world renowned, by collecting arrowheads. A second noteworthy event which occurred at Hood River was the birth, on April 29, 1884, of a second son, William.

A year later, Newcombe moved his family, collections and milk cow to Victoria, where he continued his studies and soon met John Fannin, legendary curator of the young provincial museum. The two became fast friends, Newcombe joining the Victoria Natural History Society on its regular towboat expeditions into Juan de Fuca Strait after specimens for the museum.

In his own boat, with a trawl he had designed, he made further expeditions, steadily increasing his vast collections of animal and plant life, particularly in the field of marine zoology. Some years ago, a daughter, Mrs. Harold Peck, recalled being sent with her brothers and sisters to Beacon Hill Park almost daily for fresh sea water to replenish their father's aquarium.

Dr. Newcombe then became more intrigued by Indian folklore and artifacts; sailing his open, 18-foot boat along the stormy shores of Vancouver and the Queen Charlotte Islands. Between 1895 and 1897, accompanied by sons Charles and William, he explored almost every inch of coastline about Skidegate, visiting, living with, questioning and studying the Haidas, their customs and handicrafts.

Earlier, he had advanced to a twenty-four-foot double-ended fishing craft with cabin, and now explored as far north as Alaska; shipping his vessel part of the way by steamer.

By 1904, when he organized the famous World Fair exhibition, he had become recognized as the foremost authority on northwest Indians.

In following years, Dr. Newcombe continued his studies and collections. During this period he contributed several totem poles to European museums and supervised the British Columbia Indian exhibit in Chicago's Field Museum.

Although, with advancing years, the exhausting battle to uncover nature's secrets and salvage the province's Indian heritage from extinction had of necessity to be restricted, Newcombe continued his self-appointed task.

Other duties had included, two months before his death, attending ceremonies marking the unveiling of the Captain Cook monument at Nootka, on the west coast of Vancouver Island. Once back in Victoria, he "plunged into the round of courtesies extended here to the British scientists, 400 in number, who came out to Victoria after attending the Toronto convention for the Advancement of Sciences," according to a news account.

Between field trips and his studies, Newcombe would take time to walk Victoria beaches and visit nearby Sooke in search of botanical specimens with his longtime friend, Robert Connell, the naturalists enjoying hours of discussion upon the mysteries of nature. Of all Newcombe's attributes, that which most impressed Connell, even in the scientist's last years, was his "wonderfully buoyant and boylike mind, always alert and keen, and full of fresh interest."

The end came for Dr. Charles Newcombe in 1924, when, during another upcoast sailing expedition, he caught a severe chill. By the time he reached Victoria, it was too late, and, ordered to bed, he died two weeks later, on October 19, in the family mansion on Dallas Road. He was 73.

Many mourned the gentlemanly scientist "known in every centre of learning on the continent for his extensive work in various branches of natural science in B.C." Obituaries recalled his trips in a small boat to the remote Queen Charlotte Islands with provincial museum curator Francis Kermode, in search of fossil formations, when two missionaries and two storekeepers were the only other whites for hundreds of miles.

It had been during this period that Newcombe actively studied native races of the northwest coast and gathered valuable materials for his vast anthropological collection which would be turned over to the provincial museum. Upon learning of his research, Sir Richard McBride, Premier of British Columbia, had commissioned him to "gather as much material as possible for the provincial government... as the country was being denuded of the early aboriginal relics by the leading museums of the world, particularly the United States and Germany."

In addition to being a noted botanist, Dr. Newcombe had taken up pen to write two natural history volumes and two journals concerning Captain George Vancouver's circumnavigation of Vancouver Island; not to mention his enormous contribution to the provincial fisheries department by "investigating the life histories of the sea lions along the Pacific coast...many times at great personal risk." He also had served as chairman of a commission researching the sea lions' effect upon the salmon industry. At all times, he had worked in close contact with leading institutions and scientists throughout the continent.

The Victoria *Times* noted: "In his passing this province has lost an illustrious friend whose life work will be the more remarked when the result of his labors can be collected together in review."

An editorial in the usually staid British journal, *Nature*, concluded: "To those who enjoyed Newcombe's friendship it cannot but be regretted that such a many-sided, humorous and charming personality has been lost to us without leaving an adequate memorial (referring to his not having 'published any accounts of his experiences and observations among the coast Indians'), and to those who are interested scientifically in the Pacific coast of Canada, the closing of so rich a storehouse of knowledge of a dying race is an unparallelled disaster."

But Dr. Newcombe's magnificent work was to live on, not only in memory, but in deed. Many Victorians remember the lonely figure with bushy hair and prominent nose which daily haunted Dallas Road beaches, in bygone years, salvaging driftwood. Few knew him as more than a somewhat pathetic recluse, who did odd jobs in the neighborhood for those in need, and asked for little more than a thank-you in return.

Ironically, it was not until after his death that the public learned of "Billy" Newcombe's secret.

He it was who, with brother Charles, had accompanied Dr. Newcombe on many of his upcoast expeditions in quest of artifacts and specimens. From the day he surrendered a scholarship to assist the St. Louis Fair exhibit, with the exception of military service overseas, Billy had remained at his father's side and learned all he could from his remarkable teacher.

Before long, young Billy was accepted by the scientific community as an expert in anthropology and natural science the equal of his famous father. With Dr. Newcombe's death in 1924, he had con-

tinued their ambitious program of attempting to save what remained of our native cultures.

"Untutored, but self-taught," wrote Bert Hudson some years ago, Billy "knew more about native Indian lore probably than any man in B.C. in the first half of the century. He was the man who realized the importance of the Indian culture which was fading as the white man's blight swept over the Indian villages. With dedication Willie (sic) Newcombe spent his life preserving what he could."

Unfortunately, early in his career, Billy suffered an experience which is thought by many to have driven the sensitive lifelong bachelor into solitude. After four years in the provincial museum as assistant biologist, according to one account, several items disappeared. This source suggests that Billy, stung by accusation, had retired from the world. The missing items, incidentally, turned up "some years later, hidden in an out-of-the-way place in the museum."

Another report suggests that he had been the victim of "economy."

Whatever the cause, Billy lived alone in the crumbling mansion on Dallas, acting as handyman and accepting the teasing of neighborhood children with a shy smile. One of the very few who knew the real William Arnold Newcombe was another James Bay character, Emily Carr.

Perhaps it was because both had known public scorn that this odd couple became such close friends. Billy helped her about her home, packaged her paintings for shipment in driftwood cases, and told her of Indian folklore. He also guided her to distant villages and showed her the Indian ways and artistry, that her canvases might be "correct."

Emily remembered her faithful friend, naming him an executor of her estate. From 1945, until his own death 15 years later, Billy served as trustee of the Emily Carr Memorial Scholarship Fund.

With Billy's passing, in November, 1960, a solemn ceremony was performed off Victoria's Ogden Point breakwater, when the tugboat *Island Comet*, flag at half-mast, ghosted through a rippling sea. Then, within sight and sound of the ships, bells and buoys Billy Newcombe had known and loved for 70 years, his ashes were scattered on the waves by two nephews.

Today visitors to the new provincial museum can view in amazement the internationally famous "Newcombe Collection." For, when executors had visited the old mansion, they had found one of the most complete inventories in existence of British Columbia Indian arts and crafts, including priceless books, private papers, rare photographs and documents—and almost 100 Emily Carr paintings.

These are the stories which the ancient manor at 138 Dallas Road can tell: of Dr. C.F. Newcombe, and Billy, the incredible team which contributed so greatly to our heritage, and, in so doing, to our future. ●

(Opposite page) *Chief Mungo Martin at work on a replica of a Haida memorial carving in Thunderbird Park. This carving depicts the thunderbird and the whale, a theme common to most tribes of the British Columbia coast.*
(Left) *The finished masterpiece.*

More than any other person, Mungo Martin saved his people's culture and traditions from certain oblivion. Today his great work goes on.

TEN TIMES A CHIEF

MANY were the honors bestowed upon this remarkable man during his career, but if the late Chief Mungo Martin had been asked, surely he would have replied that July 19, 1958, had been his greatest moment.

On that day the bespectacled Kwakiutl carver from Fort Rupert, guardian of his people's vanishing heritage, had been presented to Her Majesty, Queen Mother Elizabeth. It was the crowning event of a life which had spanned two centuries and two civilizations; a life of achievement which will be valued for generations to come.

Mungo's story began almost three-quarters of a century earlier when, as a youngster, he had begun his apprenticeship in the secret art of carving at his father's side. A sacred art among the Kwakiutls, totem carving was passed from father to son, like the artisans of medieval Europe.

As part of his introduction to the legendary craft, Mungo had experienced the ritual of having had four eyebrow hairs plucked and woven into a tiny paint brush to "endow him with artistic gifts," and being placed inside a wooden box drum which was then beaten to "imbue him with musical skills." The mystical ceremony must have had some effect as, by the time of his death, in 1962, Mungo had single-handedly rescued the Pacific Northwest's most distinctive native art from oblivion and made himself internationally recognized.

When his young friends had played, Mungo had whittled by himself, or listened to the old men of the village tell of days and ways long gone. Later Mungo began memorizing the legends and songs. When his father died, his mother remarried and teen-aged Mungo apprenticed with his stepfather, noted carver Charlie James.

But, as with most artists of all races, Mungo had known frustrating years. During this period, like most of his tribe, he had earned a livelihood by fishing, able to carve only in his spare time. By the 1920s, American vacationers were paying as much as $300 each for his beautiful creations.

He had gained such stature by 1947 that the University of British Columbia asked him to take charge of a totem pole restoration program. Five years later, the provincial government having embarked upon a program to "help perpetuate carving totems," Mungo was named provincial chief carver for the museum. During the next 10 years he worked diligently at his almost-forgotten craft in an open shed in Thunderbird Park, at the busy intersection of Douglas and Belleville streets, Victoria. In that time, thousands of tourists and residents had watched in admiration as the mackinawed carver with his strange looking tools had created story and song from rough cedar logs.

This productive decade had almost ended on an unpleasant note in 1955 when, applying for a suite of rooms for his family, Mungo had been rejected because he was Indian. When newspapers reported the snub, he had been beseiged with offers. Instead of returning to Alert Bay, he remained at his work in Thunderbird Park.

Actually, these had been lonely years for Mungo, far from home and family. During the potlatch which celebrated completion of Kwakiutl House in Thunderbird Park, in 1953, he told the gathered chieftains:

"Now, Nuknenes, now we are finished. That is the way I wanted you to come. Thank you. Thank you, chiefs. You have put strength into me, for I was very weak all by myself away from home. I almost cry sometimes when there is nobody to help me.

"And you have come to help, you with your famous names, you chiefs. You have strengthened me. Your fame will spread because you are here. You have strength for you know everything. You too have been left to take up the duties which have been passed on to you. So you will help me finish what I want to do."

In 1956 Mungo began his best-known creation, the "world's tallest totem." Carved from a 250-year-old cedar, it was financed through public subscription, shares selling for 50 cents each. The first went to Mungo. Six months of exhausting labor went into the 127-foot totem, Mungo being assisted by his son, David, and grandson, Henry Hunt. It was Mungo's fervent desire that David and Henry study under him and continue his work.

Today the impressive monument is among the most popular attractions of Victoria's Beacon Hill Park. A small bronze plaque set in a granite block at its base reads: "Symbolic of a proud race; memento of the nation's infancy; monument to a rare native art; proof of a united community interest; and the purest form of Canadiana."

Mungo's most thrilling moment came two years later, when the totem he had carved for British Columbia's centennial was to be presented to Queen Elizabeth at Windsor, England. Mungo was asked to dedicate the pole according to custom, then meet his sovereign. A Victoria motel owner and his wife, Mr. and Mrs. J.G. Nordal, donated $1,000 to pay expenses, and the 79-year-old carver and his grand-daughter, Mrs. Helen Hunt, flew to England.

At Windsor, wearing his crimson and white ceremonial robes, Mungo dedicated the totem before a rapt audience of thousands. Then he was presented to the Queen Mother, representing her daughter who had been confined to bed with a sinus infection. Her Majesty was "very disappointed," said the Queen Mother, at missing the unique occasion, but "most grateful" to British Columbia for the beautiful totem pole.

Before returning to Victoria, Mungo enjoyed a brief tour of the country, including a visit to the Oxford University Museum, which contains many relics of British Columbia Indians collected by Captain James Cook. Upon his return he was welcomed by hundreds, including Mayor Percy Scurrah, in an open-air ceremony held in Beacon Hill Park, home of his tallest totem.

"The world to me from the air looked like a long sandbar with lots of clams!" he exclaimed when questioned about his trip.

A month later, it was announced that Mungo would represent the province at a national handicraft show in Quebec. But September of 1959 brought tragedy. David, a commercial fisherman when not carving with his father, was lost at sea. He had but recently decided to follow in Mungo's footsteps.

Two months later, British Columbians learned the full extent of the old chieftain's tragedy. In a highly emotional rite in Kwakiutl House, the tribal house he had built in Thunderbird Park, Mungo gave all his cherished ceremonial garments to Education Minister Leslie Peterson, who accepted on behalf of the province.

"Today I am in darkness," said Mungo in a choked voice. "I cannot carry on. All my life I have worked so we would be known by the different nations. I carried on alone, when the different tribes had stopped (preserving the traditions) because I wanted to prove my love to my son."

With David's death, tradition demanded that the treasure of masks and relics be burned, thereby transporting them to the "after life." Mungo honored his people's traditions. But he had dedicated his life to the preservation of their culture.

Tearfully, he continued: "My wife and I thought night after night if it was right or wrong to give these away. With them we could not forget our son. Now he is gone. Now I am alone. I don't want to see these masks any more."

Mr. Peterson softly replied that the collection would be a "permanent memorial to you, Chief Mungo Martin, and to your son."

On May 28, 1960, a 12-foot totem bearing the family crests was erected beside a stone monument in Courtenay. Mungo had carved it in memory of David.

The following year, Mungo was invited to carve a "symbolic" pole in Times Square, "under the eyes of curious New Yorkers," by the Century 21 World's Fair management in Seattle. The offer included payment of all expenses, and Mungo joked with reporters: "Yes, I'd like to go, but once I get down to New York, I may never come back."

But Mungo's health caused negotiations to fall through. In the summer of 1962 he entered the hospital for the last time. At 7 o'clock in the morning of August 6, the weary chief passed away in his sleep. He was 83.

In a yellow cedar coffin, carved by grandson Henry, Mungo lay in state in Kwakiutl House. The casket, bearing emblems of the thunderbird and

Above) *Fort Rupert, Vancouver Island, birthplace of Mungo Martin. Here the noted Indian carver began his apprenticeship in the secret Kwakiutl art at his father's side.*

(Left) *A fine example of an almost vanished culture is this Bella Coola grave figure in Victoria's Thunderbird Park. This particular figure is a replica of the original which was obtained from the Bella Coola village of Talio in 1913. This supernatural grizzly bear, an attendant in the house of the Cannibal spirit, had an extra pair of eyes in the palms of his hands.*

grizzly bear, and surrounded by examples of his art, was open to allow relatives to clasp his hand in farewell. A tape recording of his voice, backed by a chorus singing a traditional mourning song, was played throughout the ceremony.

Among the many attending from several provinces and states was anthropologist Frederica de Laguna of Bryn Mawr College, who gave a farewell speech and prayer: "Perhaps no Canadian Indian did more than Chief Martin to secure recognition and honor for the culture of his people, and so helped to win for the Indian equal rights under Canadian laws," said de Laguna.

The Royal Canadian Navy paid unique tribute to the famous chief. Navy pallbearers carried his beautiful cedar coffin to the destroyer escort, HMCS *Ottawa*, where they were met by a guard of honor and piped aboard. Mungo's coffin, covered with flowers, was placed on the quarterdeck and guarded by four sentries with fixed bayonets for the voyage to Alert Bay.

When the *Ottawa* steamed slowly from Esquimalt Harbor into an evening mist in Juan de Fuca Strait, every ensign was dipped in salute to a great native Canadian.

Mungo's widow, Abaya, later read his last wishes to the press. She said he had changed his mind about being buried at his birthplace, Fort Rupert,

For years, Mungo Martin carried on a lonely struggle to preserve a dying way of life. Tragedy almost brought his crusade to an end in 1959 when his son David, a commercial fisherman, was lost at sea. Mourned the heart-broken chieftain: "Today I am in darkness. I cannot carry on. All my life I have worked so we would be known by the different nations. I carried on alone, when the different tribes had stopped (preserving the traditions) because I wanted to prove my love to my son."

choosing Alert Bay instead, that his family might find it easier to visit. He also asked that his proteges, Henry, and his son, Tony Hunt, be permitted by the provincial government to continue his work.

Eighty-four-year-old Abaya (Sarah Constance)

This is just a copy of one of the finest examples of Haida carvings in existence, and almost the only mortuary pole that has been preserved. The original was obtained from the abandoned village of Tanoo on Queen Charlotte Islands in 1911. It was to the preservation of this unique art form that Kwakiutl carver Mungo Martin dedicated his life.

soon joined her husband in death. Noted for her weaving of rare Chilcat blankets, one of her masterpieces had been presented to Queen Elizabeth at her coronation in 1953. Another is in the provincial museum.

Mungo was posthumously accorded yet another honor, the Canada Council Medal. This honor is granted to "persons in Canada for outstanding accomplishments in the arts, humanities or social sciences." The second Canadian to receive this coveted award posthumously, Mungo was the first Indian to be so distinguished, the council citing his "contribution to Canada's artistic, cultural and intellectual life." The council also noted Mungo's work in the "recordings of songs, ceremonies and other Kwakiutl culture."

Unable to read or write in English, Mungo had drawn upon his prodigious memory to record on tape the songs and ceremonial chants of his people; he left future generations flawlessly executed ritual masks, carved dishes, paintings, and copperwork, in addition to his famous royal and world's tallest totems. Today his 37-foot pole commemorating Mexican independence and unity stands in Mexico City, a symbol of goodwill between our nations. Another 60-foot totem stands in the national headquarters of the Boy Scouts Association in Ottawa. The same year, he carved a totem for the Royal Canadian Navy.

Further examples of Mungo's work can be found in Peace Park at Blaine, Washington; in the Vancouver Maritime Museum; in Stanley Park; and in the University of British Columbia's Totem Pole Park.

Upon his death, the British Columbia Indian Arts and Welfare Society and a committee of Victoria citizens inaugurated a Mungo Martin Memorial Fund with a goal of $5,500 to initiate a scholarship fund for promising Indian students, finance a memorial plaque to be erected in Thunderbird Park, and produce a booklet "on the life and achievements of the great Kwakiutl chief, the proceeds to go to the scholarship fund."

American anthropologist Dr. Erna Gunther said of Mungo: "He is one of the great men of the century as far as the Indian is concerned. He made a tremendous effort to keep the fine things in his culture going. I am pleased to see the establishment of the Mungo Martin Memorial Fund, particularly for what it will do to help young Indians of promise."

His had been an awesome burden. More than any other person he had saved his people's culture and traditions from certain oblivion. As he had once said, "Nobody knows now. Only me."

But of all the international and impressive honors accorded this amazing man, perhaps that which Mungo Martin most appreciated was that which was bestowed upon him by his own people. It was the title: "Naqapenkim."

It means "Ten Times a Chief." ●

BIBLIOGRAPHY

ANDERSON, Frank W. *Bill Miner, Train Robber;* Frontier Publishing Ltd., 1968.

BARLEE, N.L. *Gold Creeks and Ghost Towns;* 1970.

BEGG, Alexander *History of British Columbia From Its Earliest Discovery to the Present Time;* Ryerson Press, 1894.

CHITTENDEN *Guide of Travels Through British Columbia;* Victoria, 1882.

FETHERSTONHAUGH, R.C. *The Royal Canadian Mounted Police;* Carrick & Evans Inc., New York, 1938.

GOSNELL *British Columbia: 60 Years of Progress;* Victoria, 1913.

GREGSON, Harry *A History of Victoria, 1847-1970;* Victoria Observer Publishing Co. Ltd., Victoria, 1970.

HIGGINS, D.W. *The Mysterious Spring and Other Tales of Western Life;* Victoria, 1904.

HIND, Henry Youle *Narrative of the Canadian Red River Exploring Expedition of 1857;* M.G. Hurtig Ltd., Edmonton, 1971.

HORAN, James D. *The Pinkertons: The Detective Dynasty That Made History;* Crown Publishers, Inc., New York, 1967.

HOWAY, F.W. *British Columbia From the Earliest Times to the Present;* 1914.

McKELVIE, B.A. *Pageant of British Columbia;* Thomas Nelson & Sons (Canada) Ltd.

NICHOLSON, George *Vancouver Island's West Coast, 1762-1962;* Victoria, 1962.

PETHICK, Derek *Victoria: The Fort;* Mitchell Press Ltd., Vancouver, 1968, *James Douglas: Servant of Two Empires;* Mitchell, 1969.

RAMSAY, Bruce *Ghost Towns of British Columbia;* Mitchell Press, Vancouver, 1963.

ROBINSON, Noel *Blazing the Trail Through the Rockies;* Vancouver.

RUNNALLS, Rev. F.E. *A History of Prince George;* 1946.

WALBRAN, Captain John T. *British Columbia Coast Names, 1592-1906;* Ottawa, 1909.

Periodicals

Prince George *Progress;* Omineca *Herald; British Columbia Professional Engineer; True West* Magazine; *Alaska Sportsman* Magazine; Boundary Creek *Times;* Greenwood *Times;* Vernon *News;* Kelowna *Courier; Canada West* Magazine; *Weekend* Magazine; Terrace Omineca *Herald;* Vancouver *Daily World; Harper's Weekly; Canadian Illustrated News; American Anthropologist; Nature* Magazine; *The Victorian;* Cranbrook *Courier;* Cranbrook *Herald; Northwest Digest* Magazine; *British Columbia Outdoors* Magazine; Oregon *Spectator; Oregonian; Real West* Magazine; *The Daily Colonist;* Victoria *Daily Times;* Vancouver *Daily Province;* Vancouver *Sun;* Nakusp *Silver Standard;* Revelstoke *Review;* Nelson *Daily News;* Trail *Times; The Kaslo Kootenain;* Comox District *Free Press;* Chilliwack *Progress;* Arrow Lakes *News;* Canadian Merchant Service Guild *1954 Annual;* Oliver *Chronicle;* Salmon Arm *Observer;* Kamloops *Sentinel;* Penticton *Herald; The Western Producer; Old West* Magazine; *The West* Magazine;

Miscellaneous Sources

Vancouver City Archives; British Columbia Provincial Archives; British Columbia Division of Vital Statistics; British Columbia Department of Mines and Petroleum Resources; Victoria Press Library; British Columbia Historical Association; W. George Crisp; Guy Ilstad; Willie Hecht; Sister Mary Dorothea; Sisters of St. Ann, Victoria; Francis Dickie; National Archives and Records Service, Washington, D.C.; Smithsonian Institution, Washington, D.C. Canadian Pacific Railways; Public Archives of Canada.

Photographic Sources

British Columbia Provincial Archives; British Columbia Department of Recreation and Conservation; Guy Ilstad; Canadian Pacific Railways; Victoria Press Ltd.; Public Archives of Canada; Vancouver City Archives; George and Madelaine Larrigan.